# Research on Teacher Induction

## Teacher Education Yearbook XIV

EDITED BY JULIE RAINER DANGEL

Published in partnership with the
Association of Teacher Educators
ROWMAN & LITTLEFIELD EDUCATION
*Lanham, Maryland • Toronto • Oxford*
2006

Published in partnership with the
Association of Teacher Educators

Published in the United States of America
by Rowman & Littlefield Education
A Division of Rowman & Littlefield Publishers, Inc.
A wholly owned subsidiary of The Rowman & Littlefield Publishing Group, Inc.
4501 Forbes Boulevard, Suite 200, Lanham, Maryland 20706
www.rowmaneducation.com

PO Box 317
Oxford
OX2 9RU, UK

British Library Cataloguing in Publication Information Available

**Library of Congress Cataloging-in-Publication Data**

1–57886–383-X (cloth: alk. paper)
1–57886–385–6 (paper: alk. paper)
Control number 2005933782

♾ ™ The paper used in this publication meets the minimum requirements of
American National Standard for Information Sciences—Permanence of
Paper for Printed Library Materials, ANSI/NISO Z39.48–1992.
Manufactured in the United States of America.

# Teacher Education Yearbook XIV

## EDITOR

Julie Rainer Dangel, Georgia State University

## EDITORIAL ADVISORY BOARD

## PRESIDENT ATE 2004–2005

P. Rudy Mattai, SUNY–College at Buffalo

## EXECUTIVE DIRECTOR

David Ritchie, Association of Teacher Educators, Reston, Virginia

# Contents

## DIVISION 2: LOOKING CLOSELY AT THE MENTORING EXPERIENCE

## DIVISION 3: DESIGNING AND IMPLEMENTING QUALITY MENTORING PROGRAMS

# List of Tables and Figures

## Tables

# Figures

# Foreword

*P. Rudy Mattai*
SUNY College at Buffalo

P. Rudy Mattai, Ph.D., is professor, Educational Foundations, SUNY–Buffalo (NY) and currently serves as founding dean of the School of Education, SUNY–Old Westbury (Long Island, NY). He is currently president (2005–2006) of the Association for Teacher Educators and serves on the board of the National Association for Ethnic Studies (NAES) and the International Society for Educational Planning (ISEP). He also is a member of the Multicultural Committee (AACTE) and the Program Development Committee (ICET). He is the editor of *Educational Planning*, one of two international refereed journals on educational planning, and *Child Studies Journal*. He serves as an external examiner for graduate programs at the University of the West Indies at St. Augustine, Trinidad. His research areas are race and ethnic issues in education and urban education and he has published widely in both areas. He is co-editor of *Culturally Responsive Teacher Education: Language, Curriculum and Community*, scheduled to be published by Lawrence Erlbaum in 2006. He has received numerous awards and consults nationally and internationally on diversity issues and program development and evaluation.

I am pleased to have been invited to write the foreword for *Research on Teacher Induction: Teacher Education Yearbook XIV*, which is yet another piece in the exceptionally researched and scholarly literature that has been sponsored by the Association of Teacher Educators (ATE) over the last several years. This year's production focuses on what has perennially been an important issue in the preparation of teachers, and while being an essential ingredient in the professional preparation of P–12 teachers, it has not received the focal attention that should be accorded this phenomenon. This *Yearbook* will undoubtedly be a most welcome resource for both those engaged in the professional preparation of teachers at the tertiary level and P–12 educational institutions. The Association of Teacher Educators and particularly the editor, Professor Julie Rainer Dangel, along with her colleagues who worked tirelessly on the production, deserve special recognition.

Teacher induction and its inseparable counterpart—mentoring—has been with us for some time now. The indisputable benefits of such efforts are well touted but more often than not the political will, reinforced by financial resources to make manifest that will, have been in short supply. In a recently released report from the National Academy of Education (Darling-Hammond & Bransford, 2005) the benefits of induction and mentoring are brought to the center stage. According to the report,

> States and the federal government should sponsor high quality induction programs that will help beginning teachers gain expertise and stay in the classroom. These programs should include trained mentors who are expert teachers with released time to coach and model good instruction, reduced teaching loads, and sound performance assessment to guide learning.

The report further goes on to point out that

> teachers are much more likely to stay in the profession if they are supported in their early efforts to learn to teach. Unlike some other professions, where new entrants are formally inducted into the profession by careful supervision, mentoring, and other apprenticeship-like experiences, teachers too often are put into a classroom and left on their own without access to more seasoned teachers or formalized ways to work through with others the difficulties of any new professional confronted with the hard realities of transforming "book knowledge" into action. Although there has been a focus on support for beginning teachers and a call for induction programs to meet beginning teachers' needs, existing programs vary considerably. For some teachers, induction is merely a short nuts-and-bolts orientation: for example, where supplies are kept, where restrooms are located, and what the school rules and procedures are. Other teachers are fortunate enough to experience mentoring with experienced colleagues who have released time to coach them and model practices in the classroom and who pay careful attention to the beginning teachers' developing professional practice as they confront the hard realities of the classroom.

The contributors to this volume are indeed quite aware of the ramifications of sound practices in mentoring and induction and the range of contributions speak eloquently to the plethora of issues involved in mentoring and induction.

The import of participation by local, regional, and national policy makers in supporting induction and mentoring has indeed been a thorny issue. Linda

M. Kelley (2004, pp. 446–447), in a rather thought-provoking article, *Why Induction Matters*, concludes after a careful analysis of efforts by local, regional, and national policy makers in supporting/lack of supporting induction and mentoring that:

> Legislators and policy makers have failed to take a long view of what national, state, and local agencies might do to retain committed, effective teachers by providing the necessary financial resources and incentives for induction support and ongoing teacher development. In fact, historically U.S. school districts have paid insufficient attention to education's human resources, and this inattention has been and will continue to be financially and professionally costly. For example, NCTAF (1996) reported that induction programs are most likely to be eliminated during times of district budget reductions, decisions that inevitably produce deleterious consequences for school districts interested in retaining their novice teachers.

Maria Assunção Flores's piece, *Induction and Mentoring: Policy and Practice*, supports the findings and recommendations of the National Academy of Education and after investigating the ways in which a cohort of 14 novice teachers learned, developed, and changed over a two-year period concludes that induction is a key phase in the teacher's career which needs to be given more attention by policy makers, school leaders, teacher educators, teacher education providers and other stakeholders. Carole Basile's piece takes us down the road of possibilities when, despite the undulating support from legislators and policy makers, a collective consisting of concerned partners are willing to go beyond moral support for induction and mentoring. Basile portrays rather vividly the results of such collaborative action and based upon the research finding in one state she concludes that many organizations including school districts, institutions of higher education, businesses, NEA affiliate groups and policy groups have formed a partnership focused on comprehensive induction geared towards improving the efficacy of new teachers in the classroom.

Providing support (both morally and financially) is but one side of the equation for realizing the optimum benefits of induction and mentoring programs for new teachers. Equally important is the kind of programs that are developed. Wayne, Youngs, and Fleischman (2005, p. 76) point out that:

> Fewer than 1 percent of teachers get what the Alliance for Excellent Education (2004) calls a "comprehensive" induction package: a reduced number of course preparations, a helpful mentor in the same field, a seminar tailored to the needs of beginning teachers, strong communication with administrators, and time for planning and collaboration with other teachers. Such a package could make a real

> dent in teacher attrition, according to researchers who have investi-
> gated the variables that correlate with teacher turnover. For example,
> studies suggest that new teachers are more likely to continue teaching
> in their schools of origin when they receive mentoring from teachers
> in their subject areas. (Cohen, 2005; Smith & Ingersoll, 2004)

McIntyre, Smith, Gilbert, and Hilkirk describe a multi-layered mentorship *cum* induction teacher program that simultaneously bridges the gap that so often exists between professional teacher education programs at the tertiary educational levels and P–12 schooling. According to the results of their efforts, current and former Teaching Fellows as well as mentor teachers and school administrators reveal perceptions from each of the groups of a highly effective induction program. Similarly, Catherine K. Zeek and Carole Walker's depiction of what they refer to as a program that sees mentors as school-based educators yields promising prospects as they reflect on a program that quantitatively measures its effectiveness through high teacher retention rates, annual performance appraisals on which new teachers meet or exceed professional standards, and student achievement test results that often exceed district and state results. Qualitative measures, based on transactional inquiry, suggest that mentors take on a critical role as teacher educators, taking leadership responsibility for training novice teachers, directing professional development, and altering their school cultures.

Finally, one may argue that the *sine qua non* for effective induction and mentorship programs is the commitment and quality of those who provide leadership and execute such programs. Indeed, there are also the perceived benefits that those who provide such services receive from their engagement. Giles and Wilson (2004, pp. 90–91) point out a rather interesting notion to that effect:

> Mentors cannot be defined by a set of predetermined characteristics,
> instead "mentoring, like good teaching, should be defined by those
> who will carry it out" (Wildman et al., 1992). . . . The process of
> mentoring affords master teachers benefits, rewards, and opportuni-
> ties. Working with new teachers removes the isolation many teachers
> feel, creating one of the benefits of mentoring—a more collaborative
> environment (Ackley & Gall, 1992; Blank & Sindelar, 1992).
> Through interactions with mentees, mentors are stimulated both
> emotionally as well as intellectually (Zachary, 2000). Many mentors
> report a sense of satisfaction in their role as a mentor (Crow & Mat-
> thews, 1998; Stevens, 1999; Daresh, 2001). They enjoy sharing their
> expertise and seeing the mentees succeed (Zachary, 2000). They feel
> pride and a sense of self-worth for their efforts and are often reener-
> gized in their profession (Blank & Sindelar, 1992; Stevens, 1999).
> The questions mentees often ask cause mentors to be more introspec-
> tive and to gain new perspectives in a non-threatening arena (Abell et
> al., 1995; Crow & Matthews, 1998; Adkins, 1999; Zachary, 2000).

Mentors receive new ideas from their mentees as well as from mentor training. These new ideas help keep the mentors up to date on the latest ideas and educational theories, thus increasing their professionalism (Abell et al., 1995; Adkins, 1999; Stevens, 1999; Zachary, 2000).

Johnson and Reiman in their piece on the dispositions of mentors use an adaptation of the Flanders Interaction Analysis System and based on the findings of convergence and congruence, they make recommendations for professional development programs interested in examining mentor disposition. This piece strongly supports what is stated in the literature but goes even further to show the congruency between mentor professional judgment and professional action as constructs of disposition. Similarly, Kline and Salzman conclude in their study that qualitative analysis indicates group differences that reflect mentors' sense of collegiality and teaching efficacy while the two groups in their study performed best in communicating clear goals and procedures and worst in using questions and discussion techniques.

This *Research on Teacher Induction: Teacher Education Yearbook XIV* is especially relevant to the activities of ATE this year as it complements and is congruent with the theme I have selected for pursuit this year: Advocacy Through Engagement. I have selected this theme because despite the plethora of effort to reform teacher education and the preparation of teachers both for and in the classroom, one element still is left behind: preparing teachers and teacher candidates who genuinely understand the communities in which the majority of students spend most of their lives. More emphasis needs to be placed on genuine preparation of teachers who are fully prepared to "consider school, family, and community context in connecting concepts to students' prior experience and applying the ideas to real world problems." Indeed, what is needed is *engagement* with both the parents of students and their communities. This volume provides opportunities for learning about programs that address the issues of advocacy and engagement by teachers and teacher educators in the processes of schooling as well as how the profession may truly improve itself through collaborative relationships of induction and mentoring.

# References

Cohen, B. A. (2005). *Enhancing the "learning profession": Improving teacher retention.* Unpublished doctoral dissertation, University of Maryland, College Park.

Darling-Hammond, L., & Bransford, J. (Eds.). (2005). *Preparing teachers for a changing world: What teachers learn and should be able to do.* National Academy for Education. Draft document. Retrieved June 25, 2005 from www.nae.nyu.edu.

Giles, C., & Wilson, J. (April 2004). Receiving as well as giving: Mentors' perceptions of their professional development in one teacher induction program. *Mentoring and Tutoring, 12*(1), 87–106.

Kelley, L. M. (2004). Why induction matters. *Journal of Teacher Education, 55*(5), 438–448.

Smith, T. M., & Ingersoll, R. M. (2004). What are the effects of induction and mentoring on teacher turnover? *American Educational Research Journal, 4*(3), 681–714.

Wayne, A. J., Youngs, P., & Fleischman, F. (May 2005). Improving teacher induction. *Educational Leadership, 62*(8), 76–78.

# Introduction

*Julie Rainer Dangel*
Georgia State University

> Julie Rainer Dangel is associate professor in early childhood education at
> Georgia State University and currently coordinates the Doctoral Program.
> Her research interests include teacher development and constructivist theo-
> ries. She has published articles in a variety of journals and edited the recent
> publication by ATE: *Reframing Teacher Education: Dimensions of a Con-
> structivist Approach.*

*Research on Teacher Induction: Teacher Education Yearbook XIV* provides teachers
and teacher educators with current research, practical guidelines and thoughtful
critique as they examine the research, practice and policies related to issues of
induction. Many new teachers (about 30% nationally, with a higher rate in
most urban districts) leave the profession after one to three years of teaching,
and comprehensive teacher induction programs (including quality mentoring)
are proposed to meet the needs of new teachers, to improve teaching and student
learning, and to increase retention rates. This yearbook includes research papers
that address questions such as:

- What induction models are most successful in increasing retention rates for
  new teachers, having a positive effect on both teacher development and stu-
  dent learning?
- What are the important qualities of good mentors and good mentor training?
- What are the effects on teachers of having a quality mentor?
- What kind of school culture promotes teacher induction?

In this *Yearbook*, you will see research in three areas: (a) comprehensive approaches to induction, (b) the mentoring experience, and (c) designing and
implementing quality mentoring programs. You will find evidence of effective
models, an examination of conceptual and measurement challenges, the voices

of mentors and protégés, the effects of quality programs, and recommendations for policy-making.

There are metaphors, cross-case analyses, comparison studies, international viewpoints and longitudinal perspectives. In addition, you will find practical suggestions for improving the induction process and recommendations for improving teacher retention and performance.

# Organization of the Yearbook

The purpose of this *Yearbook* is to inform and guide teachers and teacher educators on complex issues and provide researchers interested in teacher education with current research in the area of induction. A conceptual framework, based on a triadic definition of scholarship—the production of knowledge, the interpretation and synthesis of knowledge, and the application of knowledge—is used to support this purpose. This framework also provides the organization for the yearbook. Each year, there is a call for research reports based on a significant topic and twelve manuscripts are accepted for publication in the yearbook. All research reports are blind reviewed and two to four reports in multiple divisions are published. Within the divisions, authors address a variety of issues illustrating the complex nature of the topic. A responder, a recognized scholar in the field, synthesizes, interprets, and applies results drawn from the selected research papers in each division. By providing interpretations and possible application of research, as well as the research studies, the *Yearbook* offers recommendations, raises questions and generates rich conversation around the issues of induction and mentoring. As editor of *Teacher Education Yearbook XIV*, I have the pleasure of reading all articles, providing me with an holistic perspective. I find this issue to be both informative and thought provoking and these readings leave me wondering. Just as a new baby (either born or adopted into a family) is celebrated, welcomed, nurtured and supported as they learn, why can we not think of new teachers in the same way? The authors and I welcome your thoughts, questions, recommendations, and continued research to further the conversation about the effects of teacher induction.

# Acknowledgments

I am indebted to Sujatha Bhagavati for her involvement in preparing this edition of the *Yearbook*. She makes this work manageable and enjoyable by her participation. Her initiative and organizational skills are a valuable contribution to this edition.

# COMPREHENSIVE APPROACHES TO INDUCTION

# Overview and Framework

## Leslie Huling
Texas State University–San Marcos

Leslie Huling is associate dean of education at Texas State University–San Marcos, and professor in the Department of Curriculum and Instruction. Currently she coordinates a number of collaborative initiatives involving the seven universities of the Texas State University System which are funded by the Texas Education Agency and the Houston Endowment. Recent mentoring projects include the Teacher Recruitment and Induction Program and Novice Teacher Induction Program. She is also the principal investigator for a Teacher Induction Study directed by the Center for Research Evaluation and Advancement of Teachers (CREATE), a collaborative research organization composed of the 27 teacher preparation institutions of the Texas A&M University System, the Texas State University System and the University of Texas System.

The four studies in this first division of the *Yearbook* examine the effects of various induction programs and approaches. In order to differentiate this section from the subsequent two sections, it is important to clarify the relationship between mentor programs and induction programs. While the terms "induction program" and "mentoring program" are often used interchangeably, it is sometimes helpful to distinguish between the two. A novice teacher induction program typically encompasses all of the support activities with a program, some of which do not necessarily involve the mentor teacher. For example, an orientation session for new employees, professional development specifically designed for new teachers, and support sessions with other novice teachers are all examples of induction program components that wouldn't necessarily involve the mentor teacher. Frequently, induction support can be provided more efficiently at a program level than being delivered by individual mentors. For example, a group session for novice teachers on how to use the district's "Sub-Finder" system would be more efficient than relying on each mentor to cover the topic individually with his/her mentee. This having been said, most professionals who work in the field of teacher induction believe the mentoring that occurs between an experienced teacher and a novice teacher is the most important aspect of the teacher induction program. As such, it is appropriate that two sections of the *Yearbook* be devoted to examining the mentoring experience and the implementation of mentor programs.

In this initial division, effects from a wide variety of induction programs are investigated. Studies from Colorado, New York and California, and even one from northern Portugal, are included. The New York and California studies each compare specifically defined programs, while the other two collect data from novice teachers in districts in which program approaches vary greatly. Three of the studies primarily use quantitative dimensions to guide their investigations, while the study from northern Portugal has a strong qualitative focus that reflects the novice teachers' experiences in their own words and voice. Studies of each type are important to advance our understanding of the complex phenomenon of teacher induction.

All of the studies grapple with methodological issues that are inherent in social science research. Given that randomly assigned groups are most often not a feasible option in working with novice teachers within a school or district, the New York and California studies identify paired groups to function as control groups with which to compare program effects. Such comparisons provide yet another important lens through which to examine induction program practices and effects. In each study, researchers attempt to balance the need for in-depth data with the practical reality that data requests can become overly burdensome to study participants and, in turn, can compromise data quality. Seasoned researchers recognize this fine line and the researchers in these four studies are to be commended for achieving a workable balance in this regard in their investigations.

In the respondent comments following the four studies, unique contributions of each study will be discussed as well as common themes that emerge across studies. Study results and their implications will be analyzed as they apply to both university-based and school-based teacher educators. Finally, the collective contribution of the four studies will be considered in the context of the broader field of teacher induction research to identify areas still in need of investigation and possible next steps for future researchers working in the area. Without further ado, four compelling studies of teacher induction programs and practices await your deliberation. My hope is that the reader finds these studies as intriguing and informative as this respondent has found them to be and further discussion will be resumed following the studies.

CHAPTER 1

# From Mentoring to the Colorado New Educator Consortium

## DEVELOPING A COMPREHENSIVE INDUCTION PLAN

*Carole Basile*
University of Colorado at Denver and Health Sciences Center

Carole Basile, Ed.D., is currently associate dean for teacher education and professional learning at the University of Colorado at Denver and Health Sciences Center. Her research focus is in the area of pluralistic context and the impact of context on learning. Areas of study have included environmental education, popular culture, school culture and humanity, and democracy in teacher education.

ABSTRACT

Educators agree that the need clearly exists for mentoring and supporting new teachers to bring them more purposefully and effectively into the profession. Through induction programs, districts aim to improve student learning and also retain good teachers in their schools. Unfortunately, given the lack of resources to support induction efforts, along with competing regulatory demands, induction program results remain uneven across the state. The benefits of strong programs, however, remain clear. In order for induction programs to be effective, state and local policymakers must consider new teachers' needs and the practices that best meet these needs, as well as identify the necessary resources and ensure their availability. In the spring of 2001, 1,331 teachers participated in a survey to identify the experiences of new teachers and professional staff participating in district induction and mentoring programs. As a result of the survey, many organizations including school districts, institutions of higher education, businesses, NEA affiliate groups, and policy groups have formed a partnership focused on comprehensive induction.

In 2003, the Mid-continent Research for Education and Learning (McREL) reported that in 2000 more than one in five Colorado teachers left the schools in which they were teaching and one out of ten left teaching. High-poverty and high-minority schools had attrition rates that were nine percentage points higher than low-poverty or low-minority schools. These attrition rates in high-poverty and high-minority schools contributed to the lower levels of teacher qualifications in those schools. In 2006, 18% of current teachers will be eligible to retire. Colorado hired almost 7,000 teachers in 2001, 44% of whom had no teaching experience and half of whom were trained in other states (Reichardt, 2003).

These statistics are daunting given the understanding that keeping high quality teachers in every classroom is an important factor in closing the achievement gap. Researchers show that student learning and achievement gains are influenced more by a student's assigned teacher than other factors like class size and class composition (Darling-Hammond & Youngs, 2002). Hanushek, Kain, and Rivkin (2001) and Wong (2004) find that having an effective teacher could close the gap in performance between students from low-income and high-income families. However, retaining effective teachers is a large problem (Berry, 2004).

Improving induction improves teacher quality and teacher retention (Ingersoll & Smith, 2004). Ingersoll & Smith point out that all occupations experience some loss of new entrants, but teaching consistently has alarmingly high rates of attrition among newcomers. Studies find as many as 50% of new teachers leave within the first five years of entry into the occupation (Huling-Austin, 1990; Ingersoll & Smith). Moreover, a significant negative correlation between teachers' likelihood of retention and scores on exams suggests that it is the best and brightest among the newcomers that appear to be most likely to leave (Henke, Chen, & Geis, 2000).

Organizational development literature suggests that high levels of employee turnover can cause ineffectiveness and low performance in organizations in addition to the overwhelming costs associated with replacing employees (i.e., professional development, recruiting). Therefore, induction must be a priority in high-need schools where turnover rates are exceedingly high and budgets increasingly low. Wong (2004) recommends not simply one-on-one mentoring, but induction that is "systemwide, coherent, comprehensive training and support for two to three years and becomes part of the lifelong professional development program of the district to keep new teachers teaching and improving toward increasing their effectiveness" (p. 6). In other words, induction leaders need to develop comprehensive induction programs that support new teachers, promote career learning and professional development, provide multiple support people and administrators, treat induction as part of a lifelong learning process, invest in an extensive, comprehensive, and sustained induction program, and acculturate a vision that aligns content to academic standards (Wong, 2004). These strong induction processes have the potential for increasing student achievement by increasing teacher effectiveness (Wong, 2003).

# Induction in Colorado

Colorado is a strong local-control state with its own constitution requiring local authority over education, since districts' needs and capacities differ substantially. With 178 school districts ranging in enrollment from 55 to 87,000 students and poverty levels that vary from 0% to 84% of students who are eligible for free and reduced-price lunch, Colorado's induction programs must respond to a unique set of teacher needs not seen in many other states, and induction program structures must reflect these needs. Colorado also has a diverse and unique teacher supply; more than half of all new teachers are prepared in other states, and up to 40% of the teachers trained within the state complete alternative programs (Reichardt, 2003). This variability in sources of teacher supplies results in variation in new teacher needs as they enter the Colorado teacher workforce. In 1991, the Colorado State Legislature passed new legislation for teacher licensure requiring that all districts hiring new teachers provide an approved induction program to support them during their first years of teaching. With good intentions, but no additional resources, districts set about designing induction programs and gaining Colorado Department of Education approval.

Educators agree that the need clearly exists for mentoring and supporting new teachers to bring them more purposefully and effectively into the profession. Through induction programs, districts aim to improve student learning and also retain good teachers in their schools. Unfortunately, given the lack of resources to support induction efforts, along with competing regulatory demands, induction program results remain uneven across the state. The benefits of strong programs, however, remain clear. In order for induction programs to be effective, state and local policy makers must consider new teachers' needs and

the practices that best meet these needs, as well as identify the necessary resources and ensure their availability.

# The Colorado Partnership for Educational Renewal's Induction Survey

In spring 2002, the Colorado Partnership for Educational Renewal (CoPER)
extended its efforts to understand the efficacy of district induction programs.
For two years through a U.S. D.O.E. Title II grant, CoPER had been supporting inquiry into and improvement of member district induction programs.
Through critical friends site visits in which focus groups of new teachers and
professional staff were conducted, CoPER collected valuable data, which were
then turned back to the districts to use for improving and renewing their respective programs.

To gain deeper understanding of induction efforts that would further enhance districts' ability to retain new teachers and help new and practicing teachers' continued professional development, CoPER staff then worked with a team
of researchers from its member universities to create a survey, which was sent to
approximately 2,000 new teachers and professional staff engaged in these induction and mentoring programs. The sixteen Partnership districts participating in
the effort to assess and refine induction differed considerably in size, location,
and demographics.

Ranging from slightly more than 2,000 to 88,000 students, districts clearly
brought different resources and scales to the induction effort. This variation
made it difficult to generalize or suggest that a single induction format or model
could be effective and efficient for all districts. Several common characteristics
of effective induction practice, however, emerged from the data collected, regardless of district size and characteristics of student population.

One thousand three hundred and thirty-one people participated in the survey. Ninety percent of the respondents were teachers; most were female (80%),
first-year teachers (53%), and worked in elementary schools (58%). Most were
between 22 and 30 years old (54%), and most were white (88%). A significant
majority of respondents came from two districts, Jefferson County (39%) and
Denver Public Schools (19%).

## OUTCOME MEASURES

Because the potential for educational improvement depends on the accessibility
of outcome information, great care was taken to create outcome measures (de-

pendent variables) from the data that yielded useful, reliable, and valid information. Seven outcome measures emerged from the study of 31 survey items relevant to either induction or mentoring activities. These were:

1. Structured (institutional) help from district and schools—a variable created by collapsing all of the questions (15a–h) indicating district or school activities relevant to new staff learning;
2. General mentoring help—a variable created by collapsing all of the questions (18a–h) indicating types of mentoring help provided to new staff learning;
3. Induction emphasis on district and school policies—questions 14a, 15g, 17g, and 18g;
4. Institutional efforts to promote diversity—questions 14e–g and 15a–c;
5. Mentoring efforts to promote diversity—questions 17a–c, 18a–c;
6. Institutional efforts to help boost teacher knowledge and skill—questions 14d, 15d–f, and 15h; and
7. Mentor efforts to help boost teacher knowledge and skill—questions 17d–f, 17h, 18d–f, 18h.

An eighth outcome variable, taken directly from the survey, item #25, "Overall, how do you feel about your mentoring experience?" also was used as a summary variable.

From these outcome variables, summary and individual, it was apparent that the survey distinguished between institutional efforts, conducted by school districts and individual schools, and mentor efforts, needed to address new staff needs as they learn and perform their duties in accord with state and district guidelines. Only one of the dependent variables (question 3) combined survey items both from sections relevant to the institutional efforts (questions 14 and 15) and mentoring efforts (questions 17 and 18), and so it was designated "*induction* emphasis on policies."

## DATA ANALYSIS

In addition to capturing the descriptive statistics for both the entire sample and individual district samples, multivariate analysis (MANOVA) was used initially to discern whether or not categorical variables—ethnicity, age, gender, years of experience, school district, and mentor status—had an impact on teachers' perceptions of the induction processes they experienced in the 2000–2001 school year. Results from multivariate analyses revealed that the independent variables of age, years of teaching experience, school district, and mentor status each significantly influenced this sample of teachers' perceptions with regard to two or more of the outcome measures. Subsequent analysis of variance tests (ANOVA) were then conducted to determine the effects the four categorical variables had on each of the outcome variables. Surprisingly, variables such as ethnicity, gender, and grade level failed to register sufficient levels of statistical significance (less than .05) with regard to the eight outcome variables. What follows is an explanation of the general trends that have been detected among all respondents. General trends for individual districts were reported to each of the twelve participating school districts.

Explanation of trends in this report relied primarily on the declaration of mean scores. All of the summary outcome variables, and most of the individual survey items after #13, required respondents to answer on a five-point scale, with "1" indicating the lowest rating and "5" indicating the highest rating. It is, therefore, safe to assume that: (a) "5" responses reflected respondents' perceptions of optimum effort, time, or help provided by induction staff; (b) "1" responses reflected respondents' perceptions of an absolute lack of effort, time, or help provided by induction staff; and (c) the response "3" reflected a middle position between these two extremes. For example, a mean score of 3.1 (appearing as "m = 3.1") for a group of respondents on outcome variable #3 indicated the group's perception that induction efforts to inform staff on policies were moderately helpful. Scores above this would be better. Scores significantly below this might indicate a problem area.

## RESULTS

In general, mentored younger teachers (ages 21–26) perceived general mentoring efforts to be more helpful than did older teachers (ages 32–65). Specifically, younger teachers perceived more mentor efforts to boost their knowledge and skill (m = 3.62) than did older teachers (m = 3.30). The category of teacher experience is related to the category of teacher age. Generally, first-year teachers perceived their mentors as more helpful than did all other teachers (m = 3.42 to m = 3.10). Specifically, they perceived more mentoring efforts to promote diversity (m = 3.16) than others (m = 2.80) and perceived more efforts to boost their knowledge and skills (m = 3.64) than others (m = 3.30).

Surprisingly, a relatively small percentage of teachers indicated a need for additional help in eight categories of assistance. Barely a quarter of respondents indicated they still needed help with respect to: (a) instructional strategies, (b) understanding school and district policies, (c) content and subject-area specific knowledge, (d) classroom management and student behavioral issues, (e) planning for and offering instruction to meet district and state standards, and (f) working with culturally and ethnically diverse students. However, a significantly greater percentage of teachers reported the need for additional help addressing the diversity of student learning styles (37%) and meeting the special needs of students in the classroom (42%).

**Mentor status.** The most significant results from this survey related to mentoring. Survey question 20 asked about the status of the mentor: (a) an on-site, same-content/grade-level teacher; (b) an on-site, different-content/grade-level teacher; (c) a teacher/specialist in another school; (d) a teacher who works full time mentoring new teachers; or (e) a retired teacher. The mentor-status variable that related most to outcome variables was 20d—full-time versus non-full-time mentors.

Full-time mentors were typically master teachers trained in coaching strategies, schooled in the fundamentals of adult education, and equipped to assist teachers whether they were from the same content area/grade level or not. Districts that sponsored programs for full-time or *intensive* mentoring programs were contrasted with all other forms of district and school-sponsored mentoring that depended primarily on the efforts of full-time teachers who devoted varying amounts of time and energy to the task of mentoring teachers new to the profession. Because mentor commitments can vary widely—often in response to emerging needs—*non*-full time mentors have been labeled *colleague-mentors* and their activities will be described as *colleague-mentoring.* Data from this study showed that first-year teachers who received intensive mentoring claimed to be mentored nearly every week (m = 3.86), while those with colleague-mentors claimed to be mentored somewhere between every month and weekly (m = 3.43).

Intensive mentoring led to significant differences in perceived outcomes with respect to both institutional and mentoring efforts geared toward meeting induction objectives. Those experiencing intensive mentoring, compared to those experiencing colleague-mentoring, (a) perceived more institutional help with the total induction process (m = 3.60 v 3.18), (b) experienced more mentoring help in general (m = 3.87 v. 3.17), (c) claimed to have received more information about school and district policy (m = 3.96 v. 3.59), (d) perceived more institutional help in the area of promoting diversity (m = 3.86 v 3.34), (e) claimed their mentors did more to promote diversity (m = 3.59 v. 2.92), (f) found their district and school did more to boost their professional knowledge and skills (m = 3.75 v. 3.33), (g) believed their mentors did more to boost their professional knowledge and skills (m = 4.07 v. 3.41), and (h) had more positive feelings about their experience (m = 4.70 v. 3.90). These marked differences suggest that intensive mentoring made an important difference in both the quality of induction activities and the professional development of teachers.

Intensive mentoring favorably related to the perceptions that new staff had toward their district/school. As mentors helped teachers become more knowledgeable about their content area, diversity issues, and learning standards, and as teachers became more competent regarding classroom management and instructional strategies, they were likely to promote learning more efficaciously in the school district. As mentored teachers succeeded professionally and grew in confidence *within a particular district and school,* they felt increasingly committed to that particular district/school. As such, the quality of mentoring, intensive or otherwise, could both increase teachers' sense of community and serve as a vehicle for augmenting faculty loyalty to school district and school. Moreover, individuals who felt a greater sense of community typically felt less overwhelmed and less burnt out. Intensive mentoring might prove prescriptive for school districts that suffer high staff turnover.

Data from this survey also underscored the importance of having on-site mentors assigned to protégés who share the same grade level or content area. On a 5-point scale denoting frequency of meetings—1 = not at all, 2 = 1 to 3 times total, 3 = every month, 4 = every week, and 5 = more than once a week— the mean score for teachers mentored by same content/level mentors was 3.87 v. 3.14 for all others. Proximity, coupled with similar teaching areas, appeared to relate significantly to frequency of mentor-protégé interactions. Those experiencing intensive mentoring met almost as often (m = 3.77), while those teachers matched with on-site, but different level/content-area mentors, met significantly less (m = 3.12). Additionally, the frequency of meetings related to mentoring effectiveness. Those teachers matched with on-site mentors with different level/content areas recorded significantly lower scores (m = 3.24) than did teachers mentored by same content/level mentors (m = 3.59) on outcome variable #7 (mentor efforts to help boost teacher knowledge and skill).

**District influence.** Given the differences among school districts—socioeconomic, age of staff, etc.—and given the differences in district samples and survey administration, different outcomes arose quite predictably from the data. As such, results on outcome measures viewed by individual districts must be interpreted with caution. However, in analyzing the data from this study, it was clear that teachers' perceptions of their own district's induction programs often differed considerably from the perceptions of teachers in other districts.

In general, new staff from all districts: (a) had positive, but widely ranging, feelings about their mentoring experience (m = 3.98; range means = 3.67 to 4.83); (b) perceived different amounts of institutional help with the total induction process (m = 3.25; range means = 2.66 to 3.77); (c) perceived modest to strong levels of general mentoring help (m = 3.27, range = 2.99 to 3.99); (d) experienced fewer institutional and mentoring efforts to address issues of diversity (m = 3.18 from institutions, m = 3.00 from mentors); (e) felt that induction staff were generally addressing district and school policy issues (m = 3.62); and (f) perceived that their districts and schools (m = 3.38, outcome variable #6) and mentors (3.48, outcome variable #7) were making efforts and being helpful with respect to increasing teachers' knowledge and skill.

## LIMITATIONS OF THIS STUDY

With respect to mentoring, this survey provides a cursory glance at processes that further the development of teacher knowledge and practices. It addresses, in general terms, issues tied to inclusionary practices, classroom management, content specialties, learning standards, and district and school policy. However, information about specific mentoring practices—such as the extent to which encouragement and emotional support were provided or the degree to which teachers' assumptions and behaviors were challenged—is absent. This study does not illuminate the different strategies, common practices, and emphases utilized by intensive, colleague, and other mentors. It would be enormously valuable to discern the specific and patterned mentor behaviors that engender protégé feelings of optimism with regard to the teaching profession.

Additionally, this study does not differentiate among practices occurring in different educational contexts, including different schools within districts. A particular school culture can have an enormous impact on the degree of teacher learning and the degree of collaboration, and by extension, a district culture is likely to influence the particular manifestations that either colleague-mentoring or intensive mentoring take (Bryk & Driscoll, 1988). It could be valuable to discern how facets of district or school culture augment or diminish the capacity of new staff to grow in confidence and professional competence.

Finally, this study does not directly measure the primary goal of educational improvement—increasing student learning. New staff perceptions of their experiences *suggest* what might be happening in the course of teacher growth and development, but these perceptions do not constitute empirical evidence that beneficiaries of intensive mentoring—or on-site same content/level mentors—are, in fact, increasing the learning and academic achievement of children. To address this question, an experimental design involving achievement measures of students taught by differently mentored-teachers is required.

# The Challenges for Districts

Unfortunately, given the context of a teacher shortage and the high cost of preparing and inducting new teachers who leave the profession, most districts fall short of one or more of the key elements for effective induction. These shortcomings often relate to the lack of adequate resources and the high number of new teachers requiring induction, as well as a frequent lack of understanding of what new teachers need.

Many districts lack sufficient numbers of mentors who are adequately trained to provide support to a new teacher. This can be a factor of the number of new teachers in a school or district, as well as a lack of interest and time on the part of veteran teachers. Some districts have adopted strategies such as full-time release for a small number of teachers to act as mentors, with ongoing support for the mentors during the year. This release position is similar to a sabbatical, in that it gives the veteran teachers a chance to renew their energies and acquire new skills, while at the same time providing excellent support to the new teachers. Another strategy that has been adopted is the use of recently retired teachers to act as mentors. In both cases, since these teachers do not have classrooms of their own, they are able to focus on the new teachers' needs, visit their classrooms more frequently, and meet during available planning times without scheduling conflicts. An alternative approach, using classroom teachers as mentors, requires the use of time during the school day that is gained through school-wide or district-wide strategies such as early release or late start days. These structures provide the mentor and mentee with additional time to meet without the worries of a classroom full of students.

Finally, regarding training, many districts are providing mentors with more training in strategies of teaching adult learners and peer coaching. One of the critical issues here is that a mentor, in addition to being a friend and showing the new teacher where the supply cabinet is or informing them about school traditions, needs to help a new teacher grow into a highly skilled teacher. One approach is to show the teacher "how it is done"; but this risks both perpetuating the status quo and alienating a new teacher whose personality or style may not quite match the mentor's. Another approach is to help the new teacher learn to reflect on her/his own practice, consider areas in which s/he is doing well or needs improvement, and learn where to go for resources, ideas, and help. This produces, rather than a clone of the mentor, a teacher with a fresh perspective and the tools needed to continuously reassess what s/he is doing, what is working, and what needs to change. The latter is, of course, more dynamic and better equipped to adapt to changes in the school, district, and community.

It is not surprising to find that many administrators are uncertain of how to support new teachers. Oftentimes, providing comprehensive support is not part of their preparation and many administrators themselves receive no induction for their jobs. Some districts have recently started providing principals and central administrators with more professional development in this area, recognizing that the role of the principal must go beyond that of evaluator. At the same time, the current review of principal preparation and licensure underway at the state level may help ensure that future principals see the induction of new teachers as part of their role.

# The Colorado New Educator Consortium: Moving Toward Comprehensive Induction

The Colorado New Educator Consortium (CNEC) has been created in response to the challenges and needs for comprehensive induction statewide. CNEC represents districts, institutions of higher education, and policy groups including the Colorado Partnership for Educational Renewal, the Front Range Board of Cooperative Education, the Public Education and Business Coalition, the Colorado Education Agency, the Alliance for Quality Teaching, the Colorado Principal Center, and the Center for Teaching, Learning, and Technology. The overall goal of CNEC is to build induction capacity over a five-year period within the state to implement high quality induction programs. The capacity building efforts will include:

1. State and local policymakers and community members;
2. Induction leaders and professional developers who structure and manage programs;
3. Principals who induct teachers into their schools;
4. Mentors that provide a key component of induction programs; and
5. Teacher educators and content specialists in institutions of higher education.

The work of the Colorado New Educator Consortium (CNEC) is to coordinate, research, build networks, and conduct professional development throughout the state to build the capacity to support comprehensive induction programs. Each of the participants in the induction system who has a role in creating and running induction programs faces a set of crucial challenges and decisions. The CNEC will structure its work to support participants in those decisions.

## POLICYMAKERS AND COMMUNITY LEADERS

Colorado policymakers and community leaders at both the state and district levels play an important role in structuring and supporting induction programs. In particular, they create the regulatory and legal structures for programs, allocate resources for programs, and provide oversight to programs. Currently, there are very few resources for deciding the appropriate structure and support from programs. In particular, while there have been some examples of good information on the quality of induction in Colorado, there are few tools available to Colorado policymakers to understand and evaluate the quality of their programs. The CNEC will work to support program standards and provide information on best practices around program costs to support policymaking and public engagement around induction.

## INDUCTION LEADERS

District administrators face an important set of decisions when they create induction programs and the high level of turnover in district administrators makes it difficult for school districts to develop and maintain high levels of expertise in managing induction programs (CASE, 2003). The CNEC will provide information to district administrators on effective induction practices. A network of induction leaders will serve as a professional learning community to build capacity within the group.

## PRINCIPALS

Principals play a crucial role in induction. Initial results from research on induction indicate that principals in Colorado regularly take the lead in orienting and integrating new teachers into their school operations and professional environments. Often, the principal's role in induction is expanded to include mentor selection and supervision and orientation to district procedures. At the same time, little support is available for these principals. Formal training does not exist, and much of the support they receive consists of checklists. The CNEC will work with principal preparation institutions in Colorado to develop a more robust set of supports for principals. This will include training, materials, and if appropriate, a collegial network of principals focused on induction.

## MENTORS

New teacher induction programs are required by state law to include mentors. At the same time, little guidance and support exists for districts beyond this requirement. This appears to result in wide variation in the quality, focus, and training of new mentors. In response to this issue, the CNEC will work to develop common mentor training with both materials and the professional development available through the CNEC. The intent of this training is not to supplant professional development by districts. Instead, it will be meant as a model for districts to learn from and modify as needed.

In addition, CNEC will capitalize on a group of master teachers that are part of an equity cadre. These mentors travel the state and have supported many novice and expert teachers in issues related to equity and diversity.

## INSTITUTIONS OF HIGHER EDUCATION

Jefferson County and Denver Public School district's, together with the University of Colorado at Denver and Health Sciences Center, have been involved in substantive conversations about possible models linking existing professional development schools to teacher recruitment, induction, retention, and leadership. Borrowing from the K–12 "looping" model where children stay with the same teacher for two or more years of instruction, CNEC is supporting an "induction looping" model with three critical components. The first component is that new teachers will be mentored by their previous pre-service mentors (university and school faculty) during the first several years of teaching. Like children whose learning increases because of the multi-year relationship with someone who knows their learning needs, the new teachers will benefit from the sustained relationship with their partner school site professor, site coordinator, and clinical teachers who know their learning needs in the profession. In addition, Colleges of Liberal Arts and Science also are contributing by providing access to content knowledge expertise that will assist teachers to become competent in their content area.

We believe that these efforts from the entire statewide community will create a comprehensive induction system for new teachers and create an environment in every district, no matter how large or small, urban or rural, that will build capacity for high quality teachers who remain in teaching. As one teacher put it, "I think the induction program really made me feel valued. If I were going to stay, that would be the reason."

# Acknowledgments

Thank you to Carol Wilson, Executive Director, Colorado Partnership for Educational Renewal; Robert Reichardt, Executive Director, Alliance for Quality Teaching; Elizabeth Parmelee and Chris Meager, Consulting Associates, Colorado Partnership for Educational Renewal for their contributions to this paper.

# References

Berry, B. (2004). Recruiting and retaining highly qualified teachers for hard-to-staff schools. *NASSP Bulletin, 87*(638), 5–27.

Bryk, A., & Driscoll, M. W. (1988). *The high school as community: Contextual influences and consequences for students and teachers.* Madison, WI: University of Wisconsin-Madison, National Center on Effective Secondary Schools.

Colorado Association of School Executives (CASE). (2003). *A view from inside: A candid look at today's school superintendent, 2003 Colorado school superintendent study.* Englewood, CO: Author.

Darling-Hammond, L., & Youngs, P. (2002). Defining "highly qualified teachers": What does "scientifically based research" actually tell us? *Educational Researcher, 31*(9), 13–25.

Hanushek, E. A., Kain, J. F., & Rivkin, S. (2001). *Why public schools lose teachers* (NBER Working Paper No. 8599). Cambridge, MA: National Bureau of Economic Research.

Henke, R., Chen, X., & Geis, S. (2000). *Progress through the teacher pipeline: 1992–93 college graduates and elementary/secondary school teaching as of 1997 (NCES 2000–152).* Washington, DC: U.S. Department of Education. National Center for Education Statistics, Office of Educational Research and Improvement.

Huling-Austin, L. (1990). Teacher induction programs and internships. In W. R. Houston (Ed.), *Handbook of research on teacher education* (pp. 535–548). Reston, VA: Association of Teacher Educators.

Ingersoll, R. M., & Smith, T. (2004). Do teacher induction and mentoring matter? *NASSP Bulletin, 87*(638), 28–40.

Reichardt, R. (2003). *Teacher supply and demand in the state of Colorado.* Aurora, CO: McREL.

Wong, H. (2003). Collaborating with colleagues to improve student learning. *ENC Focus, 11*(6), 9.

Wong, H. K. (2004). Induction programs that keep new teachers teaching and improving. *NASSP Bulletin, 87*(638), 5–27.

# CHAPTER 2

# Linking Teacher Induction, Teacher Development, and Student Learning

## AN EXAMINATION OF CONCEPTUAL AND MEASUREMENT CHALLENGES

*Jane Ashdown*
New York University

*Barbara Hummel-Rossi*
New York University

*Robert Tobias*
New York University

Jane Ashdown, Ph.D., is clinical associate professor in the Department of Teaching and Learning at New York University's Steinhardt School of Education. She serves as vice chair of that department. Formerly a classroom teacher in British primary schools, she currently teaches graduate courses in language and literacy development. She also directs the Ruth Horowitz Center for Teacher Development, which brings together field-based projects in New York City public schools with a focus on teacher professional development.

Barbara Hummel-Rossi, Ph.D., is associate professor of applied psychology at New York University, where she is director of the master's programs in psychological measurement and evaluation and in educational psychology in the Steinhardt School of Education's Department of Applied Psychology. She chairs the New York University Committee on Activities Involving Human Subjects, and teaches graduate level courses in research design, evaluation, measurement, and psychometrics.

Robert J. Tobias is the founding director of the Center for Research on Teaching and Learning within the Department of Teaching and Learning in New York University's Steinhardt School of Education. Professor Tobias served more than 13 years as the executive director of assessment and accountability for the New York City public schools. He has expertise in psychometrics, multivariate statistical analysis, research design, and program evaluation. He has conducted numerous evaluations of educational interventions and professional development and teacher education programs, and has authored more than 150 evaluation and research reports.

## ABSTRACT

Results from three pilot studies designed to evaluate the impact of differing induction practices on teacher development and student achievement are presented. The studies target beginning New York City public school teachers during the period 2002–2004 and employ a variety of measures and research methods. Results are mixed and attempts to establish causal relations among induction, teacher development, and student achievement prove difficult. The conceptual and measurement challenges associated with these findings are critically examined. Recent theorizing about the application of social cognitive theory to understanding schools' collective sense of agency with regard to educating students is proposed as a framework for induction research.

Several key education policy issues, such as concern about teacher shortages and teacher quality, have drawn the attention of the education community to the role of induction as it impacts the retention of new teachers in the teaching profession (NCLB, 2002). Induction typically has been treated as a dimension of teacher professional development targeted at addressing the problems associated with the beginning phase of a teacher's career. These problems include the revolving door syndrome of new teacher attrition, new teacher burnout, and the ability of the new teacher to maintain student academic progress (Gold, 1996; Ingersoll, 2001; NCTAF, 2003; Smith & Ingersoll, 2004; Strong, 1998).

Within this context, three teacher induction programs were developed and piloted in New York City public schools in 2002–2004. Although different in their design, these induction programs shared a common interest in linking the impact of the induction program directly to improved new teacher retention rates and to student achievement. However, during the evaluation of these induction programs we encountered conceptual and methodological problems common to all. Conceptually, all three programs were based on an input-output model in which the major input was some form of mentoring and the outputs were a variety of teacher behaviors and evidence of student achievement. In addition, each program emphasized some aspect of building a sense of professional community at each school site as a means of supporting and retaining new teachers. However, the evaluation designs proved inadequate for capturing these processes. This reflected a weakness in much production-function research that fails to investigate *how* programs work (Cohen, Raudenbush, & Ball, 2003). Methodologically the major problems associated with each program were related to the challenges of developing appropriate comparison groups and measures of teacher effectiveness. Again these are problems frequently encountered in educational research in meeting standards for good internal and external validity of research designs (Campbell & Stanley, 1963).

To address these difficulties in evaluating the induction programs described herein, it is hypothesized that understanding the effects of induction requires conceptualizing and evaluating induction practices as they occur within the interactions of beginning teachers, mentors, students, the curriculum, and the school community. In this chapter we propose that the concept of collective sense of efficacy as developed by Bandura (1997; 2000) and further applied to education by Goddard, Hoy, and Woolfolk Hoy (2000, 2004) provides a framework for understanding the processes that occur in a school that help to make new teachers effective in their practice. Collective efficacy is based on social cognitive theory and describes teachers' collective perceptions within a school about the extent to which their joint efforts can positively impact students' learning. This perspective on induction, as a key variable in schools' collective sense of agency, is proposed as a potential framework for the conceptual and measurement challenges encountered in the evaluation research reported herein. The concept of collective efficacy provides a means of addressing both the question of whether induction works and the question of how it works to improve teaching effectiveness in relation to student achievement.

# Objectives of the Three Induction Programs

The three teacher induction studies reported herein were implemented during 2002–2004 in New York City (Hummel-Rossi, 2005; Tobias & McCutchen,

2004; Tobias & McDonald, 2004a; Tobias & McDonald, 2004b; Tobias & McDonald, 2004c). Each induction project targeted a group of public school teachers working with a highly diverse student population. The majority of these students were receiving free or reduced-price school lunches.

In the Accelerated Teacher Preparation (ATP) program new middle and high school math or science teachers (N = 30) with undergraduate degrees in math or science, but no training in pedagogy, were enrolled in an accelerated master's degree program in either math or science education in the Department of Teaching and Learning at New York University. These ATP teachers participated in this master's program alongside their full-time teaching positions. They took classes together, including a special seminar designed specifically for the ATP program. A sense of professional community was fostered by the highly selective nature of the program, their progression through the program as a cohort, and the university-based master teachers assigned to mentor them. The master teachers observed the ATP teachers teaching in their schools and provided feedback. This constituted an induction program that included elements of teacher preparation as these teachers were in their first few years of teaching, but they had no prior experiences of coursework in pedagogy.

The Professional Development Laboratory (PDL) induction program for new middle school teachers provided in-school Resident Teachers who served as mentors for the new teachers. New teachers were observed and coached by the Resident Teachers and the new teachers observed the Resident Teachers' classrooms. Additionally, new teachers enrolled in a PDL Teacher Leadership Institute designed to assist them in developing effective teaching strategies and leadership capacity. By helping the new teacher become more competent as a teacher, the program attempted to strengthen teacher efficacy and, thus, positively impact student achievement.

The New Educator Support Team (NEST) was an induction program that operated in three elementary schools, four middle schools, and four high schools, and provided customized activities that met the specific needs of beginning teachers in the context of their school community. NEST aimed to facilitate the entry of new teachers into the school community, increase their rate of retention in their schools, and help them maintain the academic growth of their students. Services offered new teachers in these schools included study groups, peer coaching in pairs or triads, individual mentoring from a NEST coach teacher, workshops, and resource materials. More experienced teachers in the schools were also invited to participate; thus a sense of professional responsibility toward beginning teachers was fostered across each school community.

# Methods and Results

## THE ACCELERATED TEACHER PREPARATION (ATP) PROGRAM

### Objectives of the Evaluation

The evaluation of this induction program was viewed as a piloting of a new measurement instrument and of a research methodology for studying changes in teacher behavior. The specific research objective studied in this program was the extent to which new teachers, with no prior pedagogy training, improved with regard to their teaching abilities over the course of the school year. Improvement was treated as a dimension of teachers' development as reflective practitioners.

### Method

The question of how to measure teacher improvement was addressed first. A review of the available instruments revealed a plethora of teacher self-report surveys, supervisor ratings, and observation instruments with psychometric characteristics ranging from nonexistent to fairly decent, but none appropriate for the purpose at hand. It was determined that actual observation of teacher behavior by trained observers was probably the most accurate means of examining changes in teacher behavior. An observation protocol was developed from the work of Danielson (1996, adapted with permission) that offers an observation and self-assessment tool for application in four areas of teachers' professional competence: planning and preparation, classroom environment, instruction, and professional practice. A master teacher in science, a master teacher in math, and two measurement and research specialists modified Danielson's work so as to have a useable observation instrument that was consistent with the philosophy of teaching on which the induction program was based, that is, to become a reflective teacher who continually analyzed and critically reflected upon his/her behavior. The instrument development work, which included several rounds of field-testing, provided evidence of content validity. The resulting instrument, the Domain Referenced Teacher Observation (DRTO) scale, has 29 items and uses a five-point response option to reflect varying levels of proficiency for each behavior. Scores have a possible range of 29 to 145, with a high score indicating high proficiency in teaching. An inter-rater agreement study with two master teachers led to further instrument clarification and finally to inter-rater agreement of 100 percent. The instrument is intended for use by a master teacher and only has psychometric support for a professional at this level.

To determine if any changes that the teachers might exhibit were due to the induction program and not to their maturing as teachers, a constructed control group was created to compare this group's teaching behaviors to that of the program teachers. Six science teacher dyads ($N = 12$), each consisting of an ATP science teacher and a matched control, were selected. Two teacher dyads were at the middle school level, two in regular high schools, and two in alternative high schools. The primary criteria for the selection of the controls were that they were new teachers and teaching a similar science course at the same school as their matched pairs. The control teachers received a mandated mentoring service provided by each school. The ATP teachers received this same service in addition to the ATP program services, which consisted of participation in university education courses as a cohort plus intensive school-based coaching from a master teacher from the university program. Constructing the dyads required considerable effort and, as this was a pilot of the methodology, program/control dyads were not created with the math teachers. The teacher dyads were observed in the fall, mid-year, and end of year by a master science teacher using the newly developed observation protocol. After each observation the master teacher provided feedback to the program teachers on how they might improve their teaching. In his feedback, the master teacher focused on six items of the protocol that he believed were most important and most amenable to change through the coaching process. The constructed control teachers received no feedback during the year; at the end of the school year these teachers were given gift cards to use for classroom materials.

### Results

Two scores were created for each teacher at each observation time period: a total score based on all 29 items and a subtotal score based on the six target items selected by the master science teacher. The means at each time period for both groups are given in table 2.1.

Inspection of the means showed a small increase over the course of the school year for the program teachers on both the total and the subtotal scores, while the control teachers stayed relatively the same. The ATP teachers had a higher mean score at the beginning of the school year and this difference increased over the course of the school year. A nonparametric Mann-Whitney U test showed this difference not to be significant for either the beginning year total or subtotal tests, but significant for both the total and subtotal scores in midyear and end of year. This suggests that the program had a positive effect

**Table 2.1   Comparison of Mean Domain Referenced Teacher Observation (DRTO) Scale Scores for Accelerated Teacher Preparation (ATP) Program and Control Group Teachers at Three Observation Times**

| | Observation Time | | | | | |
| | Beginning of Year | | Mid-Year | | End of Year | |
| Teachers | Total Score | Subtotal Score | Total Score* | Subtotal Score* | Total Score* | Subtotal Score* |
|---|---|---|---|---|---|---|
| ATP | 58.00 | 12.00 | 59.33 | 12.33 | 60.67 | 13.00 |
| Control | 49.83 | 10.83 | 50.67 | 10.83 | 49.83 | 10.50 |

*Statistically significant difference between ATP and Control Group at p < .05, Mann-Whitney U test.
Note 1. N = 6 in each group.
Note 2. Items scored on a 5-point scale as follows: 1 Not Proficient, 2 Partially Proficient, 3 Approaching Proficient, 4 Proficient, and 5 Distinguished.
Note 3. Total Score based on 29 items with a minimum of 29 and a maximum of 145; Subtotal Score based on 6 items targeted by ATP with a minimum of 6 and a maximum of 30.

on the new ATP teachers' teaching skills. The reader is cautioned that these results are based on a small sample size and must be replicated. Note also that these teachers are at an early stage of professional development; the ATP teachers' end of year total mean of 60.67 and subtotal mean of 13.00 reflect item means of 2.09 and 2.17, respectively, which is interpreted from the response options as being at the lower end of the "partially proficient" category (table 2.2). However, these ATP teachers are doing better than the constructed control teachers whose end of year total mean of 49.83 and subtotal mean of 10.50 yield item means of 1.72 and 1.75, respectively. These means place them somewhat near the upper end of the "not proficient" category.

**Table 2.2   Mean DRTO Item Scores for ATP and Control Group Teachers at Three Observation Times**

| | Observation Time | | | | | |
| | Beginning of Year | | Mid-Year | | End of Year | |
| Teachers | Total Score | Subtotal Score | Total Score | Subtotal Score | Total Score | Subtotal Score |
|---|---|---|---|---|---|---|
| ATP | 2.00 | 2.00 | 2.05 | 2.06 | 2.09 | 2.17 |
| Control | 1.72 | 1.81 | 1.75 | 1.81 | 1.72 | 1.75 |

Note 1. See table 2.1.
Note 2. See table 2.1.
Note 3. See table 2.1 for number of items for each score. Minimum is 1 and maximum is 5 for each score.

## THE PROFESSIONAL DEVELOPMENT LABORATORY PROGRAM (PDL)

### Objectives of the Evaluation

The PDL induction program incorporated a number of service components and the overarching objective of the evaluation was to examine the extent to which these support services contributed to the retention of beginning teachers, the development of their professional competency, and their effectiveness with students. The evaluation also addressed the development of mentoring skills in those experienced teachers who served as New Teacher Facilitators and Resident Teachers. For the purposes of this chapter, only data collected to examine the development of new teachers were used.

### Method

To examine the extent to which the students of new teachers maintained similar academic progress to those students taught by more experienced teachers in the same schools, results from a state-wide, standardized assessment of students' performance in English Language Arts (ELA) were used. Data were obtained across four middle schools on 267 students taught by 12 new teachers participating in the PDL program and on 2,198 students taught by more experienced teachers who were not participating in the PDL induction program for a total of 2,465 students.

New teachers' sense of their effectiveness as teachers was assessed through the Teacher Efficacy Scale (TES) (Gibson & Dembo, 1984). The 30-item TES was developed to measure teachers' sense of efficacy as it relates to teacher behavior in the classroom and to student achievement. Individuals indicate their degree of agreement or disagreement with each item on a six-point Likert-type response. Gibson and Dembo used factor analysis to confirm the existence of two underlying factors: Personal Teaching Efficacy and General Teaching Efficacy. These two factors corresponded to their theoretical constructs of teacher self-efficacy and teacher outcome expectancy, respectively. Continued factor analytic research with the 30-item instrument found that several items loaded on both factors, leading some researchers to revise the scale to a shortened 16-item version with each item loading uniquely on one of the two factors (Woolfolk & Hoy, 1990). The questionnaire used in this study was the 16-item version of the TES consisting of nine items designed to measure Personal Teaching Efficacy and seven items to measure General Teaching Efficacy. The items are scored so that a high score indicates high efficacy; scores range from 16 to 96.

Based on the validity and reliability findings of the Domain Referenced

Teacher Observation (DRTO) scale as piloted in the ATP program, this instrument was employed to observe new teachers in their classrooms. Three master teachers were trained in use of the DRTO scale; however, after two days of training it became apparent that one master teacher did not subscribe to the philosophy of teaching on which the DRTO scale was based. This individual was removed from the study. Ten new teachers were observed twice during the spring semester of the school year in which they participated in the induction program.

## Results

Considering first the achievement of the students taught by the PDL and non-PDL teachers, means and standard deviations were obtained for each student at the end of 2002, the pre-induction year, and at the end of 2003, the induction year. Data were obtained for the sixth and seventh grade students of 12 PDL teachers and for the remaining teachers in the four middle schools who were not receiving PDL services. Data were not available for the eighth grade students as a test publisher scoring error nullified their scores for 2002. In three schools the PDL teachers' students showed greater gains than their more experienced counterparts' students, and in one school the PDL teachers' students showed a smaller gain than their colleagues' students. For the total group of 12 PDL teachers there was no statistically significant difference in gain in student achievement between those new teachers receiving PDL services and their more experienced colleagues.

To measure teachers' sense of their instructional efficacy, in fall 2002 the Teacher Facilitators gave the Teacher Efficacy Scale (TES) to 67 new teachers to complete and return in postage-paid reply envelopes. Forty-eight of the teachers (72%) completed and returned the TES. In May the Teacher Facilitators were provided with copies of the TES and return envelopes and requested to distribute the TES to the new teachers. Only 14 new teachers completed and returned the TES. Despite repeated requests to cooperate, the evaluator sensed that the Teacher Facilitators were so overwhelmed with work that they did not distribute the scale. Consequently, only fall data are reported. The fall mean on the Personal Teacher Efficacy subscale was 4.51 (SD = 1.13). This implies that these new teachers mildly agree that as individual teachers, they can impact a student's behavior and learning. The fall General Teacher Efficacy subscale mean was 3.74 (SD = 1.49) indicating mixed feelings about these new teachers' ability to influence student behavior given the impact of external elements, such as family and home environment.

Teacher observations using the Domain Referenced Teacher Observation (DRTO) scale were scheduled for the end of March and mid-June. Initially

13 teachers through their Teacher Facilitators volunteered to be observed, but scheduling conflicts did not permit the second observation of three teachers and, therefore, results are presented for ten of the new teachers. The focus of the evaluation was teacher performance on all four domains measured by the DRTO and, therefore, data for all four domains are presented as well as the six items targeted in the ATP project.

Examination of the data shows a small increase in each domain from the March observations to the June observations (see table 2.3). By mid-June these new teachers were rated as "approaching proficient" in each of the four domains of competency. On the six-item subtotal used in the ATP project the teachers showed substantial growth during the two and one-half month period between the two observations. At the end of March the item mean score on the subtotal was 3.06 (SD = .79) and by mid-June the subtotal item mean was 3.22 (SD = .87), whereas the mean for the entire scale in mid-June was 3.08 (SD = .96) (see table 2.4). However, Wilcoxon matched-pair tests on the total, subtotal, and domain scores revealed only a significant positive increase in the classroom environment domain.

## THE NEW EDUCATOR SUPPORT TEAM PROGRAM (NEST)

### Objectives of the Evaluation

The objectives of the NEST evaluation were to examine a broad range of summative effects of NEST services in participating schools to determine how NEST impacted the teachers, the schools, and the students served in those schools. Reported here are data addressing the impact of NEST on the capacity of new teachers to educate their students effectively and on the extent to which teacher retention rates were impacted in NEST schools.

### Method

The effect of NEST on the professional development of two cohorts of new teachers was assessed through classroom observations. Cohort 1 (N = 14) was composed of beginning teachers who had been served by NEST for three or four years. Cohort 2 (N = 27) included new teachers who had one or two years teaching experience in NEST schools and, consequently, had less opportunity to engage in NEST activities. In the spring semester of 2003, four trained observers (two from the PDL study) using the Domain Referenced Teacher Observation (DRTO) scale observed these 41 teachers in their classrooms.

The indirect effect of NEST upon the effectiveness of teaching and learning

**Table 2.3   Comparison of Mean DRTO Scores for Professional Development Lab (PDL) Teachers at Two Observation Times**

| Domain | Observation Time | | Mean Difference |
| | March | June | |
| --- | --- | --- | --- |
| Planning and Preparation | 40.45 | 43.33 | 2.88 |
| Classroom Environment | 21.48 | 23.45 | 1.97* |
| Instruction | 11.95 | 12.33 | 0.38 |
| Professional Responsibility | 12.38 | 12.45 | 0.07 |
| Total Score | 86.25 | 91.55 | 5.30 |
| Subtotal Score | 18.55 | 19.65 | 1.10 |

*Statistically significant difference between first and second observation mean scores at $p < .01$, for a one-tailed Wilcoxon matched pairs signed ranks test, with three cases eliminated due to ties.
Note 1. N = 10
Note 2. Items scored on a 5-point scale as follows: 1 Not Proficient, 2 Partially Proficient, 3 Approaching Proficient, 4 Proficient, and 5 Distinguished.
Note 3. Numbers of items and scoring ranges for each domain are as follows: Planning and Preparation based on 14 items with a minimum of 14 and a maximum of 70; Classroom Environment based on 7 items with a minimum of 7 and a maximum of 35; Instruction and Professional Responsibility each based on 4 items with a minimum of 4 and a maximum of 20; Total Score based on 29 items with a minimum of 29 and a maximum of 145; Subtotal Score based on 6 targeted items with a minimum of 6 and a maximum of 30.

was assessed by analyzing the results of standardized tests of English Language Arts (ELA) and math in three NEST elementary schools and one NEST middle school over a two-year period. Changes in performance of NEST school students over three test administrations (1999, 2000, 2001) were compared to changes in student performance in each NEST school's respective district. The analysis employed two metrics: mean scale scores and the percentage of students

**Table 2.4   Mean DRTO Item Scores for PDL Teachers at Two Observation Times**

| Domain | Observation Time | | Mean Difference |
| | March | June | |
| --- | --- | --- | --- |
| Planning and Preparation | 2.89 | 3.00 | 0.11 |
| Classroom Environment | 2.90 | 3.06 | 0.16 |
| Instruction | 3.08 | 3.16 | 0.08 |
| Professional Responsibility | 3.07 | 3.17 | 0.10 |
| Total Score | 2.98 | 3.08 | 0.10 |
| Subtotal Score | 3.06 | 3.22 | 0.16 |

Note 1. See table 2.3.
Note 2. See table 2.3
Note 3. See table 2.3 for numbers of items for each domain score. Minimum item score is 1 and the maximum is 5 for each domain.

meeting or exceeding New York State performance standards, i.e., scoring in performance levels three or four on a four-level scale. Data were extracted from publicly available databases reported on the New York City Department of Education (NYCDOE) website.

Finally, the retention rates of a cohort of new teachers with no more than five years of total teaching experience in each of eight NEST schools were compared with retention rates for new teachers in all other elementary and middle schools in the same school districts across two school years, beginning in September 2000. Teachers were divided into three status categories: remained in the same school, transferred to another school in the NYCDOE, or left the NYCDOE.

## Results

Table 2.5 presents the results of a comparison of the observation ratings for the two cohorts of new teachers who were observed teaching in their classrooms by trained observers using the DRTO scale. For all four dimensions of practice, the mean item ratings for Cohort 1 teachers (three or four years participation in NEST activities) were higher than those of Cohort 2 teachers (two or fewer years participation in NEST). Overall, the mean item ratings for Cohort 1 teachers were firmly in Level 3 (approaching proficient), while those for Cohort 2 were at the high end of Level 2 (partially proficient) to the low end of Level 3. The mean differences between the cohorts were not statistically significant,

**Table 2.5   Means and Standard Deviations (SD) for DRTO Item Scores of Cohort 1 and Cohort 2 New Educator Support Team (NEST) Teachers**

|  | Groups | | Mean Difference* | Effect Size |
|---|---|---|---|---|
|  | Cohort 1 | Cohort 2 | | |
| Planning and Preparation | 3.23 (0.75) | 2.87 (0.66) | 0.36 | 0.55 |
| Classroom Environment | 3.25 (0.80) | 3.00 (0.68) | 0.25 | 0.37 |
| Instruction | 3.28 (0.82) | 2.90 (0.62) | 0.38 | 0.61 |
| Professional Responsibility | 3.38 (0.86) | 3.15 (0.70) | 0.23 | 0.33 |
| Total Score | 3.29 (0.76) | 3.00 (0.61) | 0.29 | 0.48 |
| Subtotal Score | 3.39 (0.62) | 3.02 (0.57) | 0.37 | 0.65 |

*No significant differences between Cohorts 1 and 2 at $p < .05$, for t-tests for independent samples.
Note 1. Cohort 1 N = 14, Cohort 2 N = 27.
Note 2. Items scored on a 5-point scale as follows: 1 Not Proficient, 2 Partially Proficient, 3 Approaching Proficient, 4 Proficient, and 5 Distinguished.
Note 3. Numbers of items for each domain are as follows: Planning and Preparation based on 14 items, Classroom Environment based on 7 items, Instruction and Professional Responsibility each based on 4 items, Total Score based on 29 items, and Subtotal Score based on 6 targeted items.

perhaps due to the small sample size. Examination of effect size (Cohen, 1977) revealed that the differences for the planning and preparation and the instruction dimensions were moderately meaningful, while those for the classroom environment and professional responsibilities dimensions were small.

The comparison of student achievement test score changes in ELA and math for four NEST schools compared to all other elementary and middle school scores in their respective school districts over two academic years were mixed. In two districts, the NEST schools showed dramatically larger increases in both ELA and math over the two years, as compared to the other schools in their respective districts. The remaining two NEST schools had changes similar to the other schools in their districts in both ELA and math. It was clear that more in-depth case analysis was needed to investigate these differences.

Finally, the possible impact of NEST on new teacher retention was considered. New teachers (N = 329) with no more than five years experience in eight NEST schools for which data were available and new teachers in all other schools in the districts of these eight NEST schools were tracked for two years beginning in September 2000. Teacher status was classified as remaining in the same school, transferred to another school in NYCDOE or left NYCDOE employment. Differences in retention rates between NEST schools and the other schools in their districts varied widely from school to school and no clear effect of NEST on retention was identified from this analysis.

In summary, all three of these induction programs positively impacted the new teachers that they served. The ATP new teachers demonstrated greater teaching skills than their matched counterparts at the end of the school year, the PDL new teachers were "approaching proficiency" in their teaching and their students were performing as well as those of their more experienced colleagues in their districts, and the new NEST teachers also were gaining greater proficiency as teachers the longer they remained in the program.

# Lessons Learned

All three of these research studies were challenged by obstacles encountered when conducting research in the field and valuable lessons for research on teacher induction can be gleaned from them. First, from a methodological perspective, it is clear that induction is a complex process and measuring the impact of an induction program requires multiple methods. Much of the research on induction is either analyses of large databases or small sample case studies. While these methods are valuable tools in induction research, they should be supplemented by other methods capable of capturing different types of information. The gold standard in research is the randomized control group; it is unlikely that this standard can be achieved in induction research, but approximation is possible. The use of the constructed control group in the ATP study was somewhat difficult to create; however, it proved to be valuable for studying the impact of ATP on the new teacher. Hypothesizing that new teachers who experience different levels of program implementation should exhibit different behavior, as with the two NEST teacher cohorts, is another method for establishing comparison groups. As in PDL, comparing the achievement of students taught by new teachers in an induction program, new teachers not in an induction program, and experienced teachers in the induction teachers' schools or school districts provides an indicator of the effectiveness of the induction program on the ultimate criterion, student achievement.

The development of the Domain Referenced Teacher Observation (DRTO) scale and the validity and reliability evidence that was gathered in the studies described herein represents a valuable contribution to induction research methodology. Evidence of construct validity is found in the change in the expected direction of new teachers' ratings as they progressed through the programs and of the higher ratings of those teachers who were in the program the longest. For each of the programs, the substantial changes in ratings over time on the six subtotal items theorized to be most amenable to change provides further support for the construct validity. Evidence of content validity is found in the DRTO's foundation in Danielson's (1996) work and its development and field-testing by master teachers and measurement specialists. Six observers were trained to 99 to 100 percent interrater agreement and they maintained this level of agreement throughout the research. The reader is cautioned that this observation instrument can be used only by master teachers who are thoroughly informed on pedagogy and who subscribe to a theory of teaching as described by Danielson.

The evaluations for these three studies were constrained by resource limitations. For example, the return rate for the Teacher Efficacy Scale (TES) follow-up data collection was very low in the PDL program. Data collection was dependent on the cooperation of Teacher Facilitators who had many demands on their time in relation to the delivery of program services. Without adequate levels of evaluation staff it was not possible to get a full return on the TES. Similarly, limited staffing resources in the ATP program did not permit construction of a control group for the math teachers. The mixed results for the student achievement and teacher retention data in the NEST program indicated a need to examine how within school variables impacted these outcomes. Staffing limitations did not permit a multi-method design that incorporated in depth, on-site case analyses except in one site.

From a conceptual perspective, it is important for the completion of a comprehensive evaluation to clarify the theoretical underpinnings of induction models. For example, each induction program described in this chapter incorporated building a sense of professional community within its implementation. However, this concept was not well developed or articulated. The subsequent evaluations did not adequately capture how fostering a sense of professional community functioned in relation to new teacher development and retention, as well as in relation to student achievement. Yet, such data could be informative in explaining the mixed results from both the NEST and the PDL programs. While in the PDL evaluation an attempt was made to examine individual new teachers' sense of their instructional efficacy, this was not examined at the school level. Goddard, Hoy and Woolfolk Hoy (2004) observe that the construct of perceived collective efficacy in schools has received less attention from educational researchers than the efficacy beliefs of individual teachers. Measuring changes in perceptions of collective agency across a school faculty with regard to their joint capacity to support and retain new teachers, as well as to be instructionally effective with students, holds promise for evaluating how efforts to build professional community work as induction strategies. For example, attention to the role of social persuasion, such as feedback on teaching from a master teacher, as a source of information about both an individual teacher's efficacy beliefs about educating students as well as the sense of agency of all school faculty in this regard would contribute to understanding how induction works.

According to Smith and Ingersoll (2004) participation in teacher induction programs rose from about four in ten new teachers in 1990–91, to eight in ten new teachers in 1999–2000. Given this widespread implementation, it is critical that educational researchers adopt consistent methodological approaches that move beyond examining whether induction works to investigating *how* induction works to address the relations between teacher development, teacher retention, and student achievement. It can be argued that the impact of induction needs to be conceptualized and measured using data gathered from the interactions among school resources, induction practices, and school effects at both the level of the individual and at the level of the school. The application of social cognitive theory to understanding judgments about a school's collective sense of efficacy in relation to educating students, suggests that it is the empowerment experienced by teachers in fostering the success of their students that can make a significant impact on student achievement (Bandura, 1993). In conclusion, we propose that teacher induction should be examined through the lens of schools' collective efficacy beliefs, reflecting a comprehensive approach to understanding the induction environment.

# References

Bandura, A. (1993). Perceived self-efficacy in cognitive development and functioning. *Educational Psychologist, 28*(2), 117–148.

Bandura, A. (1997). *Self-efficacy: The exercise of control.* New York, NY: W.H. Freeman & Company.

Bandura, A. (2000). Exercise of human agency through collective efficacy. *Current Directions in Psychological Science, 9,* 75–78.

Campbell, D. T., & Stanley, J. C. (1963). *Experimental and quasi-experimental designs for research.* Boston: Houghton Mifflin Co.

Cohen, D. K., Raudenbush, S. W., & Ball, D. L. (2003). Resources, instruction and research. *Educational Evaluation and Policy Analysis, 25,* 119–142.

Cohen, J. (1977). *Statistical power analysis for the behavioral sciences.* New York, NY: Academic Press.

Danielson, C. (1996). *Enhancing professional practice: A framework for teaching.* Alexandria, VA: Association for Supervision and Curriculum Development.

Gibson, S., & Dembo, M. (1984). Teacher efficacy: A construct validation. *Journal of Educational Psychology, 76,* 569–582.

Goddard, R. D., Hoy, W. K., & Woolfolk Hoy, A. (2000). Collective teacher efficacy: Its meaning, measure, and impact on student achievement. *American Educational Research Journal, 37,* 479–507.

Goddard, R. D., Hoy, W. K., & Woolfolk Hoy, A. (2004). Collective efficacy beliefs: Theoretical developments, empirical evidence, and future directions. *Educational Researcher, 33*(3), 3–13.

Gold, Y. (1996). Beginning teacher support: Attrition, mentoring, and induction. In J. Sikula, T. J. Buttery, & E. Guyton (Eds.), *Handbook of Research on Teacher Education* (pp. 548–594). New York, NY: Macmillan Press.

Hummel-Rossi, B. (2005). *A case study evaluation of the Accelerated Teacher Preparation (ATP) program in mathematics and science.* (Draft paper). New York: New York University, Center for Research on Teaching and Learning.

Ingersoll, R. M. (2001). Teacher turnover and teacher shortages: An organizational analysis. *American Educational Research Journal, 38,* 459–534.

National Commission on Teaching and America's Future. (2003). *No dream denied: A pledge to America's children.* Washington, DC: National Commission on Teaching and America's Future.

No Child Left Behind Act of 2001, Pub. L. Nos. 107–110, 115 Stat. 1425 (2002).

Smith, T. M., & Ingersoll, R. M. (2004). What are the effects of induction and mentoring on beginning teacher turnover? *American Educational Research Journal, 41,* 681–714.

Strong, M. (1998). A study of reading performance among 1–3 grade students in classes taught by SCNTP teachers. *Research Paper #2.* Santa Cruz, CA: University of California, Santa Cruz.

Tobias, R., & McCutchen, R. (2004). *Report of the findings of the evaluation of the Professional Development Laboratory (PDL) programs in Community School District 20, 2002–2003.* (Tech. Rep.) New York: New York University, Center for Research on Teaching and Learning.

Tobias, R., & McDonald, E. (2004a). *Preliminary summary of findings, conclusions and recommendations for the New Educator Support Team (NEST).* (Tech. Rep.) New York: New York University, Center for Research on Teaching and Learning.

Tobias, R., & McDonald, E. (2004b, April). *Challenges in assessing teacher development and learning: The New Educator Support Team (NEST) as a case example.* Paper presented at the meeting of the American Educational Research Association, San Diego, CA.

Tobias, R., & McDonald, E. (2004c). *New Educator Support Team evaluation progress report, Evaluation year 1: 2002–2003* (Tech. Rep.). New York: New York University, Center for Research on Teaching and Learning.

Woolfolk, A. E., & Hoy, W. K. (1990). Prospective teachers' sense of efficacy and beliefs about control. *Journal of Educational Psychology, 82*, 81–91.

CHAPTER 3

# Induction and Mentoring

## POLICY AND PRACTICE

*Maria Assunção Flores*
University of Minho, Portugal

> Maria Assunção Flores is an assistant professor at the University of Minho,
> Portugal (e-mail: aflores@iep.uminho.pt). She received her Ph.D. at the
> University of Nottingham, UK. Her research interests include teacher pro-
> fessionalism, teacher education and change. She is currently working on
> teachers' professional development from a longitudinal perspective.

## ABSTRACT

This paper draws upon a broader piece of research aimed at investigating the ways in which a cohort of 14 novice teachers have learned,
developed and changed over a two-year period. A combination of
methods was used for data collection. The study highlights the key
role of idiosyncratic and contextual factors (and the interplay between them) in determining the success or failure of first teaching
experiences. It also supports the contention that induction is a key
phase in the teacher's career which needs to be given more attention
by policymakers, school leaders, teacher educators, teacher education providers and other stakeholders. Implications of the findings
for teachers and teacher educators are discussed.

Induction has been described in the literature as a key element in the professional development of teachers because the first years of teaching are crucial to
the formation and development of new teachers' attitudes, views and practices
of teaching as well as their understanding of themselves as professionals (Bolam,
1995; Day, 1999; Flores, 2001; Marcelo, 1999; Tickle, 1994, 2000). Bolam

(1987), for instance, arguing for a wide view of teacher professional development, drew attention to the "triple-I continuum of initial, induction, and in-service education and training" (p. 755). Similarly, Huling-Austin (1990) referred to induction programs as "logical extensions of the pre-service program and as entry pieces in a larger career-long professional-development program" (p. 535).

The lack of systematic attention to this period of the teacher's career has been described in the literature as the missing link (Hall, 1982), the great omission (Vonk, 1994) and the weakest link (Mahoney, 1996). Although this picture is no longer valid in some countries (e.g., USA, England, The Netherlands, Japan) where such induction programs do exist and where research into the first year of teaching has received increasing attention, it still remains the case for the contexts where this issue has not yet been addressed effectively (e.g., Portugal, Malta), in spite of recent research in this field which has highlighted its relevance (Alves, 2001; Braga, 2001; Couto, 1998; Flores, 1997; Mifsud, 1996; Silva, 1997).

Tickle (2000), in a recent book on this topic, asserted that induction constitutes "an unsolved problem" (p. 4) which he attributed to a number of pragmatic and structural reasons, which include: (a) the paradox of Newly Qualified Teachers (NQTs) "being inducted into old practices, traditions and circumstances in which behaviors are prescribed and performances assessed while expecting and being expected to participate as reformers in search of solutions to endemic educational problems" (p. 7); (b) logistical difficulties (problems in tracking NQTs as they move from different pre-service programs into diverse locations of employment); (c) the existence of different agencies in the provision of support for NQTs and, therefore, the existence of different interpretations of its role and conceptions of NQTs' needs; and (d) the varied nature of NQTs' educational background and their personal dispositions, their individual contexts of work, and the range of responsibilities they hold. A similar view is held by Fullan (1993) who contended that "induction programs to support beginning teachers are still very much in the minority, and good ones are rare, despite our very clear knowledge of needs of beginning teachers" (p. 106).

Bolam (1995) defined induction as "the process of support and training that is increasingly being seen as necessary for a successful first year of teaching" (p. 613). Schools, therefore, provide new entrants into the profession with a kind of systematic assistance and guidance which help them to deal with day-to-day difficulties inherent in teaching, fostering at the same time their professional growth through reflection. This view of induction has not been shared amongst researchers in the field; some have pointed to a more practical and sociological process of integration into the school culture (Pacheco, 1995; Schlechty, 1985), whereas others also have emphasized the need for promoting new teachers' professional autonomy and self-directed professional development (Vonk, 1993; Wilson & D'Arcy, 1987). Importantly, Tickle (2000) drew attention to the need for going beyond the "deficiency" approach and viewing novice teachers as "an enviable resource of intellectual capability, able to significantly help to transform education and to meet unforeseen challenges" (p. 2).

In a review of induction programs, Huling-Austin (1990) identified five major goals that were in general inherent in their rationale. These goals included "(a) to improve teaching performance; (b) to increase the retention of promising beginning teachers during the induction years; (c) to promote the personal and professional well-being of beginning teachers by improving teachers' attitudes toward themselves and the profession; (d) to satisfy mandated requirements related to induction and certification; and (e) to transmit the culture of the system to beginning teachers" (p. 539).

As for the strategies being put into place to provide new teachers with support and guidance, they have varied and may have included workshops, classroom observation, seminars, regular meetings with mentors, or provision of teaching material (Barrington, 2000; Huling-Austin, 1990; Marcelo, 1988; Wilson & D'Arcy, 1987; Wubbels, Créton, & Hooymayers, 1987). However, a central element in these induction programs has been the existence of a teacher-mentor at the school where new teachers work, as Huling-Austin (1990) stressed: "Probably the most consistent finding across studies is the importance of the support teacher (sometimes called the mentor teacher, the helping teacher, the peer teacher, or the buddy teacher)." (p. 542).

In this sense, the importance is to clarify the role, qualities and status of mentors, sometimes described as the "antidote" to reality shock (Marcelo, 1994). The importance of effective mentoring is well-documented in the literature, which highlights not only personal characteristics but also professional competencies (Ballantyne, Hansford, & Packer, 1995; Field & Field, 1994; Ganser, 1995; Klausmeier, 1994; Marcelo, 1994; Vonk, 1993).

Regardless of the broad or narrow view of the definition, mentors are usually more experienced colleagues who are responsible for providing help, directly or indirectly, to beginning teachers (Bolam, 1995). Their role may include giving general information, observing classrooms and feedback, promoting and engaging in discussion groups, being a liaison with other staff, Local Education Authorities or a university, evaluating new teachers' performance, and locating materials (Bolam; Huling-Austin, 1990; Marcelo, 1994). Personal and moral support has also been identified as being an important element in mentors' work (Adey, 1997; Ballantyne, Hansford, & Packer, 1995). Vonk (1994) also draws attention to the personal qualities of mentors: open-mindedness, reflectiveness, flexibility, listening skills, empathy, creativity and a helping attitude.

There is widespread acceptance of the need to promote the training of mentors (Huling-Austin, 1990; Vonk, 1993). Vonk proposes a mentoring model which is based on the dynamic understanding of the relationship between mentor and beginning teacher (or protégé). According to Vonk, in addition to personal characteristics and expertise in subject matter and in pedagogy, mentors should possess a knowledge base, which comprises three elements: (a) insight in and understanding of the process of beginning teachers' professional development, (b) knowledge of strategies of how to guide and/or give advice to help new teachers to tackle their problems effectively, and (c) insight in and understanding of the process of learning from experience. Central to this model is the notion of reciprocity, for the mentoring relationship contributes to the professional development of both the mentor and the beginning teacher, as it boosts the quality of their professional practice (Vonk).

As previously described, induction and mentoring are complex and broad processes. They need to reflect not only the personal and professional needs of the participants but also the contexts in which they work. Further research is needed to better inform the policy and practice of novice teachers' professional development in the workplace as well as the training of mentors. Also, fostering the conditions for effective continuing development of teachers in schools viewed as professional learning communities is essential.

Recently, attention has been paid to the influence of school organizational factors in shaping teachers' professional practices and attitudes toward teaching. Findings show that teacher satisfaction is affected by working conditions at school, especially in regard to administration control (Ma & MacMillan, 1999). Similarly, the quality of teachers' work life is positively related to their professionalism (Cheng, 1996) and to morale, career commitment and retention (Weiss, 1999). Furthermore, research demonstrates the effects of workplace conditions and school culture on the induction of beginning teachers (Cole, 1991; Williams, Prestage, & Bedward, 2001) and the importance of school leadership in creating and maintaining the conditions necessary for the building of professional learning communities within schools (Barker, 2001; Fernandez, 2000; Flores, 2004). Clearly, workplace conditions play a key role in reshaping teachers' understanding of teaching, in facilitating or hindering their professional learning and development, and in constructing their professional identity. Thus, gaining deeper insights into the professional world of new teachers may contribute to better understanding their needs, their expectations, and their commitment, and to provide them with meaningful opportunities for their continuing professional development, including support strategies and induction programs.

# Methodology

## PURPOSE OF THE STUDY

Understanding the ways in which beginning teachers develop professionally implies the consideration of the ways in which they learn (and have learned) to teach and the analysis of the complex personal and contextual factors influencing their professional growth. These issues led to the emergence of the following main research questions:

1. How, what, and under which circumstances do new teachers learn at work?
2. How do novice teachers develop professionally over time and what are the factors that hinder or facilitate their professional growth?
3. How and when do new teachers change (or do not change) over time and what are the factors influencing this process?

In other words, the objectives of the study included: (a) to understand new teachers' development over time; (b) to identify the variables which affect their learning in the workplace; (c) to analyze novices' change over time and the factors influencing it.

## DATA SOURCE

To capture the process-oriented and dynamic nature of professional learning, development and change over time, a longitudinal approach over a two-year period was selected. The study reported herein was carried out in 1999–2000 and 2000–2001, in northern Portugal; 18 elementary and secondary schools were involved in the research project. The schools were selected on the basis of the following criteria: type of school (rural, inner-city, and suburban) and size (large, small, and medium). See table 3.1, and note in this case that elementary schools include students aged 10 to 15. Secondary education includes the final three years of schooling before entering university (students aged 15/16 to 17/18).

Novice teachers were recruited according to the following criteria: having undertaken an Integrated Model of Teacher Training degree in a public university or institution of higher education and being in their first year of teaching without prior teaching experience. The Model presupposes that the subject area

**Table 3.1    Criteria for Selection of Schools**

| Schools | Size | Novice Teachers | Type of school | Staff | Catchment Area |
|---|---|---|---|---|---|
| A | Medium<br><br>868 students<br>78 teachers | 3 | Elementary | Young staff (including 14 trainees), new school (set up in 1997) | Suburban, working and lower-middle class |
| B | Small<br><br>527 students<br>46 teachers | 1 | Elementary | Young staff, new school (set up in 1995) | Rural, lower-middle class, poor area |
| C | Large<br><br>1,018 students<br>82 teachers | 1 | Elementary | Stable staff (large majority of them have a permanent post at the school; the school was set up in 1986) | Suburban, working lower-middle class, poor area |
| D | Large<br><br>2,120 students<br>147 teachers | 6 | Secondary | Large school, young staff (24 trainees; only 50% of the staff have a permanent post; the school was set up in 1990) | Urban, middle-upper class |
| E | Large<br><br>1,176 students<br>129 teachers | 2 | Secondary | Stable staff (large majority have a permanent post; the school was set up in 1973) | Rural, lower-middle class, poor area |
| F | Large<br><br>1,115 students<br>100 teachers | 1 | Elementary | Stable staff (large majority of them have a permanent post; the school was set up in 1968) | Urban, middle-upper and upper class |

(e.g. math, biology) and the pedagogical component are distributed simultaneously throughout the course. The latter encompasses subjects such as History and Philosophy of Education, Psychology of Development, Sociology of Education, Curriculum Development, Educational Technology, and Methods of Teaching. The Model is a five-year course including four years of full-time study at university and one year of practicum in a school. The purpose, time demands, and overall procedures of the research project were explained to all new teachers in each of the schools and volunteers were recruited. A total of 14 new teachers participated in the study. The teachers taught a variety of subjects: physics and chemistry (7 teachers), languages (3 teachers), math (1 teacher), biology (1 teacher), physical education (1 teacher) and music (1 teacher). Nine were female teachers and five were male teachers. Their ages ranged between 22 and 28 years of age. All of them were followed in their second placements to examine further the processes of professional learning, development and change.

## DATA COLLECTION

Data were gathered twice a year through semi-structured interviews (see tables 3.2 through 3.5). All the interviews were tape-recorded and transcribed verbatim. Transcriptions were returned to participants to be checked for accuracy and to have comments and/or supplementary information added. Data about the schools (such as school culture and leadership) were gathered through semi-structured interviews with the principals at the beginning of each academic year and through the administration of a questionnaire to all staff in each of the schools in which the new teachers taught. Pupils' essays were also used to elicit further information on the process of teacher change. They were asked to write a short essay describing their teacher at the beginning and at the end of the academic year, stressing the way in which he/she had changed over this period of time (such as their teaching, relationship with the students, and classes, etc.).

## DATA ANALYSIS

In the process of analysis, an inductive approach was used, and substantive themes were defined as they emerged from the data, according to the overall principles of grounded theory, as suggested by Glaser and Strauss (1967) and Strauss and Corbin (1990). The process of data analysis was undertaken in two phases: (a) a vertical analysis according to which each of the respondents' interviews was analyzed separately, and (b) a comparative or horizontal analysis, also called cross-case analysis (Miles & Huberman, 1994). In this second phase, a

**Table 3.2   Phase 1: Semi-structured Interviews**

| Topics to be covered | Interview Questions |
|---|---|
| **Personal background** | |
| Schooling Experiences | • Looking back on your own schooling background as a student, what are the most significant experiences you can remember? |
| Entry Teacher | • Why did you decide to enter a teaching career? |
| Education | • Can you identify the main influences for this decision? |
| Teacher Education | • Reflecting on your pre-service education how do you analyze your experience as a student teacher? |
| | • Could you identify the most relevant experiences during this period? |
| Teaching Practice | • And what about your teaching practice? |
| | • How do you evaluate your own experience(s) during your teaching practice period? |
| **Self-Perceptions** as a teacher (images, role, beliefs) | • Could you define yourself as a teacher? |
| | • What does it mean for you to be a teacher? |
| | • How do you see your role as a teacher? |
| **Teaching/learning processes** (images) | • How do you see the teaching/learning process(es)? |
| | • How do you define good teaching? Why? |
| **First Experiences** as a full-time teacher (expectations, former images of the school, perceptions, change) | • What were your expectations about teaching and about being a full-time teacher in a school? |
| | • Could you describe your first experiences as a teacher in this school? |
| | • Did you change your perceptions regarding your job during these first months? Why and in what way? Could you describe any particular event or events you can remember? |
| | • Could you describe a situation from which you learned during this period? In what way? How did it happen? |
| | • Among all duties required of you as a teacher, which do you find most demanding and challenging so far? What about the most satisfying ones? How did you learn to handle these duties? |
| School | • How do you define the school as a workplace? |
| | • What impressions do you have of the school in which you are teaching? |
| Colleagues | • What about your colleagues' reactions? |
| Principal | • What about the principal? And other staff? And the existing facilities? |

**Table 3.2    (Continued)**

| Topics to be covered | Interview Questions |
| --- | --- |
| Students | • What are your students like?<br>• How do you perceive your work with students? Could you describe your relationship with them?<br>• Did you change the way you interact with them?<br>• How do you think students perceive you? |
| School Policy | • Could you describe the school's policy (in terms of educational goals and staff professional development)?<br>• Is there any particular activity aimed at introducing you to this school or to your new responsibilities as a teacher?<br>• What about your colleagues teaching the same subject?<br>• What kind of support have you had so far? |

constant comparative analysis (Glaser & Strauss, 1967) was used to look for common patterns and differences. This process was undertaken iteratively and adjustments in the coding process were made where necessary. A case record (e.g., interviews, reports, questionnaires) was also kept for each of the respondents over the two-year period and an overall analysis was undertaken at the end of the research. This procedure enabled checking for recurring themes and regularities as well as contrasting patterns both in each teacher's accounts and across teachers' responses.

A wealth of data was generated over the two-year period. A discussion of all the results emerging from the longitudinal study is beyond the scope of this paper which reports on the main findings arising from the interviews conducted with the 14 new teachers over the first two years of teaching and from the interviews with the principals at the beginning of each academic year.

## LIMITATIONS

This piece of research entailed some limitations. No classroom observation was undertaken due to time and practical constraints (namely the location of the schools). It would provide some additional insights into the processes under study, especially in regard to teacher change. Nevertheless, the main purpose of this research was to examine new teachers' experiences as first and second-year teachers from their own perspectives. The inclusion of pupils' views proved to be informative in clarifying the ways in which teachers changed (or did not

**Table 3.3    Phase 2: Semi-structured Interviews**

| Topics to be covered | Interview Questions |
|---|---|
| **First Year of Teaching (Overall evaluation)** | • How do you evaluate your experience throughout the last academic year?<br>• What were the most significant experiences during the last year? |
| **Perceptions of Change**<br>An overview | • Have you changed (your behavior/performance/ understanding) since the beginning of the year until now?<br>• In what way?<br>• Why?<br>• If not, why not?<br>• Have you changed your perceptions regarding your job during the last year?<br>• Why and in what way?<br>• Could you describe any particular event or events you can remember? |
| The teacher | • Could you define yourself as a teacher?<br>• What does it mean for you to be a teacher?<br>• How do you see your role as a teacher? |
| The teaching<br>The school<br>The duties | • How do you define good teaching?<br>• How do you define the school as a workplace?<br>• Among all duties required of you as a teacher, which do you find most demanding and challenging?<br>• What about the most satisfying ones? |
| **Contexts, Processes and Nature of Learning** | • Looking back on your own experience as a teacher during the last year, what kind of learning experiences can you remember?<br>• What were the most relevant experiences during that period?<br>• Could you describe a situation from which you have learned during this period?<br>• What did you learn?<br>• How did it happen?<br>• With whom did you learn?<br>• What were the effects on your attitudes to and practices of teaching? Please give examples. |
| **Support (Induction)** | • What kind of support have you had during the last year?<br>• What were the main difficulties you have to face?<br>• How did you face them?<br>• What kind of support would you like to have had? |

**Table 3.4 Phase 3: Semi-structured Interviews**

| Topics to be covered | Interview Questions |
|---|---|
| **First Year of Teaching (Overall evaluation)** | • Looking back on your first year of teaching what are the most significant (positive and negative) experiences you can remember? Why did they occur? In what context? What was your response?<br>• How do you analyze your experience as a teacher last year?<br>• What were the main factors (positive and negative) that influenced you as a teacher and your teaching last year?<br>• Could you identify specific/different phases during your first year, for instance in terms of your own change and learning?<br>• What were the effects of your first year of teaching on your attitudes to and practices of teaching? Please give examples. |
| **Personal images/ beliefs** about being a teacher, teaching/ learning processes, school as a workplace | • Could you define yourself as a teacher?<br>• How do you see your role as a teacher?<br>• How do you define good teaching? Why?<br>• How do you define the school as a workplace? |
| **The second year of teaching**<br>First experiences at the school<br>Expectations<br>Effects of the prior learning and experience on the attitudes to and practice of teaching<br>School as a workplace | • What are your expectations about teaching and about being a teacher in your new school?<br>• What is the similarity and/or difference between your experience last year and this year?<br>• Could you describe your first experiences as a teacher in this school? What are the main (positive and negative) situations you can remember so far?<br><br>• What impressions do you have about the school in which you are teaching?<br>• What about your colleagues?<br>• What about the principal? And other staff? And the existing facilities?<br>• What are your students like?<br>• How do you perceive your work with students? Could you describe your relationship with them?<br>• How do you think students perceive you?<br>• Could you describe the school policy (in terms of educational goals and staff professional development)? |

**Table 3.4    (Continued)**

| Topics to be covered | Interview Questions |
|---|---|
| **Learning/Change** Overall evaluation of the first two months of teaching in a new school | • Among all duties required of you as a teacher, which do you find the most demanding and challenging? What about the most satisfying ones? How did you learn to handle these duties?<br>• Have you changed your perceptions regarding your job during the last months? Why and in what way?<br>• Have you changed the way you interact with your students?<br>• Could you describe any particular event or events you can remember? Could you describe a situation from which you learned during the last few months? What did you learn? In what way? How did it happen? What was difficult/easy? |

change) over time (the analysis of these data is beyond the scope of this paper). Another limitation was the relatively small number of new teachers participating in the study, which relates to the qualitative and longitudinal approach adopted. Again, the aim of this research was not to test a theory, nor to provide a generalization of the findings. Rather, it has sought to offer an in-depth description and analysis of the experience of being a new teacher from the viewpoints of the participants.

# Results

## THE CHALLENGE OF BECOMING A FIRST-YEAR TEACHER

Novices referred to their first year of teaching as not only a learning but also a tiring and stressful experience. Despite the more negative situations, some of them (8 out of 14) evaluated the year positively. Five beginning teachers referred to a positive and negative experience in equal terms, and one of them revealed a very negative picture of her first teaching experience as a full-time teacher. Several common themes emerged from new teachers' accounts: their new status as a full-time teacher, the students and their relationship with them, the atmosphere at school, the tasks performed and the working conditions. However, the opportunity to learn at work was the main positive issue reiterated throughout the interviews. They highlighted that performing new roles at school (for which

**Table 3.5   Phase 4: Semi-structured Interviews**

| *Topics to be covered* | *Interview Questions* |
|---|---|
| **Second year of Teaching (Overall evaluation)** | • Looking back on your second year of teaching what are the most significant (positive and negative) experiences you can remember? Why did they occur? In what context? What was your response?<br>• How do you analyze your experience as a teacher last year? What was similar/different from your first year of teaching? Why?<br>• What were the main factors (positive and negative) that influenced you as a teacher and your teaching last year?<br>• Could you identify specific/different phases during your second year, for instance in terms of your own learning and change?<br>• What were the effects of your first year of teaching on your attitudes to and practices of teaching? Please give examples.<br>• What were your expectations about teaching and about being a teacher in this school? How do you feel now about them?<br>• What were/are your main concerns as a teacher over your second year of teaching? Are/were they different from last year? In what way?<br>• What were the greatest challenges you faced this year? How did you deal with them? |
| **The Workplace** | • How do you describe this school? Why?<br>• What are the main differences/similarities between last year and this year in terms of work, relationship with colleagues, school atmosphere, leadership, students, etc? |
| **Leadership** | • How do you describe the leadership in this school? Why? |
| **School Culture/ Department Culture** | • What about the work with your colleagues in general? What about your colleagues within your department? Could you identify the most influential aspects of the school/department culture in relation to your teaching? |
| **Self-efficacy** | • How do you evaluate your work as a teacher in this school? Why?<br>• What went wrong? What went well? Why? What was your response? How did you feel about it? Could you identify the most influential factors in your response/feelings/point of view? What about your self-confidence? How about morale? |

**Table 3.5    (Continued)**

| Topics to be covered | Interview Questions |
|---|---|
| **Professionalism** | • How do you describe your work as a teacher?<br>• Could you identify the core issues of teaching as a profession?<br>• What makes you a professional? |
| **Professional Identity and Personal Biography** | • Could you identify the most influential aspects on your own view and practice of being a teacher? How do you see yourself as a teacher? Why? What are/were the most influential factors on your work and perspective as a teacher? |
| **Conception of Teaching (Bureaucracy versus Caring/Human Dimension)** | • How did you deal with the bureaucratic dimension of teaching? What was your response in the light of the caring/human dimension of teaching (that you described earlier – at the beginning of the year)? What was the most important/relevant one in your work over the last year? Why? |
| **Learning/Change** | • Have you changed your perceptions regarding your job during the last year? Why? In what way?<br>• Have you changed the way you interacted with your students?<br>• Could you describe any particular event or events you can remember? Could you describe a situation from which you learned during the last year? What did you learn? In what way? How did it happen? What was difficult/easy? |

they did not feel well-prepared), dealing with new tasks (which they were not expecting), and making decisions about teaching on their own (without any assistance or guidance) led to the need for a continuing and intense process of learning. For example, one new teacher stated:

> It was a year during which I have learned a lot, I have developed as a teacher. Of course, I am aware of the fact that I still have to improve, and to learn a lot. But I think that my first teaching experience was a positive one. (NT14, Interview 2, End of Year 1)

Another new teacher stated:

> It has been a year during which I have been learning a lot, because of the novelty of all the tasks I had to do . . . (NT13, Interview 2, End of Year 1).

A third novice teacher reported:

> You try to get used to the roles you have to perform, in my case as a
> tutor and as a pedagogical coordinator. I mean I was in the dark, I
> had no idea about what to do, and that was the most difficult experi-
> ence. I mean you try to learn everything you have to do. I am still
> trying to learn. You are always asking questions, trying to learn every-
> thing so you can do well. (NT9, Interview 2, End of Year 1)

In addition to the novelty of the tasks they were expected to perform was the
growing awareness of their new role at school. They emphasized the increased
autonomy and responsibility as an outcome of their new status and, consequently, of the emergence of a new perspective. The close relationship with the
students and their motivation and learning were key issues in terms of the new
teachers' sense of professional fulfillment which also accounted for the positive
evaluation of the first-year experience. For example, one teacher said: "Working
with the students was the best bit of this year." (NT2, Interview 2, End of Year
1). Another teacher stated, "From my first year of teaching I will remember my
students. I mean, my relationship with them is the most positive feature of this
year." (NT6, Interview 2, End of Year 1).

However, new teachers also identified school and job-related factors as the
most negative features of their first year of teaching. They referred to the heavy
workload, the performance of new roles for which they did not feel well-prepared, the lack of information and support, the lack of organization at school
level, the lack of adequate resources and equipment, and the existing control
over teachers. One teacher purported:

> It has been a very tough year; there were loads of new tasks to do
> and new roles to perform for which I wasn't well-prepared. It has
> been a very tiring year. For instance, the pastoral role has been a very
> demanding job. It requires much of your time . . . (NT2, Interview
> 2, End of Year 1)

Another novice teacher stated:

> The most negative experience during this year, and it really does
> disappoint me, is the existing control over teachers in this school. I
> mean, I am talking about the support staff; it seems that we depend
> on their approval. And I think this is very bad. . . . I think they
> mistrust teachers. (NT8, Interview 2, End of Year 1)

In fact, the amount and variety of tasks and the performance of other roles apart
from teaching were depicted as the greatest challenges and one of the most

demanding duties of new teachers. In addition, student lack of motivation and issues related to classroom management, in conjunction with time pressure and feelings of tiredness, were also cited as the most demanding and negative aspects of their first teaching experience. One teacher contended:

> As a student I was keen to learn, and I always enjoyed being at school. And I am shocked when I look at students who are unmotivated and just don't want to learn. . . . And you feel that your job is useless. (NT7, Interview 2, End of Year 1)

Another teacher suggested:

> Now students are very different. We spent four years at the university and we get far from the school reality. When I was at school students knew that there were rules and limits in terms of behavior, and now you realize that they behave in a way that you couldn't even dream of. (NT13, Interview 2, End of Year 1)

Some teachers reported the distant relationships among staff as one of the most negative features of their experience at school. One of them felt disappointed with the competition, hierarchy, and lack of collaboration amongst teachers. She stated:

> Last year, in my previous school, there was support among staff. I felt that my colleagues supported me because I was doing my practicum. In this school as a full-time teacher, as a new teacher I didn't feel supported. People thought "you are young, you have lots of ideas, but you cannot put them into practice. You'll see, you have to learn as time goes on." And I felt discouraged and disappointed. (NT11, Interview 2, End of Year 1)

She continued by adding:

> There is a strong competition among teachers . . . My colleagues told me that I would come across the same kind of atmosphere even if I go to a different school, but at least it would be a new experience. Here you can find several groups of teachers and there are lots of complicated situations, and it is sad . . . I had to develop a project with one of my classes, and other teachers didn't co-operate at all. So it was a one-teacher project, instead of being teamwork. Kids felt really disappointed. (NT11, Interview 2, End of Year 1)

Teachers who were employed at the same school as their peers from university and practicum reported a more positive attitude as a result of mutual support. This positive attitude was present despite the lack of guidance and assistance within the school and the negative perceptions of school culture and leadership. One teacher stated, "In terms of teaching, the support I had was my own support. . . . I guess I was lucky because three of my colleagues from the university were teaching in the same school. We supported one another" (NT5, Interview 2, End of Year 1). Another teacher revealed:

> I try to clear my doubts with a colleague of mine. He also did the same course at university and we used to be colleagues. And it is much easier to prepare the lessons, I mean we are teaching the same topics and we even prepare the written tests together. (NT9, Interview 2, End of Year 1)

## LACK OF INDUCTION AT SCHOOL

In the schools participating in this research project, no formal induction for new teachers existed. Although it has been recognized as an important phase of the teacher's career, with long-term implications for teacher learning and professional development (see legal documents regulating Teacher Education), neither the institutions of Higher Education nor the Teachers' Centers have organized specific activities for beginning teachers thus far in the Portuguese context, in spite of recent research on this field (Alves, 2001; Braga, 2001; Couto, 1998; Flores, 2000a; Silva, 1997). The principals highlighted this in the interviews I conducted with them during my first visit to the schools. One of the principals suggested:

> Maybe we should pay attention to new teachers and provide them with support and guidance. Actually I think there is something missing here, because they are "sent" to the labor market on their own. There is nobody to support them. (Principal in a large urban secondary school)

Another principal stated: "I am going to be honest with you. Maybe your visit to the school will be useful, as we may become aware of the need to think about new teachers, because we don't pay special attention to them" (Principal in a large urban elementary school). Another principal also suggested:

> I think new teachers are a bit lost, because we don't have the best conditions to provide them with the basic information and support they need. That's why I think your work will contribute to developing our understanding about the initial phase of the teacher's career. (Principal in a small rural elementary school)

New teachers corroborated this picture. In terms of guidance and support at school, they referred to the welcome meeting for all staff at the beginning of the school year, the distribution of the handbook with the schools' characteristics and regulations, a visit to the school catchment (community) area, and the existence of specific meetings for those performing other roles at school, namely pastoral duties (working with parents on their children's needs). However, according to them, these activities were not useful or relevant to their needs. One teacher explained:

> The only thing they provided was a visit to the school's catchment area . . . to get acquainted with the students' environment. But there was no support at all in terms of the duties required of you as a teacher . . . There is nobody to inform you, to support you. (NT3, Interview 1, Beginning of Year 1)

Another teacher stated, "There is no information at all. And I think that the head and his team could have a more active role in this regard" (NT14, Interview 2, End of Year 1). A third teacher contended:

> They tried to organize a welcome activity, but they failed . . . they organized a meeting for all the staff and everything . . . but, I mean everything was prepared for those who already knew what to do. And I had to try to get the information myself about what I was supposed to do, even in the case of the pastoral role, because the explanations were too vague. (NT5, Interview 1, Beginning of Year 1)

As previously stated, the lack of information and support from school leaders and colleagues led beginning teachers to adopt a personal way of coping with their duties. They emphasized that the meetings were not prepared for newcomers but for "those who already knew what to do," therefore, they had to find the information they needed for themselves. The images of being "in the dark" and "lost" are illustrative of this. For example, one teacher stated:

> At the beginning of the year the head distributed the school guidelines to each of the teachers, and we became acquainted with the school characteristics. They even emphasized the high dropout rates and other kinds of problems . . . But still I was a bit lost at the beginning, because I didn't know anyone in my department . . . and there wasn't much communication among teachers. (NT11, Interview 2, End of Year 1)

Another teacher reported:

> There wasn't specific support for new teachers, I mean for teachers teaching for the first time (and in this school we are quite a few), and we were a bit in the dark. I think there wasn't any support at all. (NT10, Interview 2, End of Year 1)

The lack of collaboration, the distant and hierarchical working relationships among teachers and the existence of two groups within the school—the new-comers and the staff with a permanent post—were also highlighted in new teachers' accounts. This depiction was also valid for the kind of interaction existing at department level. This is well-illustrated in the following quotation provided by a teacher. She stated, "There is a kind of barrier between new and old staff. As they are already integrated into the school they do not bother to welcome you" (NT12, Interview 1, Beginning of Year 1). Further in the inter-view she added:

> Well, you know that as a new teacher you go to a new school and you do not feel welcomed. You have to relate to many different and strange people who have been in the profession for many years and you feel an initial distance. . . . I mean it's very tough for a newcomer to deal with this, especially because you realize that people are to-gether in groups as they have worked in the same school for a long time. . . . At the beginning, you notice a hierarchical relationship right away, because those who have a permanent position are sat apart from those who are new at school. And then you have the trainees apart from the others . . . (NT12, Interview 2, End of Year 1)

Therefore, seeking advice from colleagues was not an easy job for new teachers. They found themselves facing a dilemma: being aware of the lack of knowledge about the tasks they had to perform and, at the same time, acting as professionals who were aware of, and knowledgeable about their duties as teachers. Some of them took the initiative and sought advice from colleagues with whom they had a closer relationship (usually former university colleagues or other young teach-ers). One stated:

> I have been learning, basically I have been asking questions to my colleagues "look, how have you done this?" or "How do you usually do this?" I mean I have been seeking advice from colleagues. At first I wasn't comfortable in doing so. Now I realize that there is no problem asking colleagues for help. I mean if you don't know you have to ask somebody else. It's not about that you don't know the stuff you should know . . . I mean, it's because no one has ever taught you, you really don't know because no one has taught you before. You have never done such kinds of tasks. I mean you don't know how to do them, so you have to ask. (NT4, Interview 2, End of Year 1)

Accordingly, another one purported, "Whenever I had a problem I sought help from other colleagues, I mean new teachers like me, because I wasn't comfortable asking for advice or help from a teacher who had a permanent post at the school" (NT3, Interview 2, End of Year 1). Only a minority reported that they asked for advice or help from the head teacher or his/her team. In the contexts described here, schools are run by a collegial team of teachers (usually three, the president/principal and two vice-presidents) elected from their peers. When they did so, they focused on problems related to bureaucratic work. One teacher stated, "When I needed guidance I asked for help from the people in the executive council and they helped me. In terms of assistance I had to take the initiative, otherwise you don't have any support at all." (NT2, Interview 2, End of Year 1). Another one reported:

> At the beginning I didn't know what to do regarding the new role I had to perform. I mean I was supposed to look after the kids, and check if they come to school and attend the classes, and everything, but I didn't know how to do it. Apparently there were a few documents I had to fill in and I didn't know. I went to see the principal and he explained to me what I was supposed to do. (NT1, Interview 2, End of Year 1)

Overall, the nature of communication within the school and its formal structures (e.g., departments, formal meetings) was guided by the taken-for-granted assumption that teachers already had the basic skills and knowledge to handle all the duties required of them. As the principals and the new teachers themselves argued, the school policy did not include the guidance of new entrants into the profession nor the assistance and training of teachers who were expected to perform other roles in addition to teaching, which, in most cases (e.g., pastoral duties, subject leader, head of department), required the mastery of a set of specific skills. Therefore, new teachers had to work out for themselves ways of coping with their new responsibilities at school, leading to the emergence of an isolated and idiosyncratic process of becoming a teacher.

Similarly, while intrinsic factors were more important in the positive evaluation of the first year of teaching (such as student learning and motivation, and the teacher/student relationship), organizational and structural issues (e.g., heavy workload, lack of resources, new roles, working conditions) and school culture (for example, leadership, nature of working relationships among staff) were crucial in determining the most negative features of the first teaching experience.

Moreover, personal biography, in conjunction with the mediating influence of school culture and leadership, seemed to play a key role in determining the success or failure of new teachers' experience. In other words, the ups and downs of the first year of teaching seemed to depend very much on: (a) the idiosyncratic way in which new teachers coped with the novelty and demanding nature of their new role and dealt with the situational and organizational constraints in the workplace (for example, their motivation toward teaching, the survival strategies they adopted even if sometimes they went against their own beliefs); (b) peer support (new teachers teaching in a school where they felt supported by colleagues, former colleagues or other young teachers, were more likely to overcome their difficulties more positively); (c) leadership (an informative and active leadership—at both school and department level—emerged as an important element in the understanding of and coping with new roles and tasks); and (d) nature (and amount) of tasks to be performed (new teachers who were expected to perform a wide variety of tasks apart from teaching—such as pastoral duties, subject leader, head of department—were more likely to have a stressful and tiring experience at the beginning of their career).

In fact, the new teachers who revealed feelings of disappointment, tiredness, and sometimes frustration were expected to perform, in addition to teaching (in most cases more than two stages of teaching), two or three different roles at school (e.g., head of department, subject leader and pastoral duties). These findings are consistent with earlier work on beginning teachers, which has demonstrated the connection between easy or painful beginnings (Huberman, 1989) and the balance between coping with difficulties and feelings of professional fulfillment (Alves, 2001). However, they also highlight the strong importance of biography, school culture, and leadership as mediating influences on new teachers' understandings and practices of teaching.

## SECOND-YEAR TEACHERS: NEW CONTEXTS, NEW CHALLENGES, NEW BEGINNINGS

Because teacher surplus and teacher recruitment policy (which occurs mainly at the national level) are important issues in Portugal, novice teachers have to move from one school to another during the first years of teaching, which was the case of the participants in this study.

Being a teacher in a different school and in most cases in rural, poor, and very isolated catchment (community) areas, had an effect on the way in which new teachers described their job and the school setting in which they worked during their second year of teaching. The metaphors of "landing" in a school, "being lost" and the "shock" of being (and living) in a new area illustrate well the way in which they perceived their new placements: being far from home, facing the unknown, and experiencing isolation and a sense of powerlessness. An example can be found in the following comment from one teacher:

> This has been a very tough year for me. It was very hard for me to
> get to know the school and this area. I feel like I've landed here. I

mean I had no idea that I would be teaching here. . . . This is a small rural school and there are loads of disciplinary problems here. . . . When I got here it was a real shock. I felt very disappointed with this place. I cried a lot during my first week here, because . . . it was a terrible shock! First of all I was given a post in this school which is very far away from home, but this is not the point. Last year I also taught in a school very far away from home, but this region is really . . . everything is so calm, so isolated; there is nothing here apart from the school itself! (NT9, Interview 3, Beginning of Year 2)

Another teacher said:

This year my experience is very different from last year. Last year I was at ease and I felt happier than I do now. At the beginning of this year I felt very disappointed, I felt lost, I didn't know anyone here. (NT1, Interview 3, Beginning of Year 2)

The isolation (not only in geographical terms but also from a social and psychological point of view) was the most negative feature emphasized throughout the interviews. Teachers stressed its effects both at the personal and professional level. One of them clearly stated:

All you can think of is . . . July; I mean the end of the school year! It's the isolation of this place and the kids are the ones who are going to pay the price for this situation. You have a very disorganized timetable and of course sometimes you are not going to turn up for the classes in order to have a break, which is understandable because of the distance. . . . I mean, all you want is to forget about this year, you don't have any projects in mind to develop over this school year. When you finish your practicum you feel enthusiastic and willing to do things but now my state of mind is very different. All I want is that this year goes as quickly as possible. (NT12, Interview 3, Beginning of Year 2)

A personal account of one of the beginning teachers also illustrated the feelings of isolation, in which the metaphor of the "big brother" house was used, "Nine of us [teachers] are from very far away, and we used to say that we are the big brother residents, because we are really isolated in this place, far away from everything . . ." (NT9, Interview 3, Beginning of Year 2). The negative perception of the new social and geographical setting, along with being far away from home, impacted negatively new teachers' predispositions and willingness to teach. Lack of motivation, low morale and commitment, and disappointment and frustration were reiterated throughout their accounts.

Overall, the second year of teaching was described as a rather negative experience by half of the teachers involved in this research project. Six of them rated their second year as a more negative experience than their first year, whereas one teacher stated that her second year of teaching was as equally tiring and negative as her first year. Conversely, three teachers reported that their second year of teaching was a better experience than their first year, whereas three other teachers stated that their second year of teaching was as equally positive as their first year. One teacher reported that his experience in his second placement was similar to his first year of teaching, being positive and negative in equal terms. The negative evaluation of the second year of teaching was related to feelings of tiredness, frustration, low self-motivation and sense of self-efficacy, which emerged from teachers' accounts. One teacher explained:

> I think this year was worse than last year. I feel that my work isn't as good as it was last year; I don't feel happy with it. . . . I don't know what's going on really. . . . They [students] just don't pay attention to me. My work is worse and I definitely don't feel motivated to teach them. I mean, I feel really unmotivated and much worse if I think of my first year of teaching . . . (NT8, Interview 4, End of Year 2)

Similarly, another teacher stated, "My evaluation of my experience this [second] year is much more negative. . . . I don't enjoy teaching. . . . I feel less happy with my work because I feel less motivated and I think that self-motivation is very important in teaching" (NT10, Interview 4, End of Year 2). In addition, a third said, "My first year was more positive than this year . . . you don't feel students' motivation and you end up feeling unmotivated too . . ." (NT2, Interview 4, End of Year 2).

Difficulties related to classroom management and dealing with disciplinary problems were also referred to by the teachers by whom the second year of teaching was seen as a negative experience. A teacher stated:

> My biggest mistake is that I am not as strict as I should be and they [students] always go too far and when I realize that it's too late, I can't change what's done. . . . I think I let them go too far. . . . I try to do that during Term one but it never works. (NT1, Interview 4, End of Year 2)

Teachers also cited issues such as isolation and distance from home, school culture and leadership, and poor working conditions as key factors in their negative evaluation of their second year of teaching. They highlighted the culture of separation within the school between the newcomers and experienced staff, the lack of support and guidance in dealing with their roles and tasks and the ineffective and badly-organized leadership. One teacher stated:

> Well, in terms of leadership this school is absolutely surreal. . . . I mean, it is chaos. They just don't have a clue how to run the school, they lack organization and they don't care and teachers end up doing the same. . . . People do their teaching and they go home . . . (NT12, Interview 4, End of Year 2)

A second teacher explained:

> I am not happy working in this school and I can't wait for the end of the school year. . . . I notice that in this school there is a gap between younger staff, newcomers and people who have worked in this school for many years. . . . I feel disappointed because you get there with expectations, willing to do things for the school and you give up because you start thinking "why do I bother, nobody cares, why should I care?" I mean you feel frustrated because the school doesn't support you . . . (NT1, Interview 4, End of Year 2)

Interestingly, five teachers reported that the initial lack of motivation and disappointment, because of the isolation and distance of the school (located in rural and poor areas) from their homes, led to a positive attitude toward teaching and, in some cases, toward a broader understanding of their role as teachers. Supportive and collaborative cultures within the school, strong and encouraging leadership, and positive feedback from students were the three major reasons behind the shift from rather pessimistic expectations toward a more committed and enthusiastic perspective. The following quotations make this point:

> It was a gradual thing . . . my relationship with the students was getting better every day . . . and the school is very nice. As time went on, coming to school wasn't an effort to me any more and the initial lack of motivation, because of the location and distance of the school, was transformed into motivation which is getting greater each day. I mean, we are approaching the end of the year and I feel more and more motivated to come to school and conduct experiments with my students. . . . Students see you as a model and you can't let them down. And I have a good relationship with my colleagues too. (NT4, Interview 4, End of Year 2)

> One of the most positive things was the close relationship among staff in the school . . . and this year I was able to have this kind of relationship that I like with students, I mean keeping order in the classroom and at the same time having a closer relationship with them, with no need to be distant. . . . I am there to help them learn something. (NT5, Interview 4, End of Year 2)

As previously mentioned, three teachers reported that their second year of teaching was even more positive than their first year. Enthusiasm, commitment and job satisfaction were recurring themes in their accounts alongside a high sense of self-efficacy and self-motivation. One teacher reported:

> This year was even more positive, I feel more motivated than last year. I woke up very happy to come here doing my teaching and I got home equally happy because the day went well, and this has been happening every single day. There are no negative experiences this year, students are motivated and committed, and staff and the principal are very supportive . . . (NT7, Interview 4, End of Year 2)

Another teacher stated, "On the whole I feel very happy here, if I forget the issue of the distance from home. I feel happier this year because I know that my work is recognized, and I feel more motivated than last year" (NT4, Interview 4, End of Year 2). A third teacher explained:

> This year is more positive than last year . . . and I feel more motivated because of the experiences I came across. There are still those students who are keen to learn and who are motivated and committed after all. . . . I mean, it has to do with the way they see the subject. If they are doing well and they are able to achieve the goals I know that I am doing a good job. (NT13, Interview 4, End of Year 2)

Again, student motivation, commitment and achievement, in addition to supportive and encouraging leadership and school atmosphere, were reiterated throughout their accounts. Conversely, the negative evaluation of the second year of teaching was related to negative perceptions of school culture, namely the lack of cooperation amongst staff and ineffective and non-supportive leadership. Along with these perceptions were students' lack of motivation and low achievement, which led, in most cases, to feelings of frustration and low morale. Overall, the second year of teaching was seen as a challenging experience for teachers whose sense of self-efficacy, self-motivation and morale in addition to, in most cases, perceptions of school culture and leadership, were key elements in determining the failure or success of their practices, and therefore their commitment toward teaching.

# Implications for Teachers and Teacher Educators

> I think that a teacher faces several difficulties when s/he starts teaching. When this happens, the teacher starts to feel alone and isolated, and s/he feels that s/he has to do everything by her/himself. Either s/

>he devotes her/himself deeply to the work (which is hard to do, be-
>cause she has to be on a permanent search for solutions), or, without
>any kind of support, she gives up. I believe that there is something
>missing in teacher education, I mean support after the practicum. . . .
>I think that there are many things one could learn, even after becom-
>ing a full-time teacher. (NT10, Interview 1, Beginning of Year 1)

This quotation from one of the participants in the study illustrates well the struggle of becoming a (new) teacher experienced by many entrants to teaching. Isolation, loneliness, lack of support, individual search for solutions, learning by trial-and-error, and feelings of "giving up" are some of the daunting situations novice teachers have to face in their first years of teaching. Having undertaken a teaching degree (involving a five-year course, inclusive of one year of practicum), did not prepare them for the reality of schools and classrooms. The mismatch between idealistic expectations and the complex and demanding nature of teaching was a key feature reiterated throughout their accounts.

This study also supports the contention that induction is a key phase in the teacher's career which needs to be given more attention by policymakers, school leaders, teacher educators, teacher education course providers, and other stakeholders. In the Portuguese context, induction is an issue that has not yet been addressed effectively despite the increasing number of studies which have highlighted its relevance and usefulness (Alves, 2001; Braga, 2001; Couto, 1998; Flores, 1997; Silva, 1997). Furthermore, support and guidance provided by school leaders in the workplace is far from being responsive to new teachers' needs, as evidence from this study also suggests.

In Portugal, references to induction do exist in policy documents. For instance, in the legal document regulating teacher education, issued in 1989, induction is referred to as follows: "In-service education of teachers is initiated by an induction period during which the institutions of teacher training provide support strategies to new teachers according to their possibilities" (Decree-Law no. 344/89, article 26). Induction is also the subject of attention in the Teacher Career Statute, first issued in 1990, but so far it has not been a priority of government in terms of its regulation. It has been recognized as a key element in linking Initial Teacher Training and In-Service Education by promoting collaborative professional learning opportunities in the workplace (Campos, 1995; Pacheco, 1995) within a career-long view of professional development (Flores, 2000b; Ribeiro, 1993).

However, up until now, induction programs have not yet been put into practice. Campos (1995) stressed the geographical distance between teachers' workplaces and corresponding teacher education institutions as one of the main obstacles. In addition to this problem are issues related to the training of mentors and the financial support that such programs would involve. A collaborative strategy, through partnerships between universities and schools, appears as a way of overcoming the practical and situational constraints related to the implementation of induction programs. Nevertheless, a political decision also needs to be made through the formal recognition of an induction program for all entrants to teaching.

High quality teaching and learning depend greatly on high quality teachers. Therefore, providing them with support deemed necessary at different phases of their careers, with resources and opportunities to develop professionally is essential. This support is even more crucial during the early years of teaching. This study provides empirical evidence of the struggles and complexities inherent in becoming a new teacher. In this respect, induction emerges as a key element in the transition from student teacher and trainee to full-time teacher. However, induction has to be framed and organized within a broad perspective of professional development of teachers. Furthermore, induction needs to go beyond the mere practical advice and socialization process whereby new entrants become members of a given professional culture, to include opportunities for self-questioning and reflection not only upon teachers' own actions, but also upon the values and norms underlying the educational settings in which they work. Crucially, Tickle (2000) argues for a "re-conceptualization" of induction and he advocates a perspective of induction which acknowledges the potential of new teachers in making a contribution to the education of students if they are empowered themselves.

From the discussion of the results, an apparent issue is that attention needs to be given to new teachers beyond the so-called induction year. As second-year teachers, the participants in this study reported more pessimistic views and experiences of teaching. Overall, their accounts of their second year of teaching pointed to a more negative picture and they highlighted the isolation, lack of support and feelings of loneliness and frustration. Therefore, the need exists for policymakers, teacher educators, in-service course providers and school leaders to recognize the intense and crucial process of learning occurring in the early years of teaching (especially if new entrants to teaching have to move from one school to another, as in the case of Portuguese newly qualified teachers) and to provide support and meaningful opportunities for professional growth. In summary, a number of key issues may be drawn from the findings, which have implications for the role of teacher educators, teachers and school leaders. These issues are:

1. The combination of idiosyncratic and contextual factors in determining the success or failure of first teaching experiences. Induction programs have to be novice-centered and context-dependent, presenting a flexible design to meet the personal and professional needs of the teachers and mentors and

the contextual challenges they face in the school settings within which they work.

2. The need to give more attention to the training of mentors and school leaders. As previously mentioned, different needs for different teachers in different contexts exist, and this existence has implications for the type of support strategies and professional development opportunities provided to teachers, especially in the early years of teaching.

3. The importance of fostering collaborative cultures within schools seen as learning communities. In this respect, leadership, both at macro and micro levels, plays a central role, which implies more attention to the kinds of characteristics of good leaders in creating and maintaining collaborative cultures at school, and therefore, the kind of training provided to them.

4. The need to invest more in the induction period and to rethink the role of teacher educators and universities in the preparation of teachers (the first phase of their career-long professional development) and in fostering the kinds of partnerships with schools conducive to a collaborative engagement to enhance the potential of both institutions, through reflection and research bringing together teacher educators, mentors and teachers.

# Acknowledgments

I would like to acknowledge Fundação para a Ciência e a Tecnologia (Programa PRAXIS XXI) for financial support.

# References

Adey, K. (1997). First impressions do count: Mentoring student teachers. *Teacher Development, 1*(1), 123–133.

Alves, F. A. C. (2001). *O Encontro com a realidade docente. Ser professor principiante.* Lisboa: Instituto de Inovação Educacional.

Ballantyne, R., Hansford, B., & Packer, J. (1995). Mentoring beginning teachers: A qualitative analysis of process and outcomes. *Educational Review, 47*(3), 297–307.

Barker, B. (2001). Do leaders matter? *Educational Review, 53*(1), 65–76.

Barrington, R. (2000). An investigation into the induction period which considers the perspectives of NQTs and their tutors. Paper presented at the Annual Conference of the British Educational Research Association, University of Cardiff, Cardiff, Wales.

Bolam, R. (1987). Induction of beginning teachers. In M. Dunkin (Ed.), *The international encyclopedia of teacher education.* (pp. 745–757). New York: Pergamon Press.

Bolam, R. (1995). Teacher recruitment and induction. In L. W. Anderson (Ed.), *International encyclopedia of teaching and teacher education* (2nd ed., pp. 612–615). Oxford: Pergamon.

Braga, F. (2001). *Formação de professores e identidade profissional.* Coimbra: Quarteto Editora.

Campos, B. P. (1995). *Formação de professores em Portugal.* Lisboa: Instituto de Inovacção Educacional.

Cheng, Y. C. (1996). Relation between teachers' professionalism and job attitudes, educational outcomes, and organizational factors. *The Journal of Educational Research, 889*(3), 163–171.

Cole, A. L. (1991). Relationships in the workplace: Doing what comes naturally? *Teaching and Teacher Education, 7*(5/6), 415–126.

Couto, C. G. (1998). *Professor: O Início da prática profissional.* (Doctoral Dissertation). Lisboa: Faculdade de Ciências da Universidade de Lisboa.

Day, C. (1999). *Developing teachers. The challenges of lifelong learning.* London: Falmer Press.

Decree-Law no 344/89, Article 26. Retrieved from www.min.edu.pt.

Fernandez, A. (2000). Leadership in an era of change. Breaking down the barriers of the culture of teaching. In C. Day, A. Fernandez, T. E. Hauge, & J. Moller (Eds.), *The life and work of teachers. International perspectives in changing times* (pp. 239–255). London: Falmer Press.

Field, B., & Field, T. (1994). *Teachers as mentors: A practical guide.* London: Falmer Press.

Flores, M. A. (1997). *Problemas e necessidades de apoio/formação dos professores principiantes. Um estudo exploratório* (Master's Dissertation). Braga: Universidade do Minho.

Flores, M. A. (2000a). *A Indução no ensino: Desafios e constrangimentos.* Lisboa: Instituto de Inovação Educacional.

Flores, M. A. (2000b). Currículo, formação e desenvolvimento profissional. In J. A. Pacheco (Org.) *Políticas de integração curricular* (pp. 147–166). Porto: Porto Editora.

Flores, M. A. (2001). Person and context in becoming a new teacher. *Journal of Education for Teaching, 27*(2), 135–148.

Flores, M. A. (2004). The impact of school culture and leadership on new teachers' learning in the workplace. *International Journal of Leadership in Education, 7*(4), 297–318.

Fullan, M. (1993). *Change forces. Probing the depths of educational reform.* London: Falmer Press.

Ganser, T. (1995). A road map for designing quality mentoring programs for beginning teachers. (ERIC Document Reproduction Service No. ED 394932)

Glaser, B. G., & Strauss, A. L. (1967). *The discovery of grounded theory: Strategies for qualitative research.* Chicago: Aldine.

Hall, G. E. (1982). Induction: The missing link. *Journal of Teacher Education, 33*(3), 53–55.

Huberman, M. (1989). The professional life cycle of teachers. *Teachers College Record, 91*(1), 31–57.

Huling-Austin, L. (1990). Teacher induction programs and internship. In R. Houston (Ed.) *Handbook of research on teacher education* (pp. 535–548). New York: Macmillan.

Klausmeier, R. L. (1994). Responsibilities and strategies of successful mentors. *Clearing House, 68*(1), 27–29.

Ma, X., & MacMillan, R. B. (1999). Influences of workplace conditions on teachers' job satisfaction. *The Journal of Educational Research, 93*(1), 39–47.

Mahoney, P. (1996). Competences and the first year of teaching. In D. Hustler and D. McIntyre (Eds.), *Developing competent teachers: Approaches to professional competence in teacher education*. London: David Fulton.

Marcelo, C. (1988). Profesores principiantes y programas de inducción a la práctica profesional. *Enseñanza*, 61–79.

Marcelo, C. (1994). *Formación del profesorado para el cambio educativo*. Barcelona: PPU.

Marcelo, C. (1999). *Formação de Professores. Para uma mudança educativa*. Porto: Porto Editora.

Mifsud, C. (1996). Preparation and competence of intending and beginning teachers in Malta. *Journal of Education for Teaching*, 22(3), 283–296.

Miles, M., & Huberman, M. (1994). *Qualitative data analysis. An expanded sourcebook* (2nd ed.). Thousand Oaks, CA: Sage.

Pacheco, J. A. (1995). *Formação de professores: Teoria e praxis*. Braga: IEP.

Ribeiro, A. C. (1993). *Formar professores. Elementos para uma teoria e prática da formação* (4th ed.). Lisboa: Texto Editora.

Schlechty, P. (1985). Induction: A framework for evaluating induction into teaching. *Journal of Teacher Education*, 36(1), 37–41.

Silva, M. C. M. (1997). O Primeiro ano de docência: o choque com a realidade. In M. T. Estrela (Org.) *Viver e construir a profissão docente* (pp. 51–80). Porto: Porto Editora.

Strauss, A., & Corbin, J. (1990). *Basics of qualitative research: Grounded theory procedures and techniques*. Newbury Park, CA: Sage.

Tickle, L. (1994). *The induction of new teachers. Reflective professional practice*. London: Cassell.

Tickle, L. (2000). *Teacher induction: The way ahead*. Buckingham: Open University Press.

Vonk, J. H. C. (1993). Mentoring beginning teachers: Development of a knowledge base for mentors. Paper presented at the Annual Meeting of the American Educational Research Association, Atlanta.

Vonk, J. H. C. (1994). Teacher induction: The great omission in education. In M. Galton & B. Moon (Eds.) *Handbook of teacher training in Europe* (pp. 85–109). London: David Fulton.

Weiss, E. M. (1999). Perceived workplace conditions and first-year teachers' morale, career choice commitment, and planned retention: A secondary analysis. *Teaching and Teacher Education*, 15(8), 861–879.

Williams, A., Prestage, S., & Bedward, J. (2001). Individualism to collaboration: The significance of teacher culture to the induction of newly qualified teachers. *Journal of Education for Teaching*, 27(3), 253–267.

Wilson, J., & D'Arcy, J. (1987). Employment conditions and induction opportunities. *European Journal of Teacher Education*, 10(2), 141–149.

Wubbels, T., Créton, H., & Hooymayers, H. P. (1987). A school-based teacher induction programme. *European Journal of Teacher Education*, 10(1), 81–95.

# CHAPTER 4

# Two Induction Models in One Urban District

## TRANSITIONING TO TEACHER CREDENTIALING

*Ann L. Wood*
California State University, Los Angeles

*Nancy Waarich-Fishman*
Glendale Public Schools

Ann L. Wood, Ph.D., is an assistant professor in the Applied and Advanced Studies of Education Division of the Charter College of Education at California State University, Los Angeles (CSULA). She teaches in the Urban Learning Program (ULRN), a blended undergraduate/teaching credential program. Her publications and research interests are in teacher development, induction, urban education, and educational reform.

Nancy Waarich-Fishman is the former director of the Glendale Beginning Teacher Support and Assessment (BTSA)/Induction Program in Glendale, California. She is now retired and operates a bed and breakfast in Napa Valley, California.

## ABSTRACT

While transitioning to a state-mandated induction/credentialing system, this urban district implemented both the Beginning Teacher Support and Assessment (BTSA) Program and the SB2042 Induction Program. This research examines these two induction models and employs a mixed method design with 13 data sources. It is a case study of elementary and secondary teachers (Group A [BTSA] and Group B [2042] matched by site and grade level/subject. It explores (a) how program participation influences performance outcomes in six professional development areas and (b) how the induction models influence teaching practices. Results show that despite differences in participant requirements, there are no statistically significant differences in performance outcomes of participants in the two models. Novice teachers in both models demonstrate high or satisfactory performance outcomes in four areas: *core curriculum, diversity, English Learners,* and *students with special needs.* They exhibit need for growth in creating supportive and healthy learning environments and using technology to support student learning.

Induction is a phase of teacher development that is characterized by survival and discovery. It is the entry period into a profession that has the potential to shape teaching practices throughout the rest of an educational career. It is a time of complex behavioral and conceptual learning, analytical thinking, and professional development (Alliance for Excellent Education [AEE], 2004; Bartell, 2004; Odell, 1990). It is no wonder that in teacher development, hardly any other phase of an educator's career is researched as much as induction (Fideler & Haselkorn, 1999; Moir & Gless, 2001; Tickle, 2000; Wood, 2001).

In California, induction programs have evolved from state policies, K–12 teachers' practices, and induction research, including the New Teacher Project (Bergeson, 1992; California Commission on Teacher Credentialing [CCTC] and the California Department of Education [CDE], 1992; Olebe, 2001). For approximately a decade, induction of California teachers into the profession was conducted through the Beginning Teacher Support and Assessment Program (BTSA), a state-sponsored induction program based on the *California Standards for the Teaching Profession [CSTP]* (CCTC & CDE 1997a), the *California K–12 Academic Content Standards* (CCTC & CDE, 1998), the *California Formative Assessment and Support System for Teachers [CFASST]* (CCCTC & CDE, 1999) or an equivalent standards-based, CCTC-approved, locally designed formative assessment system, and the *Standards of Program Quality and Effectiveness for the Beginning Teacher Support and Assessment Program* (CCTC & CDE, 1997b).

In 1998, Senate Bill 2042 mandated a state-wide review and revision of all teacher preparation and induction programs (Alpert & Mazzoni, 1998). In 2001, California induction programs were mandated to revise their programs based on the *Standards of Quality and Effectiveness for Professional Teacher Induction Programs* (CCTC & CDE, 2001). The 2042 Induction Standards dramatically changed California induction programs by mandating that they provide experiences for novice teachers in six professional development areas (Standards

15–20) and that novice teachers must demonstrate performance competencies in each standard including: (15) Core Academic Content and Subject Specific Pedagogy, (16) Using Technology to Support Student Learning, (17) Diversity, Equity & Access to the Core Curriculum, (18) Creating a Supportive and Healthy Environment for Student Learning, (19) Teaching English Learners, and (20) Teaching Special Populations. Under the 2042 law, the only way that a novice teacher can clear a Level I or Preliminary Credential and obtain a Level II or a Professional Teaching Credential is by completing a two-year 2042 Induction Program.

# Background

In Fall 2003, California districts started to implement 2042 Induction programs. Many districts, like this one, found they had to transition from an established BTSA or local program to a 2042 Induction model. Until all novice teachers completed their BTSA program or chose to join a 2042 Induction Program, some districts decided to operate parallel induction programs within one school district to meet novice teachers' needs—a tough task in tight budget times.

This study of two induction models in a large urban school district took place in one of the largest cities in Los Angeles County. Fifty percent of the city's residents were born outside the United States. The district encompassed a culturally, linguistically, and socio-economically diverse mix of K–12 students who speak over 60 languages. It had a lengthy history of providing an organized system of teacher induction and had operated the *Beginning Teacher Support and Assessment System (BTSA) Program* since the mid 1990s.

This case study involved 14 matched K–12 novice teachers who participated in two different teacher induction model programs. Group A consisted of seven teachers who participated in BTSA and Group B consisted of seven teachers who participated in the 2042 Induction Program that determines professional licensure. The distinction between the matched groups of novice teachers in Group A (BTSA) and Group B (2042) was that Group B 2042 Induction novice teachers were required to (a) attend all professional development release days, (b) participate in mandatory induction forums (two-hour after school seminars) in the six areas of professional development identified in Induction Standards 15 through 20; (c) demonstrate *teacher performance expectations (TPE)* in these teaching domains through the completion of classroom assignments, (d) meet individually with the BTSA/Induction Teacher Specialist to review their professional growth and progression in completing mandated induction assignments, and (e) complete a Teaching Portfolio demonstrating the above to clear their Level I or Preliminary Credential and attain professional licensure. Table 4.1 illustrates program components common to both induction models with additional requirements for the 2042 Induction (Group B) participants delineated in the right-hand column.

This research examines the experiences of only first-year teachers; second year teachers will be researched in a future study. In this study, "novice teacher," is used as the equivalent of the terms, "new teacher," "beginning teacher," "protégé," "apprentice teacher," and similar terms in the induction literature. Similarly, this paper refers to "support providers" as the equivalent of "mentors," "coaches," and "consulting teachers" in induction literature.

# Objectives

The objectives of the study are to determine if there are differences in (a) how participation in each of the induction models influences teacher performance in six areas of professional growth specified by SB2042 Induction Standards:

**Table 4.1   BTSA and 2042 Induction Program Requirements for First-Year Teachers**

| BTSA Program Requirements Group A | 2042 Induction Program Requirements Group B |
|---|---|
| Weekly meetings with Support Provider | Weekly meetings with Support Provider |
| Completion of 6 CFASST events | Completion of 6 CFASST events |
| Novice Teacher Orientation Meetings | Novice Teacher Orientation Meetings |
| Classroom Management Training, ASAP | Classroom Management Training, ASAP |
| TaskStream Training | TaskStream Training |
| Two Individual Induction Plans | Two Individual Induction Plans |
| Monthly Contact Logs | Monthly Contact Logs |
| Voluntary Professional Development Release Days | Mandatory Professional Development Release Days & TPEs |
| Voluntary Induction Standard Forums | Mandatory Induction Standard Forums & TPEs |
| | Mandatory Follow-Up Classroom Activities for each Release Day and Induction Forum |
| | Mandatory Meetings with Induction Program Staff to Check Professional Growth & Progress toward Induction Program Completion |
| | Mandatory Teaching Portfolio for Licensure |

- Core curriculum and subject specific pedagogy,
- Using technology to support student learning,
- Supporting equity, diversity, and access to the core curriculum,
- Creating a supportive and healthy environment for learning,
- Teaching English Learners, and
- Teaching special populations

and how novice teachers perceive these two induction programs as influencing their teaching practices in these professional growth areas.

# A Brief Overview of Research on Induction Programs

Research indicates that induction is the systematic, organized support and development of novice teachers in their initial one to three years of service (Bartell, 2004; Odell & Huling, 2000). Based on an analysis of induction research, the AEE (2004) defines "Comprehensive induction as a package of supports, development, and standards-based assessments provided to beginning teachers during at least their first two years of full-time professional teaching" (p. 11).

The last two decades of induction research reveal empirical and theoretical findings about induction's significance and essential components. It is well documented that induction works. A large percentage of teachers without induction programs leave teaching (National Commission on Teaching and America's Future, 1996; Schlechty & Vance, 1981). It is often the most academically talented ones that leave in the greatest numbers (Schlechty & Vance, 1981). With induction programs, teacher retention rates increase. In California, teacher retention is estimated at 92 percent statewide (Olebe, 2001), with some urban districts reporting higher retention rates (Wood, 2000). Research by Ingersoll and Thomas (2004) indicates that comprehensive induction programs retain teachers, even when other factors such as the school environment and teacher salaries are taken into account.

In 2003, the majority of novice teachers in the U.S. (80 percent) report participating in some form of teacher induction (Ingersoll & Thomas, 2004). In 2004, more than 30 states have induction programs; six of which are tied to credentialing and employment requirements (Wood, 2001). Now research also demonstrates that providing comprehensive induction is cost effective. Villar's research (2004) indicates that, if turnover costs represent 50% of a novice teacher's salary, an investment in an intensive teacher induction program in one district pays $1.37 for every $1.00 invested. This is encouraging, and replications of this study are warranted.

Studies show that well-designed induction programs offer a sequenced set of professional growth opportunities that are based on individual novice teacher's needs and are grounded in the school's culture (AAE, 2004; Moir & Gless, 2001; Olebe, Jackson, & Danielson, 1999). Empirical studies have shown that the key determinant of successful induction is a strong relationship between the novice teacher and an assigned and trained mentor, referred to in this study as a support provider (Feiman-Nemser & Parker, 1992; Ganser, 1999; Gehrke & Keys, 1984; Little, 1990). Support providers encourage novice teachers to plan, teach, reflect, and apply what they have learned from their present teaching to future lessons (Moir & Gless; Olebe, Jackson, & Danielson). In most quality induction programs, novice teachers continually collect evidence about their teaching throughout their first years in the profession and use it to self-assess their standards-based teaching practices (Villani, 2002; Wood, 2001).

Research shows (AEE, 2004; Bartell, 2004: Odell & Huling, 2000; Olebe, 2001; Wood, 2001) that most successful induction programs include the following key components:

- Structured observations and mentoring by trained and well-matched support providers
- Standards-based assessments of novice teachers' teaching practices
- Sustained, intensive, content-driven professional development activities related to novice teachers' needs and developmental readiness
- Common planning/meeting times for novice teachers and support
- Providers' collaborative reflections on teaching practices
- Novice teachers' ongoing collection of standards-based evidence of their practices

Both the BTSA Program and the 2042 Induction Program in this study include all of the induction components above. Although the 2042 Induction Program mandates participation, requires completion of follow-up standards-based activities, and has compulsory checks on teachers' progress toward program completion that the BTSA Program does not have, both models are structured, intensive, comprehensive induction programs that help improve novice teachers' quality of teaching by guiding them from day-to-day survival to more reflective teaching practices (Ingersoll & Thomas, 2004; Odell, 1990).

# Methodology

Using a mixed method design, this study includes survey and demographic data, as well as qualitative data. The research includes a case study (Yin, 1989) of fourteen matched elementary and secondary teachers. The study's qualitative methods facilitate an understanding of how novice teachers perceive and interpret their lived experiences in these two induction programs (Van Manen, 1990).

## PARTICIPANTS

Fourteen elementary and secondary novice teachers were purposively chosen to comprise a representative range of grade-level elementary and secondary participants. The sample included four high school teachers, four middle school teachers, and six elementary teachers with an equal number of elementary, middle, and high school teachers in A and B induction groups. Teachers in each group were matched by school site and grade level or subject. The sample of first-year teachers ranged in age from 23 to 42 with a mean age of 29. Twelve were women and two were male teachers; there were two Armenians, one Mexican-American, one Korean, and ten American-born participants. Three were second career teachers from engineering, business, and journalism.

## DATA SOURCES

To assess novice teachers' performance, five data sources were employed including (a) support providers' observations, (b) support providers' interviews, (c) novice teachers' lesson plans, (d) K–12 student work, and (e) CFASST events. CFASST is a structured formative assessment system based on the CSTP and the California Academic Content Standards. During their first year of teaching within the CFASST system, novice teachers complete six events, including CSTP-based observations, requiring lesson plans and collection of student work and explorations of one CSTP with reflection.

BTSA first-year teachers were observed by their assigned support provider at least twice during the year in 45 + minute classroom observations using the CFASST Observation Form. Observation data were analyzed according to evidence of performance levels in the CSTP (using a CFASST document called Profiles of Practice) as well as with reference to the six professional development areas represented in Induction Standards 15–20. In their first year of teaching in conjunction with CFASST events, BTSA teachers submitted at least two lesson plans and examples of student work near the beginning and toward the end of their first year of teaching. The 2042 Induction novice teachers were required to submit a minimum of three lesson plans and student work. Teacher performance was also assessed through an analysis of their completed CFASST paperwork described above. Lastly, toward the end of the year, support providers answer on-line interview questions about their assigned novice teacher's classroom performance. These included questions such as:

• What do you see as your novice teacher's strengths in teaching?
• What do you see as your novice teacher's areas for further professional growth?
• What evidence do you see that students in his/her classroom are learning?

Eight data sources were used for addressing the second research question on novice teachers' perceptions of how their induction program influenced their performance in the six areas of professional development. They included (a) a Novice Teacher Demographic Form, (b) monthly on-line novice teacher reflective questions, (c) the 2004 Novice Teachers' Induction Survey, (d) two novice teacher focus groups, (e) content analysis of BTSA Program and 2042 Induction Program documents, and (f) content analysis of site accountability report cards and other school documents.

Reflective questions were emailed to individual novice teachers monthly to query how their induction program influenced their performance in the six professional growth areas. A Likert-scale 50-question survey was designed by the authors and given to novice teachers in the matched groups. The survey asked novice teachers to assess every component of their induction program and its influence on the six professional growth areas. In addition, novice teachers were asked two open-ended questions, a self-assessment question on their professional strengths and weaknesses and a question about their overall perceptions of their induction program.

At the middle and toward the end of this study, two focus groups were conducted with Groups A and B separately. In the first focus group, novice teachers were asked specific questions about each identified professional growth area. In the second focus group, novice teachers were asked more open-ended questions about teaching and influences on their teaching practices. Table 4.2 illustrates the timeline for when the multiple data collection procedures were implemented in this study.

## DATA ANALYSIS

Descriptive statistics were compiled from the 2004 Novice Teachers Induction Survey data through the use of the *Statistical Package for Social Science (SPSS)*. Qualitative data were analyzed using a phenomenological approach described by van Manen (1990) and elaborated by Bogdan and Biklen (1992). Lesson plans and student work were analyzed with reference to CFASST requirements,

**Table 4.2  Data Collection Instruments**

| Month | NT Reflective Questions | NT Focus Groups | Lesson Plans | Student Work | NT Survey | NTSP CFASST Papers | SP Observations of NT | SP Interview Questions |
|---|---|---|---|---|---|---|---|---|
| Sept | X | | | | | X | | |
| Oct | X | | | | | X | | |
| Nov | X | | X | X | | X | X | |
| Dec | X | | | | | X | | |
| Jan | X | X | | | | X | | |
| Feb | X | | X | X | | X | X | |
| Mar | X | | | | | X | | |
| Apr | X | X | | | | X | | |
| May | X | | X | X | | X | X | X |
| June | X | | | | X | X | | |

*Notes:* NT = novice teacher; SP = support provider
The third observation, lesson plan, and student work is optional for BTSA teachers but not for 2042 Induction teachers.

as well as to the California Academic Content Standards. As state certified CFASST trainers, both authors felt comfortable conducting this analysis and checked each others' ratings and analyses of novice teachers' submitted materials.

A thematic analysis of qualitative data sources was conducted based on the constant comparative method of Denzin and Lincoln (1998). Through word counts, matrices, and the construction of participant profiles, the authors spent hours analyzing qualitative data by creating themes within and across data sources. Due to budgetary constraints, no qualitative data analysis package such as ATLAS, Nudist, Code-a-Text, Ethnograph, or AnSWR was available. The authors highly recommend use of a qualitative data analysis package for managing large qualitative data sets; it significantly shortens the time needed for data analysis.

A content analysis of written materials on the schools and induction programs was conducted and incorporated into the study's data analysis. Qualitative and quantitative data were triangulated to produce results based on performance outcomes and perceptions related to the two induction models (Denzin & Lincoln, 1998). To address the first research question, teacher performance levels were calculated based on two criteria. First, findings were triangulated across the five data sources previously identified. Second, levels of performance were based on CFASST developmental performance levels identified by the support providers and by an analysis of the novice teachers' CFASST events.

# Results

Research Question 1: Does participation in the 2042 Induction program vs. a BTSA program influence first-year teachers' performance outcomes in (a) core curriculum, (b) technology, (c) equity and diversity, (d) healthy student learning environment, (e) teaching English Learners, and (f) teaching special populations?

Triangulated data across five data sources (support provider observations, support provider interviews, lesson plans, student work, and CFASST professional development materials) yield the following findings.

## AREAS OF HIGH TEACHER PERFORMANCE OUTCOMES

Both induction groups demonstrate high performance outcomes in three of the six professional development domains: core curriculum, teaching for equity and diversity, and teaching English Learners. This finding is undoubtedly related to numerous factors. One may even be the serendipitous finding that every single teacher in the study has at least one relative who was or is a teacher. Some novice teachers have multiple relatives who are teachers, a factor worth noting because it belies a socialization process into the profession that may be different for novice teachers with no such relatives. This is definitely a question to investigate further.

### Core Curriculum and Subject Specific Pedagogy

All data sources reveal novice teachers' demonstration of core curriculum knowledge and subject specific pedagogy at high performance levels. Core curriculum is never cited as an area for growth by any support provider. Novice teachers' lesson plans and student work repeatedly demonstrate a thorough comprehension of content and a consistent use of the *California K–12 Academic Content Standards*. Novice teachers regularly reflect with their support providers on how well lessons have gone based upon how closely they have been able to adhere to these standards. In their online interviews, support providers comment on novice teachers' strengths in this area, for example, Support Provider A stated "_____ has excellent content knowledge and mastery of teaching" and Support Provider B stated "_____ demonstrates his thorough understanding of the subject matter."

### Supporting Equity, Diversity, and Access to the Core Curriculum

Second, regardless of the cultural and/or linguistic mix of students in the room, support providers often cite novice teachers' "rapport with students," and "knowledge about students." One support provider describes her beginning teacher this way, "He has a great ability to know students and encourage them to extend their knowledge and not give up."

Each pair of matched teachers has a wide variety of linguistic and culturally diverse students in their classrooms. One of the schools is 68% Latino with several other cultures represented in classrooms. Other classrooms have Korean, Armenian, Chinese, Filipino, and some American students in them. One novice teacher comments on the student diversity, "I love it. I like it that they speak more than one language. This is why I chose the _____ district."

The majority of novice teachers state that their teacher education program taught them about diversity issues. Most of the novice teachers believe that it is legitimate for the induction program to "re-emphasize this." One novice teacher, however, repeatedly labels induction in this area as "redundant," and "a replication of what her teacher education program has taught her."

## Teaching English Learners (EL)

Approximately 70% of the teachers in the study teach in classrooms with English Learners (EL). Yet, this area of professional development did not seem to be problematic in either Group A or B. All data sources confirm what support providers observe, that novice teachers use a wide variety of EL strategies appropriately. One support provider states,

> X has a lot of English learners in her class. On one observation, I noticed that one of her lowest level EL groups was doing a group discussion and presentation on *Sojourner Truth*. Not only had she expected and guided them towards research sources, she also taught them how to use bullet points on note cards to guide their discussion. They were so engaged!

In one novice teacher focus group, one novice teacher is Korean, and two are Armenian. All three use their first-hand experience of having been English Learners to enhance their teaching. Novice teachers who are not formerly English Learners speak about using the English Learner Standards frequently.

**Teacher J:** "I use the EL standards because they are a great way to teach in a different style which works for all learners. I learned the EL learning styles in my credential program."

**Teacher K:** "I try as best as I can to use the EL standards in planning lessons. I do implement as many EL strategies as I can. Some of the strategies that I use are: picture walks, realia, Total Physical Response (TPR). . . . I learned the EL Standards and strategies in my teacher prep program."

## AREAS OF SATISFACTORY TEACHER PERFORMANCE OUTCOMES

### Teaching Special Populations

Data analysis reveals one professional development area at the satisfactory performance level; this is Teaching Special Populations. Analysis of the novice teachers' observations, lesson plans, and CFASST paperwork reveals their ability to differentiate instruction and utilize appropriate pedagogical strategies. Novice teachers speak readily about the students with special needs in their classrooms. In class sizes that range from 18 to 39, novice teachers typically have two to four students with special needs. One teacher has eight of 20 students who are labeled "at-risk." Because she works closely with special-services specialists, the novice teacher does not view these students as a negative influence on her teaching nor does her support provider cite her as having difficulties in this area.

One novice teacher did mention teaching special populations as an area with which she needed help. She is, however, in a special circumstance in which one of her students has a severe psychiatric disorder, is receiving extensive mental health assistance, and is scheduled to be transferred to a residential facility. Other novice teachers comment positively about their students with special needs, their ability to provide them differentiated instruction, and the support they receive for them from a variety of specialists.

**Teacher A:** "I receive fantastic support from a specialist every day for my ADHD student."

**Teacher B:** "My deaf student reads lips so I just have to make sure I'm facing her."

**Teacher C:** "I have one visually impaired child, but the specialist comes in every day."

**Teacher D:** "I have one child who was in a car accident in which his grandfather died. . . . He sees the speech therapist and counselor. I have no problems with him or the other handful of students with special needs."

## AREAS OF TEACHER PERFORMANCE OUTCOMES IN NEED OF FURTHER DEVELOPMENT

### *Creating a Supportive and Healthy Environment for Learning*

The professional development area cited as one in need of improvement in 50% of novice teachers in both induction models is *creating a supportive and healthy learning environment*. These novice teachers are observed to have problems with "consistency in classroom rules," "implementing behavioral standards," and "conducting transitions from one activity to another."

A content analysis of what novice teachers wrote about their learning environments on their CFASST forms verifies their need for further growth in creating supportive and healthy learning environments. For instance in November, one novice teacher writes as a classroom goal, "I will stop screaming at the students as a form of management." By March 2004, her classroom management has improved. Her support provider cites her students as "being engaged" and spoke about her classroom management in terms of "more consistency in rules and procedures."

The majority of teachers in this study, including the older, second career teachers who were having trouble with behavior management, are open to learning from their support providers and others at their school site, including their principals. This is illustrated in their conversation.

**Teacher S:** "I still have some behavior problems. The kids won't follow rules."

**Teacher T:** "I tell them, if you're good, I'll put your name on the board. If you're not, you have to go up and erase it."

**Teacher U:** "Have you ever tried table points?"

**Teacher S:** "No, I hate them. Does that writing all the names on the board and erasing the naughty ones really work?"

**Teacher T:** "Yes, it does."

**Teacher S:** "O.K. I'll try it next week."

### *Using Technology to Support Student Learning*

A content analysis of novice teachers' lesson plans, support provider observations, and student work reveals novice teachers' need for growth in this teaching domain. Except for lessons by a secondary computer teacher, no novice teachers integrated technology in their lesson plans. This is particularly noteworthy since the district purchases for each novice teacher a year's membership in Task-Stream, a software package for designing lesson plans and rubrics based on teaching and academic content standards. Although all novice teachers participate in a one-day TaskStream training, when questioned about their use of TaskStream, only one computer teacher actually uses it. The other teachers in the study state that they "hadn't gotten around to using it," or they "still do not understand how to use it."

Interestingly, no novice teachers mention asking their support provider for help with TaskStream. Perhaps this is because support providers did not receive a TaskStream membership and training. Although novice teachers in both groups consider the integration of technology a weak area of professional growth, only one BTSA novice teacher signed up for a district-sponsored technology workshop. It seems clear that novice teachers do not consider utilizing TaskStream a priority amongst all that they must learn and do in their first year of teaching. Research Question 2: How do participants perceive their induction programs as helping in the six areas of professional development?

Eight data sources were analyzed to answer the second research question. They include: a Novice Teacher Demographic Information Form, monthly reflection questions, the 2004 Novice Teachers' Induction Survey, two novice teacher focus groups, BTSA and Induction Program documents and materials, and school Accountability Report Cards, as well as other site data. Findings first are presented across both induction models, Groups A (BTSA) and B (2042 Induction). Then results from a comparison of the matched groups are explored.

## POSITIVE INFLUENCES ON TEACHING PRACTICES

Novice teachers perceive their induction programs as having a positive influence on their teaching in one professional development area: creating a supportive and healthy environment for learning.

*Creating a Supportive and Healthy Environment for Learning*

Although approximately 50% of the novice teachers still exhibit problems with establishing and maintaining a healthy learning environment, specifically implementing class management strategies in the final quarter of their first year of teaching, these same teachers positively identify their induction programs as helping them in this area of professional development. In response to a question if her induction program taught her about creating a healthy learning environment, a novice teacher responded,

> We have attended at least two workshops that specifically deal with this issue and they have been very helpful. Whereas, in teacher education, we learned about theories, in the workshops, we were taught specific strategies that can be applied immediately.

## MEDIUM (SATISFACTORY) INFLUENCES ON TEACHING PRACTICES

In four of the six areas of professional development (core curriculum, diversity and equity, English Learners, and special populations), novice teachers' perceptions of their particular induction program's influence on their teaching practices is satisfactory. Many novice teachers attribute their learning or mastery of these skills and abilities to both their teacher preparation program and their induction program. Their comments frequently echo these attributions. Although one novice teacher seems frustrated by this, the rest state this confluence as something that simply "is," not a problem for them. According to Teacher L, "Induction is like a 'refresher course.' It reminds you of what you learned in your teacher preparation program."

## NEGATIVE INFLUENCES ON TEACHING PRACTICES

Half of the negative influences on novice teachers' teaching practices are unrelated to either induction program. They are (a) fear of losing one's job (100% of novice teachers were hired as *temporary* workers due to budget constraints) and (b) low salaries compared to other jobs their peers hold. Two professional development areas that are viewed as being negatively influenced by the induction programs are core academic content and subject specific pedagogy and using technology to support student learning.

## Core Academic Content and Subject Specific Pedagogy

Novice teachers' perceptions of this area of teaching differ considerably from their classroom performance as assessed by a number of measures previously described. Support providers did not mention novice teachers' lack of content knowledge or inability to teach using content standards. Yet, triangulation of data reveals that almost all novice teachers mention some concerns about knowing content and how to teach it.

**Teacher N:** I need more knowledge about _____. I'm afraid my students will know more than I do about it. I know a lot about _____ but I need more training in _____.

**Teacher 0:** What do my students need more of? I don't want to hurt them by not giving them as much as an experienced teacher would.

When asked to name a subject area with which they needed some assistance, all novice teachers name at least one subject that they needed to refine and/or learn better. Two elementary teachers report that they need assistance with science.

**Teacher R:** Science is what I need help with. I have no training in it.

**Teacher S:** I'm o.k. with math and language arts. Its science that I never get around to doing. I need more help with it.

Three secondary teachers name a certain kind of history with which they felt less competent than the major area in which they did most of their teaching. Another expressed a desire to learn more about the use of cooperative teaching techniques in mathematics. Clearly, there is a discrepancy with their rated performance in the core curriculum and their own perceptions of their content knowledge and subject specific pedagogical skills.

## Use of Technology in the Classroom

Subscriptions to TaskStream that the district purchases for novice teachers are supposed to help them plan standards-based lessons and construct rubrics. According to novice teachers, their failure to implement TaskStream or integrate technology into instruction is due to four reasons: time constraints, lack of site resources, their perception that technology is additional work, and/or their need for more instruction on how to use technology. They comment:

**Teacher D:** I feel that TaskStream can be very valuable, but I feel that I just simply have not had the time to truly put it to use.

**Teacher E:** Right now, I use technology more in the planning, organizing and communicating side of teaching, than I do as a teaching tool. This is mostly due to a lack of resources and somewhat to time.

**Teacher F:** I do not use TaskStream. I don't like it because everything we are supposed to teach is already in the adopted texts, so why, as a first-year teacher, would I want to create more work for myself and spend more time trying to figure it out?

**Teacher G:** I think that TaskStream is great, but it is a little hard to use.

## DIFFERENCES IN THE TWO INDUCTION PROGRAMS' INFLUENCE ON TEACHING PRACTICES

To compare means from the BTSA and the 2042 Induction groups, a nonparametric statistics test, the Mann-Whitney Test, was conducted. It demonstrates that there are consistent, but not statistically significant, differences when comparing ranked means from both induction groups. The 2042 Induction teachers rank their program as having greater positive influences on their practices in all professional development areas than did the BTSA novice teachers. The 2042 Induction Program participants mark 17 questions considerably higher (a minimum of two mean, but not statistically significant, points) than the BTSA program teachers' ranked means. Each question topic and difference in ranked means is listed in table 4.3.

Even when performance data are analyzed along with the self-report data, no clear demarcation of the 2042 Induction group emerges. Given the triangulation of data, one can conclude that these differences in the self-report survey results seem to be largely an artifact of inflated answers by the 2042 Induction novice teachers and do not indicate that the 2042 Induction model positively influences teaching practices more than the BTSA induction model.

# Discussion and Conclusion

Triangulation of data from a large number of data sources indicates that this urban district successfully implemented two induction models during this transition time for California teacher credentialing. Results show that novice teachers in both induction models demonstrate high or satisfactory levels of performance in four professional development areas: *core academic content and subject-specific pedagogy, supporting equity, diversity and access, teaching English Learners,* and *teaching students with special needs.* Novice teachers need further growth in two teaching domains: *creating a supportive and healthy learning environment* and *using technology for instruction.* Implications from these findings are that teacher education programs could provide some of this needed professional development offerings for and/or with this district in these identified areas of development.

**Table 4.3   Induction Program Differences in Mean Ranks of Influence**

| Research Question Number | Content of Question | Difference in Mean Ranks |
|:---:|:---|:---:|
| 49 | Induction requirements | 3.12 |
| 46 | Induction forums | 2.93 |
| 45 | CFASST process | 2.80 |
| 11 | Standards-based teaching | 2.71 |
| 15 | Short & long-term goals | 2.57 |
| 31 | Violence prevention & mediation | 2.57 |
| 33 | Accident prevention strategies | 2.57 |
| 38 | Students with special needs | 2.48 |
| 24 | Educational & web-based software | 2.38 |
| 36 | Integrated technology with instruction | 2.30 |
| 39 | Teach students with learning disabilities | 2.28 |
| 32 | Recognize own beliefs & biases | 2.20 |
| 48 | Induction orientation | 2.20 |
| 25 | Use resources on drugs, alcohol & smoking | 2.17 |
| 37 | Instruct English Learners | 2.17 |
| 47 | Release days | 2.02 |

Notes: Questions are from the Novice Teachers' Induction Survey and are listed by question number.
Readers may e-mail Dr. Wood for the novice teacher survey, interview, and reflective questions, as well as the support provider online interview questions.

In both induction groups, there are some differences between performance outcomes and novice teachers' self-assessment of their curriculum knowledge and subject specific pedagogy. Support providers in both induction programs rate novice teachers' performance in core curriculum quite highly; yet, several novice teachers express anxiety about specific subject matter content and pedagogy. They worry about knowing required subject matter so that "students learn exactly what they are supposed to." From a practical viewpoint, these data suggest that offering novice teachers more choice in professional development topics may reduce novices' anxiety and perhaps lead to greater teaching effectiveness. These results also demonstrate the significance of university/district collaborations so that districts understand exactly what teachers have covered in previous coursework, and induction extends not duplicates preservice curriculum.

Novice teachers in this study describe two strong negative influences on their teaching practices that are unrelated to any professional development domain. They are the fear of losing one's job and low teacher salaries. These negative influences cause stress among novice teachers in both induction programs. They foster insecurities that result in some novice teachers contemplating quitting teaching either in this district or altogether. Research shows that "the longer the time of uncertainty about a job, the more beginning teachers' self-esteem becomes threatened and the more they start doubting their professional competencies" (AEE, 2004, p.113). Novice teachers who start their careers with only temporary contracts may be put at higher risk for leaving the profession. This needs further investigation.

These findings indicate that for this district, like other urban ones across the United States, the greatest challenge may be retaining (not recruiting) capable novice teachers despite budget restrictions and teachers' salaries that are not competitive in a 21st century economy. These findings indicate that sociopolitical issues, such as hiring teachers as temporary employees or offering relatively low salaries can threaten the retention of some novice teachers regardless of the quality of an induction program. Ways to counteract these negative forces on novice teacher satisfaction and possibly retention should be researched further.

Based on induction group membership, there are no statistically significant differences in novice teacher performance outcomes neither between the two induction models nor in novice teachers "perceptions of the induction programs" influences on their teaching practices. Novice teachers in both programs utilize and value their support providers' assistance and suggestions to enhance their standards-based teaching and differentiation of instruction for all students, including English Learners and students with special needs. As part of a larger longitudinal study, the performance outcomes and program perceptions of these novice teachers will be researched in 2005 as they complete their second year of induction to determine if these findings change.

This study demonstrates that when designing induction programs, one should not be afraid to set high expectations or professional requirements. Although 2042 Induction novice teachers are asked to do more, they rate their program very positively and teach at a slightly higher (but not statistically significant) level of performance. Perhaps this indicates that novice teachers are like urban K–12 students; they rise to the level of expectations set for them. Regardless of the model employed, setting high expectations in a quality, structured, comprehensive induction program is the best approach an urban district can take to insure the retention and success of quality teachers (Darling-Hammond & Young, 2002).

# References

Alliance for Excellent Education. (2004). *Tapping the potential: Retaining and developing high-quality novice teachers.* Washington D.C.: Author.

Alpert, D., & Mazzoni, K. (1998). *Teacher credentialing. California Senate Bill 2042. Chapter 548, Statutes of 1998, Education Code. Section 44259.*

Bartell, C. (2004). *Cultivating high-quality teaching through induction and mentoring.* Thousand Oaks, CA: Corwin Press.

Bergeson, M. (1992). *Teaching. California Senate Bill 1422. Chapter 1245, Statutes of 1992, Education Code. Section 44259.*

Bogdan, R., & Biklen, K. (1992). *Qualitative research for education: An introduction to theory and methods* (2nd ed.). Boston: Allyn & Bacon.

California Commission on Teacher Credentialing and the California Department of Education. (1992). *Success for beginning teachers: Final report of the California Participating Teacher project.* Sacramento, CA: Author.

California Commission on Teacher Credentialing and the California Department of Education. (1997a). *California standards for the teaching profession.* Sacramento, CA: Author.

California Commission on Teacher Credentialing and the California Department of Education. (1997b). *Standards of program quality and effectiveness for the Beginning Teacher Support and Assessment program.* Sacramento, CA: Author.

California Commission on Teacher Credentialing and the California Department of Education. (1998). *California K–12 academic content standards.* Sacramento, CA: Author.

California Commission on Teacher Credentialing and the California Department of Education. (1999). *California formative assessment and support system for teachers.* Sacramento, CA: Author.

California Commission on Teacher Credentialing. (2001). *Standards of quality and effectiveness for professional induction programs.* Sacramento, CA: Author.

Darling-Hammond, L., & Young, P. (2002). Defining "highly qualified teachers": What does scientifically based research actually tell us? *Educational Researcher, 31*(9), 13–25.

Denzin, N. K., & Lincoln, V. S. (1998). *Collecting and interpreting qualitative materials.* Thousand Oaks, CA: Sage.

Feiman-Nemser, S., & Parker, M. (1992). *Mentoring in context: A comparison of two U.S. programs for beginning teachers.* East Lansing, MI: National Center for Research on Teacher Learning.

Fideler, E., & Haselkorn, D. (1999). *Learning the ropes: Urban teacher induction programs and practices in the United States.* Belmont, MA: Recruiting Novice Teachers, Inc.

Ganser, T. (1999). Joining forces: Mentors help novice teachers adjust to school life. *Schools in the Middle, 8*(7), 28–31.

Gehrke, N., & Keys, R. (1984). The socialization of beginning teachers through mentor-protégé relationships. *Journal of Teacher Education, 35*(3), 21–24.

Ingersoll, R., & Thomas, T. (2004). Do teacher induction and mentoring matter? *NASSP Bulletin, 88*(638), 30–42.

Little, J. (1990). The mentoring phenomenon and the social organization of teaching. *Review of Research in Education, 16,* 297–351.

Moir, E., & Gless, J. (2001). Quality induction: An investment in teachers. *Teacher Education Quarterly, 28*(1), 109–115.

National Commission on Teaching and America's Future. (1996). *Doing what matters most: Investing in quality teaching.* New York: Author.

Odell, S. (1990). *Mentor teacher programs.* Washington, DC: National Educational Association.

Odell, S., & Huling, L. (Eds.). (2000). *Quality mentoring for novice teachers.* Indianapolis, IN: Kappa Delta Pi.

Olebe, M. (2001). A decade of support for California's novice teachers: The beginning teacher support and assessment program. *Teacher Education Quarterly, 28*(1), 85–109.

Olebe, M., Jackson, A., & Danielson, C. (1999). Investing in beginning teachers—The California model. *Educational Leadership, 65*(8), 41–44.

Schlechty, P., & Vance, V. (1981). Do academically able teachers leave education? The North Carolina case. *Phi Delta Kappan, 63,* 104–112.

Tickle, L. (2000). *Teacher induction: The way ahead.* Philadelphia: Open University Press.

Van Manen, M. (1990). *Researching lived experience.* Albany: State University of New York.

Villani, S. (2002). *Mentoring programs for new teaches: Models of induction and support.* Thousand Oaks, CA: Corwin Press.

Villar, A. (2004). *Measuring the benefits and costs of mentor-based induction: A value-added assessment of new teacher effectiveness linked to student achievement.* Paper presented at the 2004 American Educational Research Association Annual Conference, San Diego.

Wood, A. (2000). Teaching portfolios: Tools for reflective teaching in inner city teacher induction. In D. J. McIntyre & D. Byrd, (Eds.), *Research on effective models for teacher education, teacher education yearbook VIII* (pp. 111–126). Thousand Oaks, CA: Corwin Press.

Wood, A. (2001). What does research say about teacher induction and collaborative partnerships? *Issues in Teacher Education, 10*(2) 69–81.

Yin, R. K. (1989). *Case study research: design and methods* (2nd ed). Newbury Park, CA: Sage.

# Summary and Conclusions

*Leslie Huling*
Texas State University–San Marcos

The researchers from the four previous studies use a wide variety of research approaches and the studies vary greatly on a number of dimensions including research questions addressed, sample size, data collection and analysis techniques, and methods for reporting findings. Yet, each study makes a distinct contribution to the increasing knowledge base for teacher induction, and collectively the studies more firmly establish some of the insights that are consistently emerging in the field of induction research. In this section, unique contributions of each study are discussed. Common themes and implications of study findings are explored. Finally, this section concludes with a discussion of areas still in need of investigation and how these areas might point the direction for future researchers working in the field of teacher induction.

## Noteworthy Contributions of Each Study

In addition to the collective contribution the four Division 1 studies make to the field of induction research, each study makes an individual contribution to our understanding of various aspects of induction programs and induction research.

The study by Ashdown, Hummel-Rossi, and Tobias (chapter 2) in which three New York pilot induction programs are analyzed is, in one sense, a microcosm of the problematic issues we currently face in induction research and, in another sense, models part of the solution to some of these same challenges. Among the promising aspects of this study is the fact that each of the three studies incorporates multiple data sources, examines important outcome measures (such as teacher retention, changes in teaching practices, and student achievement), and employs some common measures. Each of these aspects

89

represents movement in the right direction of advancing our understanding of the complex phenomenon of teacher induction.

On the problematic side, each of the three studies has solid outcome measures, yet it is difficult to make any comparison between the programs or the research findings. The Accelerated Teacher Preparation (ATP) program focuses on changes in teaching behaviors as compared to a control group and measured by the Domain Referenced Teacher Observation (DRTO) in beginning of year, mid-year, and end-of-year observations. The Professional Development Laboratory (PDL) program examines the student achievement of PDL teachers and of teachers not participating in PDL using a standardized assessment of English Language Arts, the efficacy of teachers as measured by the Teacher Efficacy Scale, and observations using the DRTO. Finally, the New Educator Support Team (NEST) pilot program utilizes the DRTO and examines student achievement scores and teacher retention rates. Each of the studies grapples with the issue of a constructed control group, encounters challenges in data collection, and has some subjects who, for a variety of reasons, have incomplete data sets. Finally, because the programs have differing goals and provide different services to participants, it is difficult to know which program practices actually contribute to which program effects. Collectively these challenges are representative of those faced on the broader scale by the community of researchers working in the field of teacher induction research.

The authors offer insights about these challenges when they write, "Examining the key elements of induction practices as they influence perceived collective efficacy in schools could offer a conceptual framework within which to evaluate the effects of induction on teacher development, teacher retention and student achievement." They further elaborate this point and suggest a model that incorporates School Resources, Induction Processes, and School Effects, which offers promise as the model is tested in future studies.

A similar type of study of California induction programs by Wood and Waarich-Fischman (chapter 4) had less trouble comparing programs because of strong program similarities and well-defined program components. In this study, the Beginning Teacher Support and Assessment (BTSA) program and the Senate Bill 2042 (SB2042) Induction Program are compared. It appears the programs are highly similar, with the exception that the SB2042 program incorporates the use of Teacher Performance Expectations (TPE) in various teaching domains and mandates the use of a teaching portfolio for licensure. Both programs are rated favorably by program participants and yield similar results on several measures, with the areas of "Creating & Maintaining a Healthy and Safe Learning Environment" and "Using Technology in Instruction" being the only ones identified as being in need of further development.

With both programs being so similar and yielding such similar results, it is interesting that the authors stop short of asking the obvious questions of whether there are differences in costs of the two programs and, if one is more expensive, whether there is an added benefit to offset the added cost of the program. Likely, the authors felt such a question was premature given the very recent implementation of the SB2042 program, but this question will undoubtedly arise again in the future.

A final noteworthy finding of this study relates to the negative consequences associated with lack of job security. Teachers in both programs report stress about losing one's job as all of the study participants are hired as temporary workers due to budget constraints. The insecurities about job security, as well as low teacher salaries, result in some novice teachers contemplating quitting teaching either in this district or altogether. The authors speculate, "Novice teachers who start their careers with only temporary contracts may be put at higher risk for leaving the profession." While this situation may sometimes be unavoidable, induction program facilitators would be wise to understand that such teachers are operating under additional stress and should anticipate that additional support will be needed to deal with these understandable personal concerns. It is little wonder that such teachers feel less commitment to teaching and their employers as a result of the employer's inability to commit to them.

The final two studies are almost a perfect complement for one another. The Flores study (chapter 3) clearly documents the negative consequences that result from lack of induction support and the Basile study (chapter 1) clearly documents the positive consequences of high levels of induction support.

Flores studied 14 novice teachers from northern Portugal for two years and the two-year timeframe is a strength of this study. Study participants are in schools in which "there was no formal induction for new teachers." In fact, each of the teachers in the study was moved to a different school for their second year of teaching "because of a teacher surplus and the teacher recruitment policy in Portugal" which in essence causes each participant to experience the first year of teaching two years in a row. As a group, the novice teachers report their first year of teaching as a tiring and stressful experience, but also a learning experience. By the end of their second year, six of the 14 participants rate their second year as more negative than their first year, while one states that her second year was equally tiring and negative as her first year. Three of the participants said the second year is better than the first, and three said their second year of teaching is equally positive as their first year. The author sums up the second-year experience when she writes, "As second-year teachers, the participants in this study reported more pessimistic views and experiences of teaching. By and large, their accounts of the second year of teaching pointed to a more negative picture and they highlighted the isolation, lack of support and feelings of loneliness, and frustration." As a result of these findings, Flores recommends that not only should Portugal implement a systematic novice teacher induction program, but that it should continue beyond the first year of teaching.

Another key contribution of this predominantly qualitative study is that it allows us to hear the views of first year teachers in their own words. Much (but certainly not all) of what they express is negative, and while difficult to hear, these statement are a telling affirmation of the need for induction programs. Among the negative comments are the following:

> As a student I was keen to learn, and I always enjoyed being at school. And I am shocked when I look at students who are unmotivated and just don't want to learn. . . . And you feel that your job is useless.

> There is a kind of barrier between new and old staff. As they are already integrated into the school, they do not bother to welcome you.

> I am not happy working in this school and I can't wait for the end of the school year. . . . I notice that in this school there is a gap between younger staff, newcomers and people who have worked in this school for many years. . . . I feel disappointed because you get there with expectations, will to do things for the school and you give up because start thinking "why do I bother, nobody cares, why should I care?" I mean you feel frustrated because the school doesn't support you.

> Whenever I had a problem I sought help from other colleagues, I mean new teachers like me, because I wasn't comfortable asking for advice or help from a teacher who had a permanent post at the school.

In fairness, there were some positive comments though they were certainly less frequent than the negative comments. Samples of positive comments include:

> From my first year of teaching, I will remember my students. I mean, my relationship with them is the most positive feature of this year.

> This year was even more positive. I feel more motivated than last year. I woke up very happy to come here doing my teaching and I got home equally happy because the day went well, and this has been happening every single day. There are not negative experiences this year, students are motivated and committed, and staff and the principal are very supportive.

> We are approaching the end of the year and I feel more and more motivated to come to school and conduct experiments with my students. . . . Students see you as a model and you can't let them down. And I have a good relationship with my colleagues too.

It is interesting to note the power of colleagues in both the positive and negative statements who were clearly a key factor in determining whether the teacher had a positive or negative experience. It would be difficult to find a clearer indication of the true power of mentoring than in the actual words of these novice teachers.

Flores concludes her chapter with a number of insightful implications, about the need for induction support in schools, the need to provide training for mentors and school leaders on how to support novice teachers, and the need to foster collaborative cultures within schools. Her final implication is equally applicable to educational institutions both in Portugal and the United States. She writes of "the need to invest more in the induction period and to rethink the role of teacher educators and universities in the preparation of teachers (the first phase of their career-long professional development) and in fostering the kinds of partnerships with schools conducive to a collaborative engagement in order to enhance the potential of both institutions, through reflection and research bringing together teacher educators, mentors and teachers."

Of all of the studies, the Colorado study by Carole Basile (chapter 1) has the largest sample (N = 1,331), and as such, larger variations in mentoring practices were detected. Basile conducts a statewide survey in the spring of 2001 and determines that in Colorado, like in most other states, the level of induction services provided to novice teachers vary greatly across the state. One of the most interesting findings is that the teachers who report receiving the greatest amount of induction support are those served by mentors who do not have their own classroom responsibilities, but rather are mentoring a group of novice teachers as their professional job assignment. In this study, this mentoring arrangement is called "intensive mentoring" and is contrasted with the type of mentoring that is done by another full-time teacher which, in this study, was called colleague mentoring.

In short, Basile finds that those experiencing intensive mentoring, compared to those experiencing colleague-mentoring, perceive more institutional help with the total induction process, experience more mentoring help in general, claim to have received more information about school and district policy, perceive more institutional help in the area of promoting diversity, claim their mentors did more to promote diversity, find their district and school did more to boost their professional knowledge and skills, believe their mentors did more to boost their professional knowledge and skills, and have more positive feelings about their experience. It is this final finding that illustrates the stark contrast between the findings of this study and the Flores study, where participants receive little induction support and are, as a group, discouraged about teaching and critical of those with whom they work. Considering these studies in combination, it is a very small leap to deduce that as induction support increases so do novice teachers' ability to deal with the challenges of teaching as well as their positive feelings about their experience. In turn, as these teaching abilities and positive feelings increase, so does the likelihood of teacher retention, which, in turn, is likely to result in increased student achievement. Of course, proving these links empirically is the ultimately challenge of induction research, but these two studies in combination can reasonably lead us to speculate that a causal link does, in fact, exist.

It is interesting that Basile's findings (delineated further in the next paragraph) provide evidence that this model of "full-time mentor" is resulting in increased assistance for novice teachers even though, in many instances, this mentor is only on the campus one or two days per week. This finding, no doubt, indicates the difficulty that full-time teachers experience in finding time to mentor, and many sites are currently using or are contemplating using such a model in the near future. Since large numbers of "the baby boom generation" are entering retirement and a significant portion want to continue working part-time and contribute to the teaching profession, there is an increasingly available talent pool from which to staff such a model. While on the surface, it appears that this "intensive mentoring" model would necessarily cost more than the "colleague-mentoring" model, in reality this may not be the case when one considers that there are often costs associated with mentor stipends, professional development, mentor recognition events, etc. that could be redirected to employ retired educators who, because of their retirement income and benefits, can afford to and are willing to work for very competitive rates. When policymakers and administrators factor in what services are being rendered in return for the investment, an intensive mentoring model may well be the most cost-effective model.

Other noteworthy aspects of Basile's study relate to the role of administrators and the need for extensive collaboration across entities. Basile emphasizes that administrators need preparation in how to support novice teachers. She writes, "It is not surprising to find that many administrators are uncertain of how to support new teachers. Oftentimes, providing comprehensive support is not part of their preparation, and many administrators themselves receive no induction for their jobs." What Basile's study establishes is that induction practices in Colorado are uneven across districts, and to address this issue, the Colorado New Teacher Consortium has formed a comprehensive partnership to support novice teachers. Her chapter concludes with this sentiment when she writes, "We believe that these efforts from the entire statewide community will create a comprehensive induction system for new teachers and create an environment in every district, no matter how large or small, urban or rural, that will build capacity for high quality teachers who remain in teaching."

# Study Implications for Teacher Educators

Teacher educators who carefully consider these four studies will undoubtedly see the common themes as well as a number of implications for their practice as teacher educators in universities, public schools, education service agencies, or other entities that have a stake in teacher induction. The most obvious of these, of course, is that there is a pressing need for experienced educators to provide support and assistance to those entering the teaching profession. Consequently, all teacher educators should incorporate the provision of induction support into their day-to-day professional practices. University-based teacher educators need to partner with public school practitioners in delivering these programs, and both groups, in their dealing with novice teachers, should normalize the need for and provision of induction support programs.

A second major implication from this collection of studies is that there is a pressing and ongoing need for teacher educators to take a leadership role in the preparation and development of support providers including mentors, school administrators, and other school and university-based teacher educators. Because of staff turnover, the need to provide new mentor preparation is ongoing and mentors and other support personnel need to continually improve their skills as a part of their ongoing professional development. Teacher educators, because of their background and training in teacher development, are in a key role to provide this leadership.

Another implication from these studies is that teacher educators should carefully consider the benefits of differentiated mentoring support. For example, Basile finds that younger teachers view their induction support as more helpful than teachers who enter teaching at the ages of 32–65. One explanation for this, of course, is that the older teacher group has previous experiences adjusting to workplace norms and navigating relationships with co-workers which are areas that younger novice teachers find challenging, and thus the mentoring help is perceived by younger teachers as being of greater benefit. Such a finding sheds light on the idea that program facilitators might want to consider differentiated types of mentoring as opposed to a "one size fits all" view. In addition to age of the novice teacher, other obvious considerations that could indicate the need for a differentiated approach to mentoring would be the amount and type of teacher preparation of the novice teacher, the difficulty of teaching assignment, and characteristics of the student population and school environment, just to name a few.

An additional implication of this work is that teacher educators need to think more practically and realistically about the costs involved in providing, and not providing, induction support programs. Teacher turnover has real costs, in terms of dollars, student achievement, and workplace ecology. The dollars required to support induction programs, while not insignificant, are a necessary price to pay to protect the investment that has been made in each novice teacher employed. Teacher educators and school administrators need to make sure that this reality is openly on the table in conversations with policymakers when grappling with the topics of resources, expenditures, and high stakes accountability systems.

Finally, there is a pressing need for teacher educators in all settings to aggressively pursue research in order to provide data necessary to advance the knowledge base of teacher induction and to thoroughly document the various effects of different induction programs. As elusive as they are, we must continue to purse the links between induction support, teacher retention, and student achievement. This information is critically needed to improve pre-service teacher preparation, to enhance induction programs, and to provide policymakers with data upon which to base their policy and resource decisions.

# Areas Still in Need of Investigation

Admittedly, it will likely be some time before we have a complete understanding of the relationship between induction support and student achievement. Exploring this relationship is the new frontier for teacher induction research and the field must respond with high quality studies that investigate this important relationship. However, a few words of caution are in order. It is unlikely that the relationship between induction support and student achievement will ever be as straightforward as the "hard to convince" critics of education would like it to be. Furthermore, it is unlikely that achievement effects can be understood without also considering the effects of induction support on teacher retention. Those who seek quick fixes would like evidence that the resources invested in induction support in the fall will pay off in terms of spring student achievement scores (as measured by standardized tests). While there likely is some payoff to be measured in this way, the more important achievement effect is likely to be the cumulative effect on achievement that is intertwined with induction support and teacher retention. To better understand this complex relationship, let's consider a single classroom. If a classroom has a novice teacher who, because of inadequate induction support, leaves after the one year of teaching, and this cycle repeats the following year, the classroom will likely be staffed with yet a third novice teacher the subsequent year. At this point, the instruction in this classroom is not likely to be as effective as it would be if the classroom were now staffed with a third-year teacher as opposed to a first-year teacher. In hard to staff schools this scenario repeats itself in classroom after classroom and for some children, much of their academic career is spent suspended in this revolving door of school staffing challenges. There is no denying that this situation seriously impacts instruction and achievement; yet it is difficult to disentangle the exact impact that induction support has on teacher retention and student achievement at a given point in time or as it accumulates over time. So, given these complexities, how should researchers proceed?

It will take sophisticated long-term studies to investigate these complex issues. A starting point would be to look retrospectively at student achievement at a single grade level (at a campus or within district) and to correlate this achievement with the experience of the staff at that grade level. With five or more years of retrospective data, it would be possible to extend the trend lines for both staff experience and student achievement. Where less than desirable trends are present, the setting is ripe for intervention in the form of increased induction support for novice teachers. Comprehensive studies would then be needed to document support delivered and to measure impact on teacher retention and subsequently on student achievement. It is likely that teacher retention and student achievement can be increased through induction support, but it will undoubtedly take a sustained effort over a period of years to achieve the desired effects on a large scale, and thus will require a "leap of faith" in the meantime to justify resources invested in induction support as a means to address student achievement. This point also leads to a second major area in need of further investigation by teacher induction researchers—how to effectively document induction support provided in order to accurately tie it to teacher retention and student achievement outcomes.

Most induction research to date looks at effects at the program level (i.e., how do teachers in this induction support program compare to teachers in a different program or to teachers who are not in an induction support program?) While this approach may seem reasonable, most program facilitators acknowledge the reality that some mentor-mentee pairs engage to a higher degree and function much more effectively than others. By having the unit of investigation be the program, the true effects of induction support are masked or skewed by including some subjects who, in fact, receive little or none of the "treatment" assumed to be delivered to program participants. Similarly, it is possible that a teacher who is identified as not participating in an induction support program may, in fact receive considerable induction support through informal avenues. To truly get at the effects of induction support, it will be necessary to make the unit of investigation the mentor-mentee pair and to collect detailed information at this level about what induction support was actually provided, before examining the issues of retention and achievement. Naturally, this will be a more tedious and costly investigation, but one that is likely necessary if we are to accurately measure the effects of induction support.

A similar case can be argued when attempting to relate program activities (and resources devoted to program activities) to support provided. For example, one can assume that increased amounts of mentor training are likely to result in increased amounts of induction support. However, if a specific mentor did not participate in the mentor training and yet is included in the data collection sample, it is difficult to determine the true effects of mentor training on support provided. This is not to say that this mentor should be excluded from the study, but rather that the lack of mentor training should be noted so that the practices of trained and untrained mentors could be analyzed accordingly. The inclusion of such details undoubtedly adds to the complexity of the puzzle, but at the same time, gives a much more accurate picture of what is or is not making a difference in support provided, teacher retention, and/or student achievement.

In terms of future directions, one study that is currently underway at the Center for Research, Evaluation and Advancement of Teacher Education (CREATE) is attempting to capture much of this complexity by interviewing novice teachers in great detail about the support received and mentor teachers about their individual experiences with program support structures (i.e., program training, record-keeping, ongoing contact with the program coordinator, etc.). It will be interesting to follow this study as it progresses and to see to what degree additional clarity is achieved through the inclusion of this in-depth type of investigation.

A final area in need of additional investigation relates to the resources needed to implement and maintain induction support programs. Most educators agree that induction support programs are needed, but the reality is that resources are limited and educators must make difficult choices about how to invest resources. Clearly, if induction programs can be shown to bring about substantial increases in student achievement, resources for such programs will likely be forthcoming. However, other educators argue the need for induction program resources for compelling financial reasons in addition to academic reasons. These educators contend that the financial cost of teacher turnover is greater than the resources needed to support induction programs that could dramatically decrease novice teacher attrition. Their argument is convincing when one considers the district dollars spent on teacher recruitment, the administrative cost of processing, selecting, and employing a new hire, as well as any signing bonuses and the considerable expense of providing professional development. Clearly all of these expenses become a lost investment when a recently hired teacher resigns.

The true cost of teacher turnover is the focus of the most recent study of the National Council on Teaching and America's Future (NCTAF). This prestigious organization, which has previously issued the highly acclaimed reports *What Matters Most* and *No Dream Denied*, is now focusing its attention and resources on illuminating the issue of how resources consumed by "teacher churn" could be better spent on support programs aimed at decreasing teacher attrition.

While this study will undoubtedly turn the spotlight on this resource utilization issue, the ongoing need for strong research that investigates the true cost of teacher turnover will continue for years to come. Such research will be key in convincing taxpayers and policymakers that an investment in induction support programs is good economy, even in (and perhaps especially in) an environment of declining resources.

Currently teacher induction research is in an exciting and challenging time and many large research questions loom on the horizon. Studies such as the ones in Division 1, as well as those in the subsequent two divisions, are an important part of the tapestry that is currently being woven by teacher induction researchers around the globe. As these studies advance our understanding of teacher induction practices and effects, we can expect to better serve the need of today's novice teachers and those who will enter teaching in the years to come.

Division 2

# LOOKING CLOSELY AT THE MENTORING EXPERIENCE

# Overview and Framework

*Virginia Resta*
Texas State University–San Marcos

> Virginia Resta is assistant dean at Texas State University–San Marcos and associate professor in the Department of Curriculum and Instruction. Recent mentoring projects include the Teacher Fellows Program, Teacher Recruitment and Induction Program, and Novice Teacher Induction Program. She is currently serving on her second ATE Commission on Mentoring.

Since the 1980s interest in ways to improve beginning teachers' first experiences in the profession have grown steadily, spurred on by teacher shortages, ever increasing student populations, and alarming teacher attrition rates. It was widely reported that 20 to 30% of new teachers leave the profession within the first 3 years; 9.3% don't make it through their first year of teaching; and after 5 years approximately 50% of beginners have left the field (Ingersoll, 2001). High teacher turnover leads to less stable and less effective learning environments for students. It places greater demands on teachers and other school staff members and increases the amount of money and time that must be spent in recruiting, hiring, and training replacements (DePaul, 2000 as cited in Brewster & Railstack, 2001). In response to these trends, mentoring programs have increased dramatically since the 1980s in the hopes of retaining promising teachers in the profession and increasing the effectiveness of beginning teachers as they transition from their role as preservice teacher to full-fledged accomplished classroom teachers. Research demonstrates that districts such as Rochester, New York, Cincinnati, Columbus, and Toledo, Ohio have reduced attrition rates of beginning teachers by more than two-thirds by providing expert mentors with release time to coach beginners in their first year on the job (NCTAF, 1996).

The effectiveness of the teacher is the major determinant of student academic progress. In today's environment of the No Child Left Behind Act and its requirement of high-stakes testing there is a renewed sense of urgency to bring beginning teachers up to speed as quickly as possible. This is especially important since beginning teachers are disproportionately assigned to teach students in low-income, high minority schools and students in lower track classes who have the greatest need for skilled teachers in order to succeed (National Commission on Teaching and America's Future [NCTAF], 1996). Consequently, teacher turnover is 50% higher in high-poverty than in low-poverty schools (Ingersoll, 2001). A large share of students in high-turnover schools are consigned to a continual parade of ineffective teachers (Darling-Hammond, 2003). These students, like all others, are entitled to sound instruction and cannot afford to lose a year of schooling to a teacher who is ineffective or learning by trial and error on the job (Darling-Hammond & Bransford, 2005). Teacher effects on student achievement are been found to be both additive and cumulative with little evidence that subsequent exposure to effective teachers can offset the effects of earlier ineffective ones (Sanders & Horn, 1998). In contrast to this trend, there is evidence that beginning teachers who experience high-quality mentoring not only stay in the profession at higher rates, but also become competent more quickly than those who must learn by trial and error (Darling-Hammond, 2003). Based on these findings, an increasing number of states and school districts have initiated efforts to create mentoring programs. For example, the number of mentoring programs has increased from seven states in 1996–1997 to 33 states in 2002.

The programs, however, vary significantly in quality, commitment of resources, and level of support provided to novice teachers. These programs will produce benefits for beginning teachers and ultimately for their students only if they are well designed, well supported, and invest substantially in the professional development of mentors. Previous research describing critical components of mentoring programs and the roles of those working in them has been invaluable in helping leaders design the infrastructure for mentoring programs. Having managed to get such a large number of programs underway to support beginning teachers, it is now important to closely examine what happens in the context of the mentoring experience. Recent studies provide evidence to inform stakeholders, policymakers, administrators, and teacher educators of aspects of the mentoring experience that yield the greatest benefits to novice teachers. Although mentor teachers have an important role to play, all mentoring programs do not yield the same results; careful attention must be paid to their practices of mentoring.

The framework for the research studies in this section of the yearbook examines the quality of the mentoring experience novices receive and reveals the complexity of the mentor's role. The following four chapters provide examples and research findings, drawn from close examination of the mentoring experience. In chapter 5, Yendol-Hoppey and Dana provide a year-long case study through which they reveal how differences in the perceptions and expectations of a novice and a mentor teacher may weaken or reduce the quality and effectiveness of the mentoring experience. The authors highlight the importance of mentor selection, matching, and proximity and provide important insights and suggestions for matching mentors and novices.

Wang, Odell, and Strong, in chapter 6, drawing on conversations recorded from three novice-mentor pairs in an induction context over a two-year period, analyze the content and focus of novice-mentor conversations about novice teachers' lessons. The authors raise important questions about the effectiveness of novice-mentor conversations in supporting novice teachers' focus on standards-based teaching. Johnson and Reiman, in chapter 7, demonstrate how mentor-mentee interactions are influenced by mentors' dispositions. The authors tested promising tools for measuring mentor dispositions, and provide recommendations for professional development programs interested in examining mentor dispositions and their influence on novice teachers.

Finally, in chapter 8, Kline and Salzman compare mentor teachers and their non-mentoring colleagues in the domains of planning and preparation, classroom environment, instruction, and professional responsibilities. The authors illustrate the need to consider how mentors' performance in critical areas of practice impacts the novice teachers with whom they work and suggest serendipitous professional development benefits to mentor teachers.

As is demonstrated in the chapters that follow, mentor teachers have an important role in the induction of beginning teachers. These researchers provide important insights about the mentoring experience and provide suggestions that can improve the mentoring process for mentors and their protégés.

# References

Brewster, C., & Railstack, J. (2001). *Supporting beginning teachers: How administrators, teachers and policymakers can help new teachers succeed.* Portland, OR: Northwest Regional Educational Lab. By Request Series.

Darling-Hammond, L. (2003). Keeping good teachers: Why it matters, what leaders can do. *Educational Leadership, 60*(8), 6–13.

Darling-Hammond, L., & Bransford, J. (Eds.). (2005). *Preparing teachers for a changing world: What teachers should learn and be able to do.* Hoboken, NJ: John Wiley & Sons.

Ingersol, R. (2001). Teacher turnover and teacher shortages: An organizational analysis. *American Educational Research Journal, 38*(3), 499–534.

National Commission on Teaching and America's Future (NCTAF). (1996). *What matters most: Teaching for America's future.* New York: Author.

Rowley, J. (1999) The good mentor. *Educational Leadership, 56*(8), 20–22.

Sanders, W., & Horn, S. (1998). Research findings from the Tennessee value-added assessment system (TVAAS) database: Implications for educational evaluation and research. *Journal of Personnel Evaluation in Education, 12*(3), 247–256.

CHAPTER 5

# Understanding and Theorizing Exemplary Mentoring through the Use of Metaphor

## THE CASE OF BRIDGETT, A GARDENER

*Diane Yendol-Hoppey*
University of Florida

*Nancy Fichtman Dana*
University of Florida

Diane Yendol-Hoppey is an assistant professor in the School of Teaching and Learning. Her area of research focuses on understanding the complexity of teacher learning. As a result she teaches classes in supervision and professional development. Her research has focused on understanding the power of a variety of tools for teacher learning including teacher inquiry, professional learning communities, mentoring, teacher leadership, the development of school-based teacher educators, and professional development schools. She has published numerous articles in referred journals focused on understanding teacher thinking about the complexity of teaching, capturing the role of context in teacher learning, and identifying the development of pedagogical content knowledge.

Nancy Fichtman Dana is currently a professor of education and director of the Center for School Improvement at the University of Florida. Prior to her appointment at the University of Florida, she served on the faculty of Curriculum and Instruction at Pennsylvania State University, where she developed and directed the State College Area School District–Pennsylvania State University Elementary Professional Development School program. She has published numerous articles in professional journals as well as authored *The Reflective Educator's Guide to Classroom Research* with Diane Yendol-Silva (now Yendol-Hoppey).

ABSTRACT

This case study enhances our understanding and theorizing about exemplary mentoring through the use of metaphor. As a result, the case of Bridgett offers the metaphorical work of a gardener to give mentors insight into the types of activities that promote prospective teacher growth. This eighteen-month study draws on a variety of data including field notes, interviews, documents, journals, and e-mail. Data analysis consists of ongoing readings of collected data, sorting data by work or interaction activity, and searching for patterned regularities in the data. Like the gardener, Bridgett gives careful attention to a variety of spaces where her intern grows. Through this activity she intentionally cultivates five different spaces within her classroom: space to be, space to explore, space to raise questions, space to improve, and space to celebrate. The case study suggests that mentoring is indeed a complex and dynamic activity that requires attention to the dispositions of both the mentor and mentee.

The last decade has brought heightened interest in mentoring. In fact, teacher education reformers "regard the mentor-novice relationship in the context of teaching as one of the most important strategies to support novices' learning to teach and, thus, to improve the quality of teaching" (Wang, 2001, p. 52). Concurrent to the heightened interest in mentoring during the last decade is the Professional Development School movement. Professional Development Schools facilitate reform and renewal by building partnerships between public schools and colleges of education to prepare the next generations of teachers (Lieberman and Miller, 1990). The professional development school often offers an intense field placement or internship for prospective teachers, a context where reform and simultaneous renewal can occur. Since 1990, almost every commission and report on teacher education advocates the PDS as a strong vehicle for teacher preparation and educational change (Goodlad, 1990; Holmes, 1986, 1990; Levine, 1992). As a result, literally hundreds of PDSs have emerged across the country.

Unfortunately, across the nation, as schools have become PDSs and prospective teachers have been placed in PDSs to be mentored into the profession, assumptions have been made that if teachers are good in the classroom, they will be good mentors. Yet, research tells us that outstanding teaching does not readily and intuitively translate to outstanding mentoring. For example, in an extensive research study comparing mentor teachers in the United States, UK, and China, Wang (2001) finds that:

Relevant teaching experience, though important, is not a sufficient condition for a teacher to be a professional mentor. Mentors who are practicing or moving toward practicing the reform-minded teaching may not develop the necessary conceptions and practices of mentoring that offer all the crucial opportunities for novices to learn to teach in a similar way. Thus, when selecting mentor teachers, not only is it important to consider the relevant teaching experiences of mentors but it is also important to identify how mentors conceptualize mentoring and their relevant experience in conducting the kind of mentoring practices expected. (pp. 71–72)

Given the essential call made by Wang (2001) to identify how mentors conceptualize their mentoring, coupled with the proliferation of Professional Development Schools across the nation, this study is conducted to capture the way an exemplary mentor teacher understands and enacts her mentoring role in a professional development school setting. Research questions include: (a) How does a mentor conceptualize her work with a novice teacher? (b) What metaphor(s) does she utilize to conceptualize her mentoring role? (c) What are the theoretical underpinnings of a mentor's work that leads to novice teacher development? And (d) How does a mentor's practice and dispositions intersect with novice teacher learning?

# Theoretical Framework: The Use of Metaphor to Understand Mentoring

Most people view metaphor as an abstraction of language, associating metaphor mainly with the reading and writing of literature and poetry. With the work of many philosophers and linguists, however, metaphor has come to mean much more than "icing on the cake of literality, but is instead ingrained into the way that human beings think and perceive" (Gregory, 1987, p. 101). For example, according to Lakoff and Johnson (1980), metaphor:

is pervasive in everyday life, not just in language but in thought and action. Our ordinary conceptual system, in terms of which we both think and act, is fundamentally metaphorical in nature. The concepts that govern our thought are not just matters of the intellect. They also govern our everyday functioning, structure what we perceive, how we get around in the world, and how we relate to other people. Our conceptual system thus plays a central role in defining our everyday realities. If . . . our conceptual system is largely metaphorical, then the way we think, what we experience, and what we do every day is very much a matter of metaphor. (p. 3)

With this insight into metaphor, many in the field of education have gone from viewing metaphor as a mere literary device taught in English classes to a powerful conceptual tool that can be used to understand the current state of educational practices. If metaphors govern the way we think, what we experience, and what we do in everyday life, then an understanding of metaphors utilized by mentor teachers in professional development schools can be at the heart of understanding and facilitating the professional growth of teachers as mentors.

Existing literature on mentoring offers an assortment of metaphors characterizing alternative conceptions of the work of teachers who help induct new teachers into the teaching profession. For example, contemporary mentor definitions include the following:

- Coach, positive role model, developer of talent, opener of doors, protector, sponsor (Schien, 1978)
- Trusted guide, counselor, teacher-guardian (Galvez-Hjornevik, 1986)
- Colleague teacher, helping teacher, peer teacher, support teacher (Borko, 1986)

Additionally, Goldsberry (1998) defines mentor as "an experienced practitioner who guides the development of an inexperienced one" (p. 438). Zimpher and Grossman (1992) define a mentor as a "master of the craft of teaching and personable in dealing with other teachers; an empathetic individual who understands the need for a mentorship role" (p. 145). Harris (1998) explores the work of mentoring in his review and concludes that the mentoring role lacks clarity and a conceptual model. The existing definitions of mentoring are indeed ambiguous and do not offer much guidance in defining and knowing the work of a mentor of prospective teachers in a professional development school. As a result, the empirical literature would benefit by not only involving mentors in the naming of the metaphor that represents their work but empirical study of the conceptual underpinnings that support that metaphor.

# Methodology

This study was interpretive (Erickson, 1986) in nature and drew on case study methodology (Stake, 1995) informed by both ethnographic (Wolcott, 1994) and phenomenological (Denzin & Lincoln, 1994) lenses. This methodology focused the spotlight on the ways one mentor teacher came to know and carry out her work with a prospective teacher over a ten-month period that spans the first year of work in a PDS. In this particular PDS, interns were placed in the classroom every day for an entire school year to teach and inquire into teaching alongside the mentor teacher (Yendol-Silva & Dana, 2004; Silva & Dana, 2001).

Using a unique case selection procedure, the mentor teacher was selected from a pool of six veteran teachers serving as mentor teachers for the first time in a newly formed professional development school. In this case, the unique attributes included: (a) the mentor's willingness to actively engage in creating a year-long internship with an inquiry component and (b) the intern/mentor dyad's negotiation of a successful and exemplary learning context as perceived by intern, mentor, and university faculty. Through this process, one teacher, Bridgett, and her intern, Angela, (pseudonyms) were selected for participation in this study, and their story is the focus of this paper. Both participants were white females. Bridgett had been teaching for nearly twenty years and had received no formal mentor training. Angela was completing her senior year of a four-year teacher education program. Yet, it is important to note that this case study of Bridgett was a part of a larger study exploring the work lives of mentor teachers in a newly formed PDS. This larger study yielded data and interpretation of other exemplary forms of mentoring (Yendol-Hoppey, in press; Silva, 1999) as well as issues veteran teachers face as they assume the role of teacher educator in PDS work (Yendol-Silva & Dana, 2004).

The data sources used to understand Bridgett's work as a mentor teacher included: (a) 26 journal entries written by Bridgett and her intern Angela, (b) weekly fieldnotes of conversations with Bridgett and Angela, (c) one formal interview at the end of the school year with Angela, (d) e-mail between interviewer and participants, (e) meeting minutes, (f) weekly classroom teaching observation notes, and (g) three semi-structured interviews with Bridgett focused on her experiences working as a mentor. Each of these sources offered insight into Bridgett's daily work as a mentor and Angela's experiences being mentored. Specifically, the semi-structured interviews drew on Seidman's (1991) interview schedule which began by exploring Bridgett's prior experiences and then inquired into Bridgett's mentoring experiences at multiple points across the course of a school year. The tape recordings of each interview were transcribed, allowing for accurate reporting of the participants' responses and enabling the researchers to interpret specific responses in the context of the entire transcript. The researcher assumed the role of participant observer as she captured Bridgett's work, while simultaneously serving as a field advisor responsible for guiding Angela's growth as a teacher.

After reviewing the data set multiple times utilizing Wolcott's (1994) methodological structure of description, analysis, and interpretation, themes emerged within this case that outlined the components or "spaces" present in Bridgett's mentoring work (Stake, 1995). As themes emerged, systematic searches of the data for disconfirming and confirming evidence to support the themes were conducted (Erickson, 1986). Based on the emerging themes, the metaphor of gardener was selected in consultation with Bridgett to capture, explicate, and theorize her work as a mentor teacher. Once the report of the Bridgett's metaphor was written, it was member checked to ensure trustworthiness (Patton, 2002). The remaining sections of this paper present a description, analysis, and interpretation of Bridgett, "The Gardener" and her work with her intern, Angela, as it unfolded throughout one entire school year in an elementary (kindergarten) classroom.

# Bridgett, the Gardener

The work of a gardener entails overseeing a plot of land intentionally and deliberately divided into unique spaces targeted for specific types of plants to grow. Similarly, for Bridgett, her work as a mentor entails intentionally planning, plotting, and creating many types of "spaces," both *physical* and *psychic* (Oberg, 1989), within the classroom for her intern to develop.

Oberg's (1989) concept of "space" acknowledges the need for "times and places for teachers to contemplate what it means to be educators in their situations" (p. 63) and argues that:

> More crucial than the physical space and time for reflection is the psychic space where it can happen. Teachers who feel that a supervisor knows better than they themselves do what they should be doing or who feel they will be held to behavioral specifications of their jobs are not likely to ask the kinds of penetrating questions that reach down to the very ground of their practice." (p. 64)

Oberg's conception of cultivating space during field experiences to pose questions that reach down to the very ground of practice correlates metaphorically with the gardener's careful attention to cultivating the soil that reaches down to the roots of a plant. Skilled gardeners know optimal plant growth and development occurs only when care is given to the space within which the plant grows. Like the gardener, Bridgett gives careful attention to the space her intern grows, in her intentional cultivation of five different spaces within her classroom: space to be, space to explore, space to raise questions, space to improve, and space to celebrate.

## SPACE TO BE

Bridgett offers the idea of "feeling like a teacher" or "being a teacher" as a necessary first space to create for and with her intern. Unlike many cooperating teachers who are accustomed to maintaining the role of "head teacher" in the classroom until the traditional "takeover" period, Bridgett believes that her intern, Angela, will need to feel equally like a teacher right from the start:

> Initially I feel like I am there to make it as successful an experience as possible. I think that they need to feel like they can grow and stretch. . . . I like for the intern to have as much opportunity to feel like a teacher and work with children more informally to get their comfort level as a teacher. (Bridgett, interview B, 203–207)

By providing the space for Angela to be and feel like a teacher, Bridgett encourages Angela to assume the role of teacher, rather than student, and to begin cultivating the stance of a professional engaged in learning about her own practice.

Bridgett's focus on providing Angela a "space to be a teacher" connects to the notion of efficacy (Costa & Garmston, 1994). By being a teacher, Angela begins believing she can make a difference with her students and becomes more willing to challenge herself. In fact, research suggests that teachers with efficacy are likely to expend more energy in their work, persevere longer, set more challenging goals, and continue in the face of barriers or failure (Costa & Garmston). According to Garmston, Lipton, and Kaiser (1998), "efficacious people regard events as opportunities for learning, believe that personal action produces outcomes, control performance anxiety by accessing personal resources, and recognize what is not known by the self and seek to learn. They are self-modifying" (p. 266). Thus, feeling like a teacher is a keystone behavior to professional growth and Bridgett's focus on helping Angela gain an early sense of efficacy as an intern is a central feature in building Angela's capacity as a learner. This space to "be a teacher" is a prerequisite necessary for successful exploration of each of the other spaces.

## SPACE TO EXPLORE

Consistent with her work as a kindergarten teacher, Bridgett's belief system honors the importance of learning by doing:

> Understanding that people learn best by doing—No matter what the age of the student, having the actual experience facilitates the best and longest lasting learning. (Bridgett, Journal, 5/99)

As a result of this belief system, Bridgett also cultivates "space to explore" as a way of learning to teach in her classroom. Angela occupies this space to explore by observing Bridgett in action, and translating what she is learning through observation into her own developing teaching practices. Angela describes this process:

> I learned a lot from (Bridgett's) modeling. I would observe, try, think about it, try, observe, reflect. We did a lot of talking about things I observed. (Angela, interview, 104–106)

Although evidence suggests that Bridgett's modeling offered rich opportunities for Angela to learn, Angela's ability to learn through observation also centered on her own ability to independently identify and practice powerful elements of Bridgett's instructional practice. Thus, an intern's ability to identify, replicate, critique and adjust powerful practices contributes substantially to growth within the space to explore.

Additionally, an important component of "space to explore" is Bridgett's willingness to allow Angela to develop her own teaching identity:

> I think you need to be flexible because there is no guarantee that the intern you have will be a perfect match personality-wise, style-wise, and you need to be able to let that intern develop her own strengths and not have to fit into your mold. So I can't think of anything more important than that because being a mentor teacher means that you are there to try and make sure this new teacher is as successful as possible and let her grow and stretch as much as she possibly can. (Bridgett, interview A, 332–338)

Bridgett's accepting tone sets the stage for Angela's freedom and space to learn through exploration:

> She gives me a lot of room to explore and figure things out on my own . . . She has given me the freedom that I wanted and I have been able to go in directions I have wanted. Much like she is with her students, she leaves lots of room to take risks and fail and I know she is going to be there for me no matter what, if it is a flop or not. (Angela, interview, 18 and 25–28)

The space to explore encourages Angela to take risks as she grows and learns about herself as a teacher.

Hence, inherent in this space of exploration is the importance of risk-taking. This risk-taking necessitates mentor support but also prospective teacher willingness to engage in risk taking. This is consistent with Hall's (1996) study of the Indiana State Professional Development School, where risk-taking was identified as a critical value and belief system in the culture of the schools. As the year progressed, Bridgett increasingly encourages Angela to share her new ideas and take risks as she implements them:

> So when I asked her what she was thinking about doing for social studies, Angela said, "Well, how about if I use the pen pal exchange?" Then I suggested that maybe we could add a foreign exchange puppet and Angela picked up on it and is constantly infusing things that we have started with her ideas. I am hoping it continues to go this way. (Bridgett, interview A, 318–323)

Also inherent in this space for exploration is the importance of confidence. Without confidence, the risk taking to share ideas as described in the above quote could not happen. Bridgett indicates that Angela's confidence to take risks within the exploratory space Bridgett cultivated for this purpose grew over time:

> I think that it took Angela a long time to feel comfortable to explore in the classroom. I can tell she is one of those very obedient children who has probably done what her parents have expected her to do . . . It took a while for her to share her opinions, even her sense of humor. But I don't think of this as horribly negative, it is just adjusting to each other's personalities and that I wanted her to start to give me more ideas. (Bridgett, interview B, 441–449)

Indeed, the longevity of this mentoring relationship (over an entire school year) affords Angela the opportunity to develop the confidence and trust necessary to utilize the space Bridgett created for exploration of teaching.

Finally, although Bridgett believes that exploration is a key to learning to teach, she does not believe that exploration without reflection is productive. Angela describes the importance of reflection:

> After my lesson, Bridgett asked me to reflect on what I thought went well, what I thought didn't go so well and what changes I might make next time. When I sat down to reflect it wasn't as easy as I thought it would be. (Angela, Triad journal, 2/99)

Bridgett's insistence on exploration paired with reflection encourages Angela to think seriously about her work with children.

## SPACE TO RAISE QUESTIONS

Bridgett's garden encourages Angela to raise two types of questions as she prepares and reflects on her work, instructional and philosophical. The most frequently posed questions are typically instructional and tend to center around when and how she should implement instruction. In the beginning of the year, these instructional questions are initiated by Bridgett but as the year progresses and Angela begins assuming more responsibilities, Angela initiates more of these questions. These questions often center on timing, materials, and types of strategies she is considering in her planning.

As gardeners utilize essential tools, such as hoes, rakes, and hedgers, to shape the growth of plants, Angela and Bridgett find a tool during the second half of the internship year to maximize the use of "space to raise questions"—the triad journal (Silva, 2002). This journal is an outgrowth of the traditional supervisor and student teacher journal assignment used at the university. However, the journal naturally evolves into a three-way dialogue journal initiated by the intern with contributions from both the supervisor and mentor. Angela reflects on their use of the triad journal:

> I kind of wish we would have done this sooner. I think there are questions that I should ask her but I don't. But in the triad journals she can see my thinking coming out about children and situations. I think it is a good way for everyone to see what each other is thinking. I bring up questions and those bring up more thoughts for me, more things of concern. I think it is because I have a close relationship with her. (Angela, interview, 218–223)

Bridgett also shares the following thoughts about the journal as a forum for Angela to raise questions:

> You just learn so much about how (the interns) are feeling about things. Even the fact that Angela and I are together all day, have conversations and visit, chit chat and everything else, it is still another way to get to know her, get to look at her thinking and see what she considers important. (Bridgett, interview B, 438–441)

Bridgett writes to Angela in the journal:

> Angela, I am so enjoying your journal. It's helping me to understand issues you feel are important. You share a wonderful variety of insights and from reading it I don't feel that the journal is drudgery for you. I hope you are able to continue as your teaching load increases. (Bridgett, triad journal, 1/99)

Jerelyn Wallace (1999) who also works with a similar three-way dialogue journal describes the journal as a "forum for observations, questions, and reflections that chronicled the year's teaching practice as well as the evolving relationship between mentor and teacher candidate" (p. 35). Wallace finds that, like Bridgett and Angela, many mentors view the dialogue journal as a tool:

> The exchange may take on a life of its own, become a welcomed place to record the joys and frustrations of teaching practice, and provide a forum through which communication among teacher candidates, mentors, and university colleagues is greatly enriched. Additionally, the journal is a reflective instrument, in both the long and short term, gives incredible insight into the process of the year—the progress of students, personal growth as an educator, the evolution of relationships and connections all the way around. (p. 35)

Because Bridgett and Angela are so focused on their teaching of the children during the day, dialogue journals provide the space for raising questions and collaboratively reflecting on the questions raised.


## SPACE TO IMPROVE

In very concrete ways, space to improve is naturally created in Bridgett's kindergarten because of the opportunity to teach similar lessons in both the morning and afternoon:

> I think, for an intern, teaching in kindergarten is a wonderful experience because you can make that adjustment immediately and try again right away that same day. It gives you a lot more room for experimentation in working out your own teaching. (Bridgett, interview B, 539–543)

Bridgett believes that Angela will improve and retain more if she discovers the changes she needs to make herself and that by trying, thinking, making adjustments, and trying again she will learn more. This is consistent with the work of Joyce and Weil (1980) who believe ownership of a learning experience is enhanced when learners experience new information in a way that makes the learning theirs by discovery. Bridgett shares her initial concern with Angela teaching her afternoon class as she believed them to be a more challenging group of children and she feared the challenges might inhibit Angela's ability to feel like a teacher.

> My husband and I were talking and he said that he didn't know if I should be allowed to be a mentor if I am not allowing the intern to actually try out some strategies and not be there to try to fix things all of the time. He said that I didn't know what her class would be like next year and that I really wasn't helping her. I agreed and have tried to let Angela practice on her own. (Bridgett, interview B, 223–227)

Angela shares how she and Bridgett discuss the differences in her teaching between the morning and afternoon class in an effort to make explicit why the afternoon looks different than the morning instruction:

> After the children would leave, we might talk about why I used the puppet in the morning and how that went and then why I didn't use the puppet in the afternoon . . . (Angela, interview, 112–114)

The opportunity to teach the same lesson to both the morning and afternoon class affords Angela the opportunity to adjust and improve within a single day.

Bridgett describes Angela's greatest challenge as classroom management and believes that the way she will get better is by having "space to improve." Bridgett's belief that Angela will learn most effectively by practicing is consistent with Kolb's (1984) cognitive style model. Kolb's model "is based on Dewey's focus on experience-based learning, Lewin's focus on active learning, and Piaget's focus on intelligence as the result of the interaction of the person and environment" (p. 472). Angela's "learning by doing" continues within this space to improve throughout the year:

> As Angela moves through the year she is accepting more and more responsibility for the children. For me it is to help facilitate giving her more and more opportunities to teach. . . . I just feel that I have to offer her opportunity. (Bridgett, interview A, 208–212)

As the year progresses, Angela continues identifying spaces to improve and Bridgett continues creating them for Angela. Underpinning the success of this space is Angela's personal disposition toward ongoing improvement and lifelong learning and Bridgett's modeling of that same disposition.


## SPACE TO CELEBRATE

Celebration as a learning space completes a cycle of learning that Bridgett believes is key to Angela's growth in her garden.

> Most of the time, Bridgett would ask me how things went and I would tell her I thought that they went ok. But then she would say I think it went great and then she would talk about why it was so successful. (Angela, interview, 108–111)

Angela also has learned to celebrate her own growth as she reflects in her own journal:

> My relationship with my mentor is growing stronger everyday. I feel that my ideas are really valued and that my mentor has placed a lot of confidence in me. In responding to that entry Bridgett adds, "Absolutely!" (Triad journal, 2/99)

Another example of celebration is the enthusiasm that Bridgett shows for Angela's teaching. She frequently shares with Angela's supervisor the clever lessons that she is doing or highlights the special skills that Angela brings to her work with children. Angela feels this same enthusiasm from Bridgett as evidenced in the following:

> Bridgett really shows enthusiasm for my lessons. She is always pushing me to my fullest potential and then helping me see my successes. (Angela, interview, 23–25)

Throughout Angela's internship, Bridgett highlights Angela's many accomplishments and frequently celebrates her successes. Angela's growing confidence in her teaching helps her feel even more like a teacher and leads to increasing her success as she re-enters each of the other spaces throughout her internship. Celebration is a necessary space for building a sense of efficacy that strengthens Angela's ability to grow within each of the other spaces.

In creating this professional relationship and cultivating spaces for Angela to learn to teach, Bridgett adopts an organic frame of mind as she mentors. This organic frame of mind is similar to that discussed by Garman (1982):

> A heightened sense of collegiality is possible when I can imagine myself as a member of an organic unit, when the distinction between supervisor and teacher is less discernible and I can transcend my conventional role status. . . . As an organic member I'm aware of the individual and collective possibilities when members are involved in the flow of the experience toward common goals. As a member of an organic unit I am active and reactive, inductive and productive during the life of the experience. I can be most effective when I imagine how other members might contribute. I'm able to see that much of the activity and results of the involvement will unfold in a manner that will lead to new and unpredictable states. I can be energized by seeing others and myself make important contributions, discovering potential we never imagined ourselves. (42)

Bridgett uses this organic frame as she provides spaces for Angela to grow in her own unique directions and celebrates her teaching. Bridgett views Angela as a colleague who has developed sophisticated "ways of knowing" as an intern. As a result, Bridgett feels confident that Angela will not simply replicate her teaching practices but rather use the spaces to develop her own teaching self and the dispositions of lifelong learning.

# Implications for Working in Bridgett's Garden

Throughout the internship year, Bridgett acts as a gardener, nourishing the growth of her intern through careful cultivation of the "soil" in which she grows. Bridgett deliberately and intentionally divides her "learning to teach" garden into five separate spaces that Angela cycles through numerous times during her internship year: space to be a teacher, space to explore teaching, space to raise questions about teaching, space to improve teaching, and space to celebrate teaching successes. As the year progresses, Bridgett's garden becomes a successful learning context for Angela, as she develops teaching confidence and competence, as well as the skills of an independent lifelong learner.

In deconstructing Bridgett's garden metaphor, an espoused supervisor platform (Sergiovanni & Starrat, 2002) can be identified as guiding Bridgett's work. An espoused platform is the stance, created by a set of beliefs about mentoring that underpin the way Bridgett works with Angela. To begin with, a mentor using a gardener approach to mentoring must feel comfortable sharing her classroom space with her intern. Additionally, the mentor must consider her intern a colleague who has important contributions to make to the children. Third, the mentor must also feel comfortable allowing her intern to assume increasingly challenging teaching experiences. Fourth, the mentor must allow herself to be vulnerable and open to intern's questions even when they are about one's own practice or classroom. Fifth, the mentor must be able to identify and build on every intern success much like a good teacher celebrates each child's success.

Each element of a mentor's espoused supervisory platform and the overarching metaphor she utilizes to conceptualize her mentoring practice has ramifications for the intern as well. In Bridgett's garden consisting of five different types of mentoring spaces, specific intern dispositions must be present in her mentee for each of the spaces to be useful, and powerful learning to occur. First, the intern must want to assume the roles and responsibilities of a teacher. Second, the intern must be able to identify questions and be willing to raise these questions for conversation. Third, the intern must be willing to take risks, make mistakes, brainstorm adjustments, and approach the task again with increased confidence. Fourth, the intern must be able to acknowledge her own successes and accept the compliments of others. Hence, through this case study of Bridgett, it becomes clear that mentoring is a highly complex and dynamic endeavor involving critical interplay between mentor and mentee, rather than a technical enterprise.

When mentoring is understood as a dynamic and complex relationship between mentor and mentee, what happens if an intern does not possess the learning to teach dispositions that mesh successfully with the mentor's approach to mentoring? The degree to which a future intern possesses the four dispositions described above may determine whether she will benefit from Bridgett's particular approach to mentoring, as Angela did. Since each intern brings a unique set of dispositions to the internship, these dispositions may or may not fit with the way a mentor defines her work. As a result, opportunities for mentors and interns to better understand their platforms, make their platforms and needs explicit to each other, build bridges between their platforms, and adjust platforms to accommodate each other's needs will strengthen the learning to teach context. Metaphors may be a powerful conceptual tool to articulate platforms.

With this insight into mentoring, teacher educators and state policymakers could benefit from re-examining and reconceptualizing activities such as clinical educator training and other technical approaches to mentoring that often communicate mentoring as a "one-size fits all" activity. Palmer (2000) identifies mentoring as a partnered experience:

> Mentors and apprentices are partners in an ancient human dance, and one of teaching's greatest rewards is the daily chance it gives us to get back on the dance floor. It is the dance of the spiraling generations in which the old empower the young with their experience and the young empower the old with new life, reweaving the fabric of the human community as they touch and turn. (25)

If mentoring is indeed a complex, dynamic, and partnered activity, as indicated in this case study, then more attention must be given to the dispositions of both the mentor and mentee. Partners need to adjust to each other in an effort for the dance to flow to the music. In this case, Bridgett and Angela offer us one example of a powerful dance that allowed Angela to grow within the multiple spaces cultivated in the garden.

# References

Borko, H. (1986). Clinical teacher education: The induction years. In J. V. Hoffman and S. A. Edwards, *Reality and reform in clinical teacher education* (pp. 42–52). New York: Random House.

Costa, A. L., & Garmston, R. J. (1994). *Cognitive coaching: A foundation for renaissance schools.* Norwood, MA: Christopher-Gordon.

Denzin, N. K., & Lincoln, Y. S. (1994). *Handbook of qualitative research.* Thousand Oaks, CA: Sage.

Erickson, F. (1986). Qualitative methods in research on teaching. In M. C. Wittrock

(Ed.), *Handbook on research of teaching* (3rd ed.) (pp. 119–161). New York: Macmillan.

Galvez-Hjornevik, C. (1986). Mentoring among teachers: A review of the literature. *Journal of Teacher Education, 37*(1), 6–11.

Garman, N. (1982). The clinical approach to supervision. In T. J. Sergiovanni (Ed.), *Supervision of teaching* (pp. 35–52). Alexandria, VA: Association for Supervision and Curriculum Development.

Garmston, R. J., Lipton, L. E., & Kaiser, K. (1998). In G. R. Firth and E. F. Pajak (Eds.), *Handbook of research on school supervision* (pp. 242–286). New York: Simon & Schuster Macmillan.

Goldsberry, L. (1998). Teacher involvement in supervision. In G. R. Firth and E. F. Pajak (Eds.) *Handbook of research on school supervision* (pp. 428–462). New York: Simon & Schuster Macmillan.

Goodlad, J. I. (1990). *Teachers for our nation's schools.* San Francisco: Jossey-Bass.

Gregory, M. (1987). If education is a feast, why do we restrict the menu?: A critique of pedagogical metaphors. *College Teaching, 35*(3), 101–106.

Hall, J. (1996). A qualitative look at the Indiana State University professional development school program. *Contemporary Education, 67*(4), 249–254.

Harris, B. M. (1998). Paradigms and parameters of supervision in education. In G. R. Firth and E. F. Pajak (Eds.), *Handbook of research on school supervision* (pp. 1–34). New York: Simon & Schuster Macmillan.

The Holmes Group. (1986). *Tomorrow's teachers: A report of the Holmes Group.* East Lansing, MI: Author.

The Holmes Group. (1990). *Tomorrow's schools: Principles for the design of professional development schools.* East Lansing, MI: Author.

Joyce, B., & Weil, M. (1980). *Models of teaching* (2nd ed.). *Englewood Cliffs, NJ: Prentice-Hall.*

Kolb, D. A. (1984). *Experiential learning: Experience as the source of learning and development.* Englewood Cliffs, NJ: Prentice-Hall.

Lakoff, G., & Johnson, M. (1980). *Metaphors we live by.* Chicago: The University of Chicago Press.

Levine, M. (1992). *Professional practice schools: Linking teacher education and school reform.* New York: Teachers College Press.

Lieberman, A., & Miller, L. (1990). Teacher development in professional practice schools. *Teachers College Record. 92*(1), 105–122.

Oberg, A. (1989). Supervision as a creative act. *Journal of Curriculum and Supervision, 5*(1), 60–69.

Palmer, P. (2000). *The courage to teach: Exploring the inner landscape of a teacher's life.* San Francisco: Jossey-Bass.

Patton, M. Q. (2002). *Qualitative evaluation and research methods* (2nd ed.). Newbury Park: Sage.

Schien, E. (1978). *Career dynamics: Matching individual and organizational needs.* Reading, MA: Addison-Wesley.

Sergiovanni, T. J., & Starrat, R. (2002). *Supervision: A redefinition* (2nd ed.). Boston: McGraw-Hill.

Seidman, I. E. (1991). *Interviewing as qualitative research: A guide for researchers in education and the social sciences.* New York: Teachers College Press.

Silva, D. Y. (1999). *Telling their stories: Mentor teachers' ways of being and knowing in a professional development school.* Unpublished doctoral dissertation. The Pennsylvania State University, University Park.

Silva, D. Y. (2002). Triad journaling: A tool for creating professional learning communities. *Teacher Education Quarterly, 28*(3). 23–34.

Silva, D. Y., & Dana, N. F. (2001). Collaborative supervision in the professional development school. *Journal of Curriculum and Supervision, 16*(4), 305–321.

Stake, R. (1995). *The art of case study research.* Thousand Oaks, CA: Sage.

Wallace, J. (1999). The dialogue journal. In P. Graham, S. Hudson-Ross, C. Adkins, P. McWhorter, & J. M. Stewart (Eds.), *Teacher mentor: A dialogue for collaborative learning* (pp. 51–74). New York: Teachers College Press.

Wang, J. (2001). Contexts of mentoring and opportunities for learning to teach: A comparative study of mentoring practice. *Teaching and Teacher Education, 17,* 51–73.

Wolcott, H. (1994). *Transforming qualitative data: Description, analysis, and interpretation.* Thousand Oaks, CA: Sage.

Yendol-Hoppey, D. (in press). Mentor teachers' ways of being and knowing. *Teachers College Record.*

Yendol-Silva, D., & Dana, N. F. (2004). Encountering new spaces. *Journal of Teacher Education, 55*(2), 128–140.

Zimpher, N. L., & Grossman, J. E. (1992). Collegial support by teacher mentors and peer consultants. In C.D. Glickman (Ed.), *Supervision in transition* (pp. 141–154). Alexandria, VA: Association for Supervision and Curriculum Development.

CHAPTER 6

# Conversations about Teaching
## LEARNING FROM THREE NOVICE-MENTOR PAIRS

*Jian Wang*
University of Nevada, Las Vegas

*Sandra J. Odell*
University of Nevada, Las Vegas

*Michael Strong*
University of California, Santa Cruz

Jian Wang is an associate professor of teacher education in the Department of Curriculum and Instruction at the University of Nevada, Las Vegas. Dr. Wang's research interests include teacher learning and mentoring and the comparative study of teaching and learning across cultures. Recent publications include articles in *Review of Educational Research*, the *Elementary School Journal*, and *Teacher's College Record*.

Sandra J. Odell is a professor of teacher education and coordinator of doctoral studies in the Department of Curriculum and Instruction at the University of Nevada, Las Vegas. Dr. Odell maintains career-long research interests in teacher development, teacher induction, and mentoring in the context of collaborative university/school district programs. Recent publications include articles in *Review of Educational Research*, the *Elementary School Journal*, *Teacher's College Record*, and *Journal of Research on Technology in Education*.

Michael Strong is director of research at the New Teacher Center, University of California, Santa Cruz. His current research interests include the development of beginning teacher practice, the effects and process of new teacher mentoring, and alternative mentoring approaches via the Internet. Recent publications include articles in *Teaching and Teacher Education* and *Teacher's College Record*.

*Note:* This study is based on data from the research project, "The Effects of Mentoring on New Teacher Development and Student Outcomes," conducted by the Research Division at the New Teacher Center, University of California at Santa Cruz. The authors acknowledge researchers and teachers in the project for their participation in collecting and transcribing the data for this study. The views expressed in this paper do not necessarily represent those of the New Teacher Center.

ABSTRACT

Novice-mentor reflections about teaching are thought to be crucial to the development of novices' professional knowledge. However, few studies have actually examined the content of novice-mentor discussions or how the focus of these discussions changes over time. Drawing on conversations recorded from three novice-mentor pairs in an induction context over a two-year period, this study analyzed the content and focus of novice-mentor conversations about novices' lessons. A primary finding was that the focus of novice-mentor lesson-based discussions did not change substantially over time. It was concluded that novice-mentor conversations alone might not be effective in supporting novice teachers' focus on standards-based teaching.

# Introduction and Objectives

Novice-mentor conversations about teaching are presumably important for the development of teachers' professional knowledge (Wang & Odell, 2002) and, thus, to the improvement of teaching. These novice-mentor interactions are assumed to be important in helping novices teach in ways consistent with reform-minded curriculum standards (Austin & Fraser-Abder, 1995). Such theoretical assumptions need to be verified empirically by examining novice-mentor conversations about novices' lessons. Of particular interest is how such conversations influence novices' teaching practice in the context of teacher mentoring where reform standards are encouraged and promoted. Drawing on conversations from three novice-mentor pairs in induction contexts, this study aims to determine the content and focus of novice-mentor conversations and whether these change over time.

# Teachers' Professional Knowledge and Novice-Mentor Interaction: Theoretical Framework

Over the past decade, national curriculum and teaching standards have been established in different subject-matter areas. In spite of questions about the efficacy of teaching standards on teaching reform (Apple, 1996; Berliner & Biddle, 1996), these standards are being incorporated into curriculum and teaching requirements at state and school levels presumably to help transform teaching practice and improve student learning (Cochran-Smith, 2001; Darling-Hammond & Ball, 1998).

It is assumed that for teachers to teach in ways consistent with reform standards, they need to develop a deeper understanding of subject matter (Ball & McDiarmid, 1989) and how to represent such understanding in classrooms (Shulman, 1987). Teachers also need to understand how children from different cultural backgrounds and different developmental and intellectual levels learn, and what influences their learning (Grimmett & MacKinnon, 1992; Ladson-Billings, 1999). The assertion is that teachers need to analyze their teaching, reflect about alternative teaching strategies, and apply themselves in diverse teaching contexts (Floden, Klinzing, Lampert, & Clark, 1990; Kennedy, 1991a).

Teacher mentoring relationships, particularly those involving novice-mentor lesson-based discussions, are thought to help novices develop the professional knowledge necessary for them to teach in ways consistent with reform standards (Cochran-Smith & Lytle, 1999; Feiman-Nemser, 2001; Wang & Odell, 2002). It is assumed that such relationships and discussions offer novices opportunities to develop a deeper understanding and better representation of subject matter (Austin & Fraser-Abder, 1995; Feiman-Nemser & Parker, 1990), connect their knowledge to different students (Kennedy, 1991b), and develop important attitudes and skills for analyzing and transforming teaching (Cochran-Smith, 1991). Indeed, these assumptions have helped shape the policy framework for teacher development (Holmes Group, 1986; Holmes Group, 1990) and the standards that guide the formation of teacher induction and mentoring programs (Interstate New Teachers Assessment and Support Teaching Consortium, 1992; Odell & Huling, 2000), including those at the state and district levels (Feiman-Nemser, Schwille, Carver, & Yusko, 1999; Sweeny & DeBolt, 2000).

The assumed influences of mentoring relationships and novice-mentor lesson-based discussions on novice teachers' learning to teach have roots in sociocultural learning theory. The practice of holding novice-mentor discussions about specific lessons is consistent with the premise that all knowledge is situated in and grows out of a context (Brown, Collins, & Duguid, 1989; Rogoff, 1984). The development of a unique relationship between mentors and novices rests on the premise that novices have opportunities to access and internalize higher-order-social functions that they did not hitherto possess and that will then gradually become internalized (Lave & Wenger, 1991; Vygotsky, 1994). Through interactions with novices, experienced teachers are able to identify the zone of proximal development of novices and to provide the necessary scaffolding to help beginners move to a level beyond their extant learning (Tharp & Gallimore, 1988; Vygotsky, 1978).

These assumptions about teacher mentoring are both supported and challenged by two separate lines of research. The supportive line of research suggests that lesson-based teacher interaction is important in helping teachers develop professional knowledge and transform existing teaching practice (Hiebert, Gallimore, & Stigler, 2002). Research on the differences between expert and inexperienced teachers shows that teachers' knowledge is event-structured, context-based, and practical in nature (Carter, 1990; Elbaz, 1983); therefore, learning to teach should be situated in the context of teaching (Cochran-Smith & Lytle, 1999; Richardson, 1996).

For example, Chinese mathematics teachers are found to have a deeper understanding of mathematics concepts and flexible representations of these concepts in teaching as a result of their observations and discussion of one another's teaching (Ma, 1999; Paine & Ma, 1993; Wang & Paine, 2003). Lesson-based interactions among Japanese teachers also are found to be important in helping them develop effective teaching practices closer to those envisioned by the U.S. reform standards (Hiebert & Stigler, 2000; Lewis & Tsuchida, 1998). However, these studies rely on interview and survey data focusing on teachers' knowledge and relationships instead of on direct observation of novice-mentor relationships and conversations.

A second line of research challenges the efficacy of lesson-based novice-mentor conversations in developing professional knowledge and relevant reform-minded teaching practice. It suggests that teacher mentoring is a conservative force that helps reproduce the existing culture and practice of teaching instead of transforming it (Cochran-Smith & Lytle, 1999; Cochran-Smith & Paris, 1995).

Wang (2001) shows that mentor teachers from the U.S., UK, and China hold different beliefs about teaching and mentoring depending on the nature of the curriculum system and teaching organization in which they work. Little (1990a; 1990b) indicates that mentoring and discussion about teaching, structured in an individualist culture of teaching, does not help form effective and collaborative teacher relationships crucial for developing professional knowledge. However, these studies again rely on interview and survey data collected in traditional mentoring contexts without direct observation of the specific nature and forms of novice-mentor conversations in reform settings.

In spite of the potential importance of direct observation of novice-mentor lesson-based discussions and their consequences in program-reform contexts, the direct observation method of studying mentoring and its impact is just emerging. Strong and Baron (2003) analyze the types of suggestions that mentors offer to novices in their lesson-based discussions. Achinstein and Barrett (2003) focus on the role and function of mentor teachers' conversational frames and frame changes in their discussions with novices about the role of teaching in shaping novices' perspectives about children's diversity. Understanding the foci and speech acts of both Chinese and U.S. novice-mentor lesson-based discussions and the learning opportunities that these discussions offer novice teachers in learning to teach is also a subject of research (Wang, Strong, & Odell, 2004).

The above direct observation research does not examine the ways in which discussions between mentors and novices change focus and conversational form over time. Exploration of these changes can provide data relevant to the role of novice-mentor lesson-based discussion in helping novice teachers develop useful professional knowledge. It also permits the development of an empirical base upon which effective mentoring programs can be designed to guide both mentors and novices in working effectively together in learning to teach. Drawing on conversation data from three U.S. novice-mentor pairs, the present study explores these issues. In particular, the following two questions are addressed: (a) What topics and forms of expression occur within novice-mentor pre-lesson-based planning discussions? (b) Do these discussion topics and forms of expression change over time?

# Method

## PARTICIPANTS AND CONTEXTS

Three novice-mentor pairs were randomly selected from 20 such pairs in a database that were made available by the Research Division at the New Teacher Center, University of California, Santa Cruz. They were not in any relevant manner atypical from the other pairs in the database according to a related study (Strong & Baron, 2003). The participants were three novice-mentor pairs in California: Kevin and Tanya, Elaine and Peggy, and Lisa and Kathy. (All the names used here or in the other places related to this paper are pseudonyms.)

All novices were first-year teachers working in different public elementary schools. Kevin and Elaine taught fifth grade while Lisa taught third grade. Kevin and Lisa graduated from an undergraduate teacher education program and each taught 24 ethnically diverse students. Elaine held a Master's degree in language arts and went through a post-baccalaureate teacher education program. She taught 30 Caucasian students in a mixed suburban rural community on California's central coast. In spite of these contextual differences, however, all novices were in schools where they were urged to teach according to national and state curriculum standards, although such curriculum standards were not always consistent with the textbooks and other curriculum materials (Cohen & Spillane, 1992).

All mentors (Tanya, Peggy, and Kathy) had more than 15 years of elementary teaching experience, were released from teaching to be full-time mentors, and mentored 12–15 novices at various grade levels in different elementary schools. They were required to meet with novices weekly, to observe teaching, and to provide formative feedback. The novices were made aware that mentors were not responsible for providing summative assessment information to their supervisors as part of the feedback process. All assessment conversations were between the mentor and novice only. In addition to meeting formally with novices at least weekly, mentors had additional informal contact through telephone and e-mail conversations.

These novice-mentor pairs worked in a mentoring program designed to help new teachers learn to teach consistent with national and state professional standards. The mentors participated in an Induction Institute that focused on building the capacity of participating teams to develop and implement an intensive model of beginning teacher support based upon the principles and practices of the highly successful Santa Cruz New Teacher Project. The project is guided by the belief that learning to teach is a career-long cycle of planning, teaching, and reflecting. The work is centered on responding to each new teacher's individual and contextual needs through ongoing examination of classroom practice for the purpose of promoting high achievement for all students.

The program required mentor teachers to have pre-lesson conversations to review the novice's lesson plans, make suggestions based on the novice's questions/concerns and the California Standards for the Teaching Profession, and determine what to observe during the novice's lessons. Mentors were also asked to have a post-lesson reflection conference to help the novice review the lesson, ponder the success of the original plan and any deviations from it, provide feedback, and discuss next steps. Because the mentors were released from classroom teaching to work full time as mentors, the observations and interactions with novices could occur during school hours.

The program also provided a weekly professional-development seminar for mentors and mentoring resources, tools, and protocols. While the mentors would come to these sessions with an agenda of questions to ask and areas to cover, the actual interactions allowed ample opportunity for the mentor and novice teachers to discuss whatever was on their minds.

## DATA SOURCE

The data for the current study were made available by the Research Division at the New Teacher Center, University of California, Santa Cruz. The data for the current study consisted of four, randomly selected, audio-taped pre-lesson discussions about novices' lessons for each of the three novice-mentor pairs. The pre-lesson discussions ranged from approximately 20 to 50 minutes in duration. Two of these pre-lesson discussions were collected during the first year, and the other two were collected during the second year of the induction program.

This study has obvious limitations. First, the study presents data from only three novice-mentor pairs. Given the labor-intensive nature of transcribing conversational data and coding these data along several dimensions, it is difficult to complete studies with a large number of participants in this area of research. Moreover, while each sentence in the novice-mentor conversations was transcribed and coded, the micro level of analysis was not such that the initiator of each sentence or phrase was preserved. Unfortunately, this study only had available for current analysis a set of rather formal pre-lesson conversations related to novice's teaching. We recognize that different content and linguistic forms may have characterized other more spontaneous conversations, but such conversations were not recorded and hence were not available for analysis. Another limitation is that we do not include here the analysis of post-lesson conversations between mentors and novices. Such analysis could shed light on whether the post-lesson mentor/novice conversations, as compared to the pre-lesson mentor/novice conversations, impacted the novices' teaching in significant ways. The transcripts of the post-lesson conversations have yet to be analyzed but will be included in a future follow-up publication.

## DATA COLLECTION AND CODING PROCEDURES

The four audio-taped novice-mentor pre-lesson discussions for each novice-mentor pair were transcribed. The transcriptions were then coded along multiple dimensions. First, major content topics were identified. Fourteen content-topic categories emerged from the data that encompassed the vast majority of the novice-mentor discussion sequences and included: *instruction* (teaching strategies and events stressing what the teacher needed to do or did); *activity* (teaching strategies and events stressing what students need to do or did); *standards* (curriculum or teaching standards encouraged by the induction program and the school); *goals* (lesson objectives or goals); *lesson topic* (content to be addressed in the lesson); *subject matter* (specific discipline knowledge); *materials* (manipulative materials and resources for the lesson); *understanding* (students' understanding of concepts or content); *students* (individual students in the class); *needs* (a focus on needs of students in general); *feelings* (issues related to student feelings or emotions in general); *management* (how to manage and control the class with special attention to what a teacher needed to do or did); *assessment* (students' progress, in general, and students' work, specifically); *learning to teach* (issues related to the induction program and how to observe, assess, and support teaching and learning to teach); and *other* (issues not belonging to any of the above or that were unclear).

These statements in each conversation were also coded with respect to their reference, that is, whether they referred to present, prior, or future lessons. Next, the statements were labeled with respect to their interconnectedness, that is, whether the participants discussed the content topics in isolation or whether they connected them to one another.

Statements were further coded for surface form. The first category of surface form was *Questions*. These were divided into *what* questions, *yes/no* questions, *how* questions, and *why* questions. Further categories involved *explanations*, *agreements* or *disagreements*, *criticisms*, *justifications*, *confirmation*, *compliments*, or *suggestions*. An additional category called *other* was used when the surface form did not fit well into one of the established surface-form categories.

Finally, each statement was coded for elaboration. The codes used included: *unelaborated* (statement unaccompanied by example, reason, or detailed description; *concrete* (statement accompanied by a concrete example or a detailed description); *reasoned* (statement accompanied by reasons and/or analysis); *referred* (statement unelaborated but referred to another statement); or *other*.

The first author did the initial coding and the second author performed a check and a re-coding. Both authors discussed any questions and problems in the coding process in weekly research meetings until agreement was reached. The three authors then reviewed the work and made final revisions.

# Results and Conclusions

The results obtained were analyzed to address two research questions. The first concerned the content of novice-mentor discussions. Specifically, we were interested in determining what topics were discussed, whether statements referred to previous or future lessons, whether topics were connected to other teaching topics, what surface forms conversational statements took, and whether the statements were elaborated. The second research question asked whether there was a change in the nature of the conversations between each mentor and novice from the novice's first year of teaching to the second.

Inasmuch as there were no consistent differences obtained among the coded dimensions between the two conversations from each novice-mentor pair in year one or in year two, the data for each novice-mentor pair were combined for each year and are presented as a percentage of the number of statements on the coded dimension separately for Year 1 and Year 2 in the subsequent data tables. The data tables also present the two-year percentage of the total number of statements for the coded dimension (total) for each novice-mentor pair. Data are not presented for instances where this total percentage metric for a data category was less than five percent for each of the pairs.

Looking first at the total percentages across the two years, it can be seen in table 6.1 that the mentors and novices discussed teaching strategies focusing on the novices' instruction and student activities about half of the time on average. This was to be expected since the purpose of the pre-lesson conversation was to focus on the upcoming lesson. It is interesting to note that more of the teaching-strategy discussions for each novice-mentor pair stressed what the students needed to do (*activity*) rather than what the novice needed to do (*instruction*).

Given previous work, for example, by Kagan (1992) who suggested that management issues dominate teachers' attention in their first year, and because of the stress that the induction program put on the California Standards, it was anticipated that management issues would be a frequent topic in novice-mentor conversations. While table 1 shows that management issues comprised 10% of the total conversations between Kevin and Tanya, the overall percentage of management topics for the three novice-mentor pairs was not substantial. Generally speaking, the novice-mentor conversations focused more on specific subject-matter knowledge and the assessment of students' performance than on management issues. Despite the focus on subject-matter knowledge, very little attention was paid to students' understanding of concepts or content and general lesson topics that tied subject concepts together. The conversations also did not focus on materials for the lesson. Even though substantial but uneven attention was given to the assessment of students' performance, relatively little attention was paid to individual students or their feelings and needs in the conversations.

Categories that constituted less than five percent of the total conversations across the three novice-mentor pairs included the needs of students in general, and issues related to students' feelings or emotions. Likewise, lesson goals and issues related to learning to teach were topics of discussion less than five percent of the time. Finally, there was little discussion of the curriculum or teaching

**Table 6.1    Percentage of Different Topics Occurring in Novice-Mentor Conversations over Two Years**

| Topic | Year 1 | Year 2 | Total |
|---|---|---|---|
| **Instruction** | | | |
| K&T | 28 | 12 | 20 |
| E&P | 29 | 17 | 23 |
| L&K | 14 | 23 | 18 |
| **Activity** | | | |
| K&T | 29 | 24 | 26 |
| E&P | 42 | 42 | 42 |
| L&K | 30 | 35 | 32 |
| **Subject Matter** | | | |
| K&T | 9 | 6 | 8 |
| E&P | 15 | 14 | 14 |
| L&K | 7 | 6 | 7 |
| **Assessment** | | | |
| K&T | 12 | 5 | 8 |
| E&P | 5 | 8 | 6 |
| L&K | 13 | 8 | 10 |
| **Management** | | | |
| K&T | 3 | 16 | 10 |
| E&P | 1 | 0 | 1 |
| L&K | 9 | 6 | 7 |
| **Students** | | | |
| K&T | 4 | 2 | 7 |
| E&P | 1 | 4 | 2 |
| L&K | 7 | 6 | 6 |
| **Understanding** | | | |
| K&T | 0 | 0 | 0 |
| E&P | 4 | 8 | 6 |
| L&K | 4 | 2 | 3 |
| **Lesson Topic** | | | |
| K&T | 10 | 8 | 9 |
| E&P | 1 | 1 | 1 |
| L&K | 0 | 0 | 0 |
| **Material** | | | |
| K&T | 0 | 11 | 6 |
| E&P | 0 | 3 | 2 |
| L&K | 7 | 2 | 5 |

standards encouraged by the induction program and school. Consequently these categories were not included in table 6.1.

Table 6.2 presents the extent to which the novice-mentor conversations referred to present, prior, or future lessons. This analysis was an attempt to determine the extent to which novice-mentor discussions tended to locate the current lesson within a broader cycle of instruction. As can be seen, this was not frequently done inasmuch as approximately 80% of the total conversations of the three novice-mentor pairs were devoted to the present lesson, with the balance of the conversations referencing prior lessons and, to a lesser extent, future lessons.

Literature on teacher learning has stressed the importance of helping novice teachers learn to plan lessons while giving careful consideration to connecting what students are currently learning to other learning (Dewey, 1938; Feiman-Nemser & Buchmann, 1987; Kennedy, 1991b). In the present research, the metric of interconnectedness was intended to reflect the extent to which novice-mentor pairs discussed teaching topics in isolation as opposed to linking them to one another within a single conversation. The total percentages displayed in table 6.3 reveal that 60% of the conversation topics were connected. This dominance of connected over isolated statements was a consistent feature of each of the novice-mentor conversations. This is in contrast to the data in table 6.2 that showed most references were not connected to prior or future lessons.

How mentors and novices discuss lessons is an area that is not well understood in the existing literature of teacher mentoring but has the potential to impact what and how novices learn from novice–mentor conversations

**Table 6.2    Percentage of Statements in Novice-Mentor Conversations That Referred to Present, Prior, or Future Teaching Lessons over Two Years**

| Reference | Year 1 | Year 2 | Total |
|---|---|---|---|
| **Present Lesson** | | | |
| K&T | 82 | 82 | 82 |
| E&P | 67 | 88 | 77 |
| L&K | 83 | 85 | 84 |
| **Prior Lesson** | | | |
| K&T | 8 | 13 | 10 |
| E&P | 9 | 9 | 9 |
| L&K | 15 | 13 | 14 |
| **Subject Matter** | | | |
| K&T | 10 | 2 | 6 |
| E&P | 24 | 3 | 14 |
| L&K | 2 | 2 | 2 |

**Table 6.3    Percentage of Connected or Isolated Statements in Novice-Mentor Conversations over Two Years**

| Statements | Year 1 | Year 2 | Total |
|---|---|---|---|
| **Connected** | | | |
| K&T | 67 | 38 | 53 |
| E&P | 67 | 52 | 59 |
| L&K | 60 | 74 | 67 |
| **Isolated** | | | |
| K&T | 33 | 62 | 48 |
| E&P | 34 | 48 | 41 |
| L&K | 40 | 27 | 33 |

(Wang & Odell, 2002). Given the context of a veteran mentoring a novice, it was anticipated that the primary surface forms of the conversational statements would reflect the novice seeking advice by asking questions of the mentor, who would respond by offering explanations. With respect to the surface forms that were questions, *why* questions were virtually absent, *how* questions were infrequently used, and as shown in table 6.4, *yes/no* questions were more prevalent than *what* questions. This distribution of different types of questions reflects the fact that, contrary to expectation, questions originated most often from the mentor, not from the novice. Table 6.4 further shows that the most common surface form for each novice-mentor pair was *explanation*, usually uttered by the novice in response to the mentor's questions. On average one-third of the total surface forms across the three novice-mentor pairs were *explanations*. In general, after the initial sequence of mentor question and novice explanation, the mentors would usually confirm or agree with the novice as reflected in the percentage of *confirmations* and *agreements* in table 6.4, or they would pose more questions. As would be predicted by previous work (Strong & Baron, 2003), the mentors infrequently offered direct advice or concrete suggestions to the novices.

It is notable that none of the other categories of surface forms occurred at a rate of more than five percent. This included the surface forms of *criticism*, *disagreement*, and *justification*, suggesting that novice-mentor conversations involved a rather low level of polemical dialogue.

It is assumed that novice teachers will learn to teach effectively as mentors help novices reflect about their practice in the classroom context and that mentors will model such reflection (Feiman-Nemser & Remillard, 1996; Schon, 1987). In order to understand whether mentor and novice teachers in our study were able to develop reflective conversations, we looked at the level of elaborations, that is, whether a statement was elaborated with examples, reasons, or both.

Table 6.4    Percentage of Different Surface Forms Occurring in Novice-Mentor Conversations over Two Years

| Surface Form | Year 1 | Year 2 | Total |
|---|---|---|---|
| **Explanation** | | | |
| K&T | 32 | 36 | 34 |
| E&P | 26 | 34 | 30 |
| L&K | 26 | 25 | 26 |
| **Yes/No Questions** | | | |
| K&T | 15 | 15 | 15 |
| E&P | 16 | 20 | 18 |
| L&K | 17 | 22 | 19 |
| **What Questions** | | | |
| K&T | 18 | 11 | 15 |
| E&P | 7 | 7 | 7 |
| L&K | 6 | 4 | 5 |
| **Confirmations** | | | |
| K&T | 9 | 9 | 9 |
| E&P | 17 | 17 | 17 |
| L&K | 14 | 13 | 13 |
| **Agreements** | | | |
| K&T | 9 | 9 | 9 |
| E&P | 16 | 9 | 12 |
| L&K | 14 | 15 | 15 |
| **Suggestions** | | | |
| K&T | 6 | 4 | 5 |
| E&P | 4 | 3 | 4 |
| L&K | 7 | 11 | 9 |

The greatest variability among the three novice-mentor pairs occurred in the total number of statements that were unelaborated. An unelaborated statement was considered to be one that was unaccompanied by example, reason, or detailed description, and did not refer to another statement. Table 6.5 shows that unelaborated statements ranged from 24% for Kevin and Tanya to 54% for Lisa and Kathy. It is not possible to conclude whether a high percentage of unelaborated statements meant that a pair readily understood one another, so that no elaboration was needed, or whether the unelaborated statements indicated that the conversation did not stimulate additional reflection. As can be further seen from table 6.5, where elaborations did occur, the vast majority involved concrete examples as opposed to elaborated reasons or analysis.

By way of overall summary of the total percentage data, the principle topics of the novice-mentor conversations involved what students and teachers need

Table 6.5    Percentage of Different Kinds of Elaboration Statements in Novice-Mentor Conversations over Two Years

| Elaboration | Year 1 | Year 2 | Total |
|---|---|---|---|
| **Unelaborated** | | | |
| K&T | 24 | 24 | 24 |
| E&P | 44 | 38 | 42 |
| L&K | 53 | 55 | 54 |
| **With Concrete Examples** | | | |
| K&T | 68 | 66 | 67 |
| E&P | 54 | 55 | 54 |
| L&K | 34 | 38 | 36 |
| **With Reasons** | | | |
| K&T | 6 | 6 | 6 |
| E&P | 3 | 7 | 5 |
| L&K | 13 | 8 | 10 |

to do. Secondarily, the conversations focused on subject matter and student assessment. Notably, classroom management and student-focused issues such as student understanding, needs, or feelings constituted less than 10% of the total topics. The majority of novice-mentor conversations focused on present lessons rather than prior or future teaching lessons. For the most part, novice-mentor conversations were linked to other teaching topics. Still, approximately 40% of the total conversations involved isolated teaching topics. With respect to surface forms, almost 30% of novice-mentor conversations involved *explanations*, primarily by the novice, in response to *yes/no* or *what* questions posed primarily by the mentor. This was most frequently followed by *confirmations* and *agreements* and less frequently by direct *suggestions*, *criticisms*, or *justifications*. Statement *elaborations* by example, reason, or description varied considerably among the novice-mentor pairs. However, in all instances where statements were elaborated, more than 70% of the elaborations involved concrete examples rather than the provision of abstract reasons or description.

At the outset of the research, a second research question was posed to investigate the hypothesis that novice-mentor discussions would be dynamic and change over time as both mentors and novices gained additional experience. For the most part, we did not observe consistent developmental changes expected from the literature on novice teacher needs (Kagan, 1992) suggesting that experience did not exert a strong influence on the novice-mentor conversations. For example, we did not find that issues such as classroom management or individual student behaviors received considerable attention during a novice's first year, with instructional issues gaining focus during the second year. This is reflected in the year-to-year percentage data in table 6.1 that demonstrate there was no consistent pattern of changes in management or instruction across the two years for the three novice-mentor pairs. Indeed, the same lack of consistent year-to-year trends characterized each of the topic categories. This is not to say that individual novice-mentor pairs showed no successive year variations in the percentages of topics covered in their conversations. Indeed, there is considerable variability among the yearly changes between the three pairs. However, in the absence of consistent between-pair changes, the authors do not think a more micro-analysis of the individual pair changes was merited by the current data given its inherent limitations and general variability. Still, it must be acknowledged that further consideration of contextual factors would likely suggest explanations for the individual novice-mentor patterns of response.

We hypothesized that novice-mentor conversations might begin by focusing on present lessons and then show an increase in the percentage of references to prior and future lessons in the second year. No such trend was apparent. Indeed, as shown in table 6.2, there was a greater consistency among the novice-mentor pairs in referring to the present lesson during the second year than there was in the first and, if anything, a decrease in references to future lessons in the second year.

Another unconfirmed expectation was that, as novice-mentor conversations continued, a larger percentage of the statements would be linked to or interconnected with other teaching topics. This expectation followed from the notion that novice-mentor conversations would be the foundation for a broader framework about teaching. Table 6.3 shows, surprisingly, that two of the three novice-mentor pairs actually showed a decrease in the percentage of connected statements from year 1 to year 2.

Table 6.4 shows that there was a remarkable consistency from year 1 to year 2 in the percentage of surface forms. While there was a tendency for the percentage of *explanations* to increase from year 1 to year 2, the best characterization of the overall data in Table 4 is that within the mentoring program the novice-mentor pairs fostered conversations that were consistent in surface form across time.

Finally, we anticipated developmental trends where novice-mentor conversations across the two years would show increases in the percentage of elaborated and reasoned statements. This follows from the argument that elaboration and reasoning can be regarded as higher-order skills that novices internalize over time with the support of mentor teachers (Tharp & Gallimore, 1988). Table 6.5 did not confirm the existence of any developmental changes in the percentages of unelaborated statements for any of the novice mentor pairs from year 1 to year 2 and, if anything, the data suggest an increase in elaborations involving concrete examples and a decrease in elaborations with reasons.

# Implications for Teachers and Teacher Educators

In the teacher learning and development literature, learning to teach by beginning teachers is often conceptualized as a developmental continuum (Feiman-Nemser & Remillard, 1996) in which attention to classroom management is reported as a necessary first step in learning to teach (Kagan, 1992). According to this perspective, teacher mentoring is a situated support for beginning teachers' learning first to manage classrooms and students. Thus, teacher mentoring should be guided by the assumptions of the teacher-learning continuum that reflect the needs of beginning teachers in different stages of their development (Moir et al., 2001). However, our study suggests that the topics, reference, connectedness, surface forms, and elaboration across novice-mentor pre-lesson conferences in a two-year period tended to be quite constant, and that classroom management was not a central issue or concern in the first year or anytime throughout the two-year pre-lesson conferences. Such a finding questions the conceptual assumption and practical application of applying this developmental continuum to novice-teacher learning.

Teaching according to current educational standards requires teachers to develop a deeper understanding of the subject matter that they teach (Ball, 2000; Ball & McDiarmid, 1989) and flexible representations of such understanding to various groups of students (Grossman, 1990; Shulman, 1987; Wilson & Berne, 1999). To help teachers develop such subject-matter knowledge, it has been assumed that teachers need opportunities to observe and discuss each other's lessons. Over time, such discussions will help develop a culture where subject-matter knowledge is developed through public examination and reflection on teacher's teaching (Hiebert et al., 2002; Hiebert & Stigler, 2000). In the current study, however, subject matter was not often the topic of teachers' conversations. The infrequency of discussion about standards as well as the lack of articulation, reflection, and connection to prior and future lessons, and the substantial percentages of isolated and unelaborated statements obtained, leads us to question whether the quality of subject-matter discussions between novices and mentors can be achieved solely through adjusting the structure and length of mentoring relationships.

In order to develop teaching as envisioned by the reformers, teachers need skills of inquiry to reflect on their teaching and to pose questions, interpret different situations, develop constructive criticism, and come up with useful ideas to solve various problems in their teaching practice (Cochran-Smith, 1991; Cochran-Smith & Lytle, 1999). Teacher mentoring relationships that are committed to the reform of teaching would foster the novices' development of these important skills. However, in spite of the reform agenda of the current induction program, the fact that few *how* and *why* questions were asked, and few *criticism, disagreement,* and *justification* statements were made in the novice-mentor lesson-based conferences over time does raise the question as to whether novice-mentor discussions automatically lead to novice-mentor learning in ways envisioned by reformers.

In addition, an important element of teachers' professional knowledge is the ability to conduct contextualized reasoning about subject matter and pedagogy, arguing the alternatives, and applying their thoughts to uncertain and irregular contexts of teaching (Floden et al., 1990; Kennedy, 1991a; Schon, 1987). However, in the present novice-mentor conversations, opportunities for novices to develop reasoning skills were limited since many of the exchanges were unelaborated or were elaborated with concrete examples rather than elaborated with abstract reason or description.

Keeping in mind the limitations of the study that were discussed earlier (limited number of formal pre-lesson conversations with a small sample of participants), it would appear that novice-mentor conversations alone, even in induction programs, are unlikely to be fully effective in supporting novice teachers' focus on standards-based teaching. Substantial mentor preparation that focuses on how mentors can address the developmental continuum of learning to teach, how to promote the acquisition of flexible subject-matter knowledge, and engender inquiry, problem solving, and contextualized reasoning by the novice apparently must be included as an integral part of an induction program.

# References

Achinstein, B., & Barrett, A. (2003, April). *(Re)Framing classroom contexts: How new teachers and mentors understand and are influenced by diverse learners.* Paper presented at the Annual Meeting of American Educational Research Association, Chicago, IL.

Apple, M. W. (1996). Being popular about national standards: A review of "national standards in American education: A citizen's guide." *Education Policy Analysis Archives, 4*(10), 1–6.

Austin, T., & Fraser-Abder, P. (1995). Mentoring mathematics and science preservice teachers for urban bilingual classrooms. *Education and Urban Society, 28*(1), 67–89.

Ball, D. L. (2000). Bridging practices: Intertwining content and pedagogy in teaching and learning to teach. *Journal of Teacher Education, 51*(3), 241–247.

Ball, D. L., & McDiarmid, G. W. (1989). *The subject matter preparation of teachers* (Issue Paper 89–4). East Lansing: National Center of Research on Teacher Learning, Michigan State University.

Berliner, D. C., & Biddle, B. J. (1996). Standards amidst uncertainty and inequality. *School Administrator, 53*(5), 42–44, 46.

Brown, J. S., Collins, A., & Duguid, P. (1989). Situated cognition and the culture of learning. *Education Researcher, 18*(1), 32–34.

Carter, K. (1990). Teachers' knowledge and learning to teach. In W. R. Houston (Ed.), *Handbook of research on teacher education* (pp. 314–338). New York: Macmillan.

Cochran-Smith, M. (2001). Constructing outcomes in teacher education: Policy, practice, and pitfalls [Electronic version]. *Education Policy Analysis Archives, 9*(11), 68 pages.

Cochran-Smith, M. (1991). Learning to teach against the grain. *Harvard Educational Review, 61*(3), 279–310.

Cochran-Smith, M., & Lytle, S. (1999). Relationship of knowledge and practice: Teacher learning in communities. *Review of Research in Education, 24*, 249–298.

Cochran-Smith, M., & Paris, P. (1995). Mentor and mentoring: Did Homer have it right? In J. Smith (Ed.), *Critical discourses on teacher development* (pp. 181–202). London: Cassell.

Cohen, D. K., & Spillane, J. P. (1992). Policy and practice: The relations between governance and instruction. *Review of Research in Education, 18*, 3–49.

Darling-Hammond, L., & Ball, D. L. (1998). *Teaching for high standards: What policymakers need to know and be able to do* (CPRE Joint Report Series No. JRE-04). Philadelphia, PA: National Commission on Teaching and America's Future Consortium for Policy Research in Education.

Dewey, J. (1938). *Experience and education.* New York: Collier Books.

Elbaz, F. (1983). *Teacher thinking: A study of practical knowledge.* London: Croom Helm.

Feiman-Nemser, S. (2001). Helping novices learn to teach: Lessons from an experienced support teacher. *Journal of Teacher Education, 52*(1), 17–30.

Feiman-Nemser, S., & Buchmann, M. (1987). When is student teaching teacher education? *Teaching & Teacher Education, 3*(4), 255–273.

Feiman-Nemser, S., & Parker, M. B. (1990). *Making subject matter part of the conversation or helping beginning teachers learn to teach* (Research Report 90–3). East Lansing, MI: National Center for Research on Teacher Learning.

Feiman-Nemser, S., & Remillard, J. (1996). Perspectives on learning to teach. In F. B. Murray (Ed.), *The teacher educator's handbook* (pp. 63–91). San Francisco: Jossey-Bass.

Feiman-Nemser, S., Schwille, S., Carver, C., & Yusko, B. (1999). *A conceptual review of the literature on new teacher induction* (The NPEAT Report). East Lansing: Michigan State University.

Floden, R. E., Klinzing, H. G., Lampert, M., & Clark, C. (1990). *Two views of the role of research on teacher thinking* (Paper 90–4). East Lansing, MI: National Center for Research on Teacher Education, Michigan State University.

Grimmett, P., & MacKinnon, A. (1992). Craft knowledge and the education of teachers. *Review of Research in Education, 18*, 385–456.

Grossman, P. L. (1990). *The making of a teacher: Teacher knowledge and teacher education.* New York: Teachers College Press.

Hiebert, J., Gallimore, R., & Stigler, J. W. (2002). A knowledge base for the teaching profession: What would it look like and how can we get one? *Educational Researcher, 31*(5), 3–15.

Hiebert, J., & Stigler, J. W. (2000). A proposal for improving classroom teaching: Lessons from the TIMSS video study. *Elementary School Journal, 101*(1), 3–20.

Holmes Group. (1986). *Tomorrow's teachers*. East Lansing, MI: Holmes Group.

Holmes Group. (1990). *Tomorrow's schools*. East Lansing, MI: Holmes Group.

Interstate New Teachers Assessment and Support Teaching Consortium. (1992). *Model standards for beginning teacher licensing and development: A resource for state dialogue*: The Council of Chief State School Officers.

Kagan, D. M. (1992). Professional growth among preservice and beginning teachers. *Review of Educational Research, 62*(2), 129–169.

Kennedy, M. (1991a). *An agenda for research on teacher learning* (NCRTL Special Report). East Lansing, MI: National Center for Research on Teacher Learning, Michigan State University.

Kennedy, M. M. (1991b). Some surprising findings on how teachers learn to teach. *Educational Leadership, 49*(3), 14–17.

Ladson-Billings, G. J. (1999). Preparing teachers for diverse student populations: A critical race theory perspective. *Review of Research in Education, 24*, 211–247.

Lave, J., & Wenger, E. (1991). *Situated learning: Legitimate peripheral participation*. Cambridge: Cambridge University Press.

Lewis, C. C., & Tsuchida, I. (1998). A lesson is like a swiftly flowing river: How research lessons improve Japanese education. *American Educator, 22*(4), 12–17, 50–52.

Little, J. W. (1990a). The mentoring phenomenon and the social organization of teaching. *Review of Research in Education, 16*, 279–252.

Little, J. W. (1990b). The persistence of privacy: Autonomy and initiative in teachers' professional relationship. *Teachers College Record, 91*(4), 509–536.

Ma, L. (1999). *Knowing and teaching elementary mathematics*. Mahwah, NJ: Lawrence Erlbaum.

Moir, E., Freeman, S., Petrock, L., Baron, W., Stobbe, C., & St. John, L. (2001). *A developmental continuum of teacher abilities*. Santa Cruz, CA: University of California, Santa Cruz, New Teacher Center.

Odell, S. J., & Huling, L. (Eds.). (2000). *Quality mentoring for novice teachers*. Indianapolis, IN: Kappa Delta Pi.

Paine, L., & Ma, L. (1993). Teachers working together: A dialogue on organizational and cultural perspectives of Chinese teachers. *International Journal of Educational Research, 19*(8), 667–778.

Richardson, V. (1996). The role of attitude and beliefs in learning to teach. In J. Sikula, T. Buttery, & E. Guyton (Eds.), *Handbook of research on teacher education* (2nd ed., pp. 102–119). New York: Macmillan.

Rogoff, B. (1984). Introduction: Thinking and learning in social contexts. In B. Rogoff & J. Lave (Eds.), *Everyday cognition: Its development in social context* (pp. 1–8). Cambridge, MA: Harvard University Press.

Schon, D. (1987). *Educating the reflective practitioner*. San Francisco: Jossey Bass.

Shulman, L. (1987). Knowledge and teaching: Foundations of the new reform. *Harvard Educational Review, 57*(1), 1–22.

Strong, M., & Baron, W. (2003, April). *An analysis of mentoring conversations with beginning teachers: Suggestions and responses*. Paper presented at the Annual Meeting of the American Educational Research Association, Chicago, IL.

Sweeny, B., & DeBolt, G. (2000). A survey of the 50 states: Mandated teacher induction programs. In S. Odell & L. Huling (Eds.), *Quality mentoring for novice teachers* (pp. 7–106). Indianapolis: Kappa Delta Pi.

Tharp, G., & Gallimore, R. (1988). Assisting teacher performance through the ZED: A case study. In Tharp & Gallimore (Eds.), *Rousing mind to life: Teaching, learning, and schooling in social contexts* (pp. 217–248). Cambridge: Cambridge University Press.

Vygotsky, L. S. (1978). Interaction between learning and development. In L.S. Vygotsky, *Mind in society: The development of higher psychological processes* (pp. 79–91). Cambridge: Harvard University Press.

Vygotsky, L. S. (1994). The problem of the environment. In Rene van der Veer & J. Valsiner (Eds.), *The Vygotsky Reader* (pp. 338–354). Cambridge, MA: Blackwell.

Wang, J. (2001). Contexts of mentoring and opportunities for learning to teach: A comparative study of mentoring practice. *Teaching and Teacher Education, 17*(1), 51–73.

Wang, J., & Odell, S. J. (2002). Mentored learning to teach and standards-based teaching reform: A critical review. *Review of Educational Review, 7*(3), 481–546.

Wang, J., & Paine, L. W. (2003). Learning to teach with mandated curriculum and public examination of teaching as contexts. *Teaching and Teacher Education, 19*(1), 75–94.

Wang, J., Strong, M., & Odell, S. J. (2004). Mentor-novice conversations about teaching: A comparison of two U.S. and two Chinese cases. *Teachers College Record, 106*(4), 775–813.

Wilson, S. M., & Berne, J. (1999). Teacher learning and the acquisition of professional knowledge: An examination of research on contemporary professional development. In A. Iran-Nejad & P. D. Pearson (Eds.), *Review of Research in Education, 24,* 173–209.

# CHAPTER 7

# Studying the Disposition of Mentor Teachers

*Lisa E. Johnson*
Winthrop University

*Alan J. Reiman*
North Carolina State University

Lisa E. Johnson, Ph.D., is an assistant professor at Winthrop University in Rock Hill, South Carolina. In addition to being a nationally board certified teacher and a teacher educator, Dr. Johnson's research interests include examining the dispositions of preservice and practicing teachers specifically in the moral/ethical domain.

Alan Reiman, Ph.D., is an associate professor in the Department of Curriculum and Instruction at N.C. State University. His current scholarship examines teacher moral and reflective dispositions from a cognitive-developmental perspective. Among his recent publications is "Promoting Teacher Professional Judgment" (with Lisa Johnson) in the *Journal of Research in Education* (2003).

## ABSTRACT

This study explores the congruency between mentor professional judgment and professional action as constructs of disposition using three mentor/beginning teacher dyads. Professional judgment was assessed using the Defining Issues Test-2 (moral/ethical judgment), the Sentence Completion Test (ego judgment) and the Paragraph Completion Method (conceptual judgment). Professional action was measured using an adapted form of the Flanders Interaction Analysis System. In addition, a matrix, derived from cognitive-developmental theory, was used to qualitatively analyze mentor professional judgments and actions as expressed in interview transcripts, self-assessment and reflection, and videotapes of conferences with beginning teachers. Convergence between the two methods of data collection was first investigated followed by an examination of the congruence between judgment and action. Based on the findings of convergence and congruence, recommendations are made for professional development programs interested in examining mentor disposition.

Typically, schools of education and teacher professional development programs concentrate on the knowledge and skills that are requisite for high quality teachers, however, little is being done to promote the dispositional development of preservice, initially licensed, or mentor teachers (Raths, 2001). Dispositions, trends of a teacher's professional judgments and professional actions in ill-structured contexts, are not seen as a priority in teacher education programs or programs focused on developing effective beginning teachers and mentors (Katz & Raths, 1985; Reiman & Johnson, 2003). Developing high quality mentors is imperative as high quality mentoring is a prime factor in teacher retention. However, like teaching, knowing what should be done in the processes of mentoring, having the judgment to decide on a course of action, and actually taking action are very different aspects of mentor dispositions that need to be investigated. This study addresses this challenge in the context of mentor judgment and action. Case study methodology is used to explore the congruence between mentors' professional judgment and professional action while engaged in a professional education program. Analysis focused on how the mentors' disposition influenced interactions with the beginning teacher to whom they were assigned. The research is guided by two main questions:

1. How do the observed patterns of professional judgment in mentor teachers converge with predicted patterns?
2. How does the professional judgment of mentor teachers correspond to their professional action as they assist in beginning teacher development?

# Defining Constructs and Theoretical Framework

## DEFINING DISPOSITIONS

Definitions of disposition found in standards governing accreditation of teacher education programs remain confusing and ambiguous to many college professors and teachers alike (Johnson, 2003). However, much can be learned from Lee Shulman's work (1998) of the shared characteristics between teaching and other professions. Acknowledging over a century of scholarly thinking, Shulman notes that teaching is built on cognitive constructs in the moral and reflective domains (Dewey, 1904; Mentkowski & Associates, 2000; Oser, Dick, & Patry, 1994). Second, he describes disposition as being both an action and an underlying judgment. Where many professional organizations will not argue that judgment and action are paramount, definitions for dispositions include a cadre of other aspects such as beliefs, values, and attitudes absent a theoretical framework (NCATE, 2002).

Recognizing the need to accommodate these professional organizations as well as maintain a definition grounded in a framework of cognitive development of judgment and action, Reiman and Johnson (2003) propose the following definition: Dispositions are attributed characteristics of a teacher that represent a trend of a teacher's judgments and actions in ill-structured contexts (situations in which a multitude of perspectives exist in how to address issues). Further, it is assumed that these dispositions, trends in teacher judgments and actions, develop over time in deliberate professional education programs. This conception of disposition is grounded in a theory of adult cognitive development.

## ASSUMPTIONS OF ADULT COGNITIVE DEVELOPMENT

Basic assumptions underlie the theory of adult cognitive development and are summarized by Reiman and Thies-Sprinthall (1998). First, all experience is processed through cognitive structures and is organized from less to more complex stages of growth. Next, a shift in change from one stage to the next represents a major transformation in how a person makes meaning from his or her experience. Such a transformation, however, is not automatic. Significant experiences and interactions with the environment are needed to promote shifts in stages. Finally, a person's behavior can be predicted by his or her stage of cognitive development.

Three specific domains of adult cognitive development adhering to the above conditions are examined in this study: the moral/ethical, the conceptual, and the ego. Reiman and Thies-Sprinthall (1998) describe these domains as connected but independent; interacting as a coherent whole and having significant impact on the teaching profession whether in classroom teaching or mentoring practices. First, the mentor is an epistemologist, understanding educational foundations, and an instructional manager able to consider various perspectives when solving problems (conceptual domain). Second, the mentor acts as a representative of democratic values and makes judgments based upon principles of social justice and diversity (moral/ethical domain). Finally, the mentor is self-aware while being responsible for the needs of learners and colleagues (ego domain) (Reiman, 1999; Reiman & Watson, 1999). These three domains are now described in more detail.

## CONCEPTUAL DOMAIN

David Hunt's (1975) theory of conceptual judgment is based largely upon Piaget's premise of a developmental progression in cognition from concrete to more abstract conceptual understanding. The theory, considered an interpersonal maturity model, has unique applications to teaching. Hunt postulates that teachers at a higher stage of conceptual judgment are better able to "read and flex" with their students (O'Keefe & Johnston, 1989) and exhibit conceptual understanding of the teaching/learning process. Translated into the mentor context, mentors are better able to "read and flex" to the needs presented by the beginning teacher. First the mentor can "read" cues given by the beginning teacher such as frustration or misunderstandings. Second, the mentor must "flex" the communicative approach used in response to the information presented by the beginning teacher. Hunt's work inspired Karen Kitchener and Patricia King to study reflective judgment or how persons form judgments about ill-structured problems (King & Kitchener, 1994). They are particularly interested in the justifications persons used to form such judgments. Those at higher levels of reflective judgment as measured by the Reflective Judgment Interview (King & Kitchener) are better able to understand and appreciate varied perspectives and can tolerate high levels of ambiguity and frustration.

The conceptual/reflective domain theorized by Hunt and King and Kitchener encompasses three levels:

**Pre-Reflective.** This level is characterized by thinking that is concrete. Knowledge is fixed and all problems have a solution. There is a high need for structure at this stage with little tolerance for ambiguity.

**Quasi-Reflective.** A growing awareness for alternative solutions increases at this level. Individuals are more open to other ideas and perspectives, although there is limited use of such when making decisions. An increased tolerance for ambiguity is evident. This is the modal level for most adults.

**Reflective.** Individuals at this level are able to weigh and balance alternative solutions. They value collaboration and are able to synthesize and integrate complex intellectual and interpersonal functions. There is openness to criticism stemming from a belief that judgments made should be open to debate. A high tolerance for ambiguity exists (King & Kitchener, 2001, p. 41).

As individuals progress from pre-reflective to reflective thinking, they progressively develop tolerance for ill-defined situations and are able to be more self-analytical.

## MORAL/ETHICAL DOMAIN

Neo-Kohlbergian theory (Rest, Narvaez, Bebeau, & Thoma, 1999) is used to interpret mentor construction and understanding of moral/ethical problems. Neo-Kohlbergian theory emphasizes, "basic human rights, equal individual moral status, and rational, autonomous individuals who are free to enter into contracts and obligations" and assumes "some ways of thinking are better at supporting respect for individual human rights than are other ways of thinking" (Narvaez, 2002, p. 2). It is based upon a three-schema conception of moral judgment. Narvaez and Bock (2002) describe schemas as the supervisors of decision making and reasoning, acting for the most part without one's awareness. The integration of schema into the theory of cognitive development acknowledges the presence of other ideologies (i.e., religious or cultural) interacting with moral structure. Socialized values act in conjunction with deeper cognitive structures versus acting independently. Rest and his associates suggest three schemas as a way of understanding moral development in a "sociomoral perspective" (p. 36):

1. First, the Personal Interest Schema describes individuals lacking in sociocentric perspective. Decisions are based primarily in the personal stake of the decision-maker stressing notions such as survival and getting ahead (Narvaez & Bock).
2. The Maintaining Norms Schema signifies an increase in an individual's ability to recognize society-wide cooperation. It emphasizes rules that are clear and consistent and applying to everyone. The social system is imperative (i.e., the hierarchical nature of a school) along with maintaining the established norms.
3. Finally, the Postconventional Schema includes four specific components: (a) There is a primacy of moral criteria, social norms are not set, but are alterable and relative; (b) Idealized ways exist for humans to interrelate; (c) Ideals are both shareable and open to justification and scrutiny; and (d) There is recognition of full reciprocity of social norms. They must be uniformly applied and unbiased.

Research on moral development using the Neo-Kohlbergian approach spans 25 years and amounts to more than 400 publications. Recent studies focus on a deeper understanding of moral judgment across the professions with emphasis on examining correlations between judgment and action (Bebeau, 2002).

## EGO DOMAIN

Ego, according to Loevinger (1976) acts as an executive, "a frame of reference that structures one's world" (p. 9). It is viewed as a construct of personality that works to make sense of experience through an integration of interpersonal and intrapersonal understanding, similar to theories of emotional intelligence. Loevinger's theory of ego personality suggests that ego is manifested in one of ten stages. Individuals can be successful at various stages; higher is not always better, just qualitatively different (Hy & Loevinger, 1996). For the purpose of this study, the ten levels are compiled into three categories theoretically similar to Loevinger's original conception of ego (Hy & Loevinger).

**Preconventional.** Includes the impulsive and self-protective stages. Adults at this stage may use judgments and show actions that are "opportunistic, deceptive, and preoccupied with control and advantage in relations with other people" (p. 17). Teachers and/or mentors at this stage lack empathy for their students or colleagues and have a strong need to minimize controversy, thus placing blame on others (or external factors) or not recognizing problems in general.

**Conventional.** Includes the conformist, self-aware, and conscientious stages. There is a strong urge at the beginning of the conventional stage to comply with the rules and norms of the group with an emphasis on respecting authority. As self-awareness increases, rules and norms remain important, however, there is a trend to accept other perspectives and an ability to be self-critical. Mentors at the beginning of the conventional stage view themselves and their colleagues in stereotypical roles and view learning as adhering to a mandated curriculum (Cummings & Murray, 1989; Hy & Loevinger, 1996). Self-reflection and analysis emerge later in the conventional stage as mentors develop their own standards for achievement (for both themselves and their colleagues) and exhibit a freer expression of emotion.

**Postconventional.** Includes the individualistic and autonomous stages. There is an ability to assume multiple perspectives at this stage. An increased tolerance for frustration and ambiguity is evident and a goal of self-fulfillment exists. Mentors at more complex levels of postconventional reasoning view education as a process of discovery acknowledging the importance of mistakes as part of learning (Hy & Loevinger, 1996). There is a pattern of increased sensitivity towards others as well as an interest in self-development in various life roles (i.e., mother, teacher, partner, etc.).

Significant efforts have been made to validate Loevinger's theory of ego development with studies being employed in clinical studies, education intervention studies, and cross-cultural studies in Japan, Europe, Australia and more (Loevinger, 1998).

# Review of Literature

Limited research exists relating teacher or mentor professional judgment and action to the domains previously described. However, reviews of literature in the moral domain and conceptual domains contend that judgment and action are connected (Blasi, 1980; Miller, 1981). Acknowledging that no perfect means exists by which to assess direct correlation between an action and an underlying behavior, trends have emerged. For example, Chang (1994) found teachers at a higher level of moral reasoning held a more "humanistic-democratic view of student discipline" and were able to consider different viewpoints, held more tolerance for student disturbances, and stressed student understanding of the purpose of rules (p. 73). In a review of over sixty studies, Miller found a direct relationship between higher conceptual reasoning and behavior such as reduced bias and prejudice, increased empathy, greater use of indirective approaches to instruction, and more intrapersonal control. Thies-Sprinthall (1980) and Reiman and Watson (1999) found that the judgment level of instructional supervisors had significant impact on their actions in reference to evaluating student and beginning teachers. In a study by MacCullum (1993), 24 high school teachers were tested on the Defining Issues Test (measure of moral judgment) and interviewed about various discipline issues. During the study, participants were tested two times using the DIT, during which time they attended staff development focused on a cognitive-developmental approach to reconceptualizing teachers' roles in discipline situations. Repeated measures analysis of variance (2 − moral group × 4 − story) was used to determine teacher response to hypothetical discipline incidents. The group mean on the DIT was 39.5 (SD = 19.55 with a range from 3.3 to 76.7). Participants in the higher range of principled reasoning (over 46) approached three out of the four dilemmas presented during the interviews from more varied perspectives, viewed their role as more facilitative, and provided more information/rationale (the fourth involved fighting, which most thought should be handled by someone such as an administrator). A major implication of the study was to further explore the variations in information interpretation based upon moral judgment level.

# Methodology

Case study methodology was used to explore the dispositions of mentor teachers. Yin (2003) described case study research as "an empirical inquiry that investigates a contemporary phenomenon within its real-life context, especially when the boundaries between phenomenon and context are not clearly evident" (p.

13). It is virtually impossible to study professional judgments and professional actions outside the real-life context of mentoring. They are embedded within each other.

## SETTING

The program in which the study took place involved examining the mentors and beginning teachers as developing adult learners. It adhered to several conditions. Summarized, the conditions acknowledged the context of the learner and use new role-taking and guided inquiry to support a framework for learning. The mentor provided an environment that is both supportive and challenging in which the beginning teacher could optimize learning over time. A more extended discussion of the conditions can be found in Reiman and Johnson (2003).

The conditions were being used as a foundation for a university program to establish high-quality mentoring programs and retain beginning and lateral-entry teachers in a rural Southeastern county experiencing high rates of teacher attrition. The school system lost 22% of its teachers each year and 42% of all teachers in the school system are initially licensed or lateral-entry teachers. The school system had one of the highest teacher turnover rates in North Carolina, which had been correlated with higher percentages (44%–60%) of students performing below grade level within the county. The retention rates and mentoring strategies were examined by school leaders, community leaders, and business representatives, leading to a call for new innovative approaches to mentoring and new teacher development.

## PARTICIPANTS

Six participants agreed to be a part of the study, three mentors and the three beginning teachers to whom they were assigned (denoted as dyads). These participants were purposely chosen after all members of the program were administered the DIT-2 (Defining Issues Test), a measure of moral judgment. Three mentors were identified as representing an above average (58), average (46), and low (28) score on the DIT-2 and were chosen to be part of the study. The beginning teacher to whom each mentor was assigned prior to the study then agreed to participate. *Dyad one* consisted of two female high school teachers. Logan was a foreign language teacher for eight years and Sherry, a science teacher, was starting her second year (teachers in their first through third years are considered beginning teachers within the county and state). *Dyad two* consisted of two middle school teachers. Linda, a math teacher, was just starting her seventh year and Joseph was in his first year of teaching language arts and social studies. Thomas and Susan were *dyad three*. Thomas was in his eighth year of teaching high school art while Susan had just started her career as a teacher in secondary science. Sherry, Joseph, and Linda were all lateral entry teachers. The three dyads were teaching in the same county, but in separate schools. All mentors met as a group on a weekly basis to participate in the same mentoring training.

## SOURCES OF DATA

### Quantitative Data

**Judgments.** The ethical judgment of the program participants was evaluated using the DIT-2 (Rest & Narvaez, 1998) during the first session of the course. Chang (1994) suggested that the average score for teachers on the DIT-2 began in the 40s for postconventional moral reasoning.

Once the participants were chosen they were administered an assessment of ego judgment and conceptual judgment. The WUSCT (Washington University Sentence Completion Test) (Hy & Loevinger, 1996) was developed as a projective measure of one's level of ego development, or how an individual derives meaning from experience. Using sentence completions, the WUSCT allowed for the subject to use his or her own frame of reference to complete 36 sentence starters. Each stem is then scored according to the stages of ego development with a method of averaging used to attain a final score. The PCM (Paragraph Completion Method) (Hunt, Butler, Noy, & Rosser, 1977) was used to assess conceptual judgment and the ways in which individuals understand the self and others. On the PCM, individuals responded to six paragraph stems, each scored from zero to three based upon the stage of conceptual judgment demonstrated. A final score is attained by averaging the top three scores. Data on the reliability and validity of the three instruments are shown in table 7.1.

**Actions.** Quantitative data on the professional actions of each mentor were collected using an adapted form of the Flanders Interaction Analysis System known as the GIAS (Guided Inquiry Analysis System) (Flanders, 1967; Reiman, 1999). Both systems supply a means by which to estimate the balance of teacher-student behavior in classroom interactions. In the case of this study, the GIAS was used to measure interaction during conferences conducted between the mentor and the beginning teacher, hence the language was changed from "student" to "learner" denoting the beginning teacher. The system consisted of three categories: direct mentor interaction, indirect mentor interaction, and be-

**Table 7.1  Psychometric Summary of Three Instruments**

| | Reliability | Content Validity | Construct Validity | Predictive Validity | Concurrent Validity |
|---|---|---|---|---|---|
| Defining Issues Test (Rest, 1986) | Test-Retest = .75<br>Internal = .75 | Moderate to High | Moderate (.60) | Moderate | Ego (.65)<br>Moral (.65) |
| Paragraph Completion Method (Hunt, 1971) | Inter-Rater = .80—.95<br>Test-Retest = .45—.56<br>Internal = .70 | Moderate | High in terms of cognitive complexity | Moderate | Ego (.23)<br>Moral (.34) |
| Sentence Completion Test (Loevinger, 1979) | Inter-Rater = .94<br>Test-Retest = .72—.79<br>Internal = .77 – .91 | High | Moderate (.58–.61) | High | Conceptual (.40)<br>Moral (.60) |

ginning teacher talk. Research has shown that mentors using less direct and more indirect styles of coaching were able to hold more learner-centered conferences in which the beginning teacher was able to express more feelings, engage in deeper analysis of instruction, and become more independent in solving classroom dilemmas (Reiman & Watson, 1999).

### Qualitative Data

Qualitative data were gathered from a cycle of mentor assistance conducted by each mentor with his/her beginning teacher. A cycle of assistance was composed of three steps taken by the dyad: (a) identifying a teaching behavior focus on which the beginning teacher would like to work (i.e., positive reinforcement, lesson planning, etc.); (b) engaging in discussion and mentor demonstration of the behavior, which included a pre- and post-conference before the demonstration; and (c) conducting pre- and post-observation conferences around the beginning teacher's utilization of the behavior. Observations of conferences with the beginning teacher took place over a six-week period. In addition, observations of lessons by the beginning teacher, analysis of artifacts asking the mentor to self-analyze and reflect on his or her role (weekly during class sessions as well as following each conference with the beginning teacher), and interview data with the mentor and beginning teacher were collected, transcribed, and coded for judgments and actions. Focused interview questions were designed for mentors based upon their role as well as to address questions specific to each domain (moral, conceptual, and ego) and were conducted either in person or via telephone (for interview schedules see Johnson, 2004). Interviews were held with each participant on two occasions, before the cycle of assistance began as well as once it was completed. One of the main purposes of using an interview was to discover those judgments and actions in participants that were not directly observable (Merriam, 1998). The qualitative data were coded according to a list of indicators or "decision rules" (Miles & Huberman, 1984, p. 246) for each theoretical domain (moral/ethical, conceptual, and ego). Table 7.2 illustrates an abbreviated version of the coding matrices that were derived from general trends in the literature (Yin, 2003). Note that table 7.2 includes the category or levels for a domain, and descriptors of teacher judgment and teacher action. As well, table 7.2 illustrates each of the cognitive domains: moral/ethical; conceptual, and ego.

Although the matrices described in table 7.2 are based on three separate domains of cognitive development (i.e., moral, conceptual, and ego), they share common characteristics of adult cognitive theory including delineation of categories of less to more complex reasoning (vertical axis) and a premise that actions

**Table 7.2   Overview of Coding Matrices**

| Category/Level | Judgment | Action |
|---|---|---|
| MORAL/ETHICAL DOMAIN | | |
| Personal Interest Schema | Personal stake in outcome | Made without considering others |
| Maintaining Norms Schema | Rules and norms apply to everyone | Made out of respect for social system |
| Postconventional Schema | Norms are relative; there are idealized ways in which persons should interact | Ideals are shared, scrutinized, and constantly reevaluated |
| CONCEPTUAL DOMAN | | |
| Pre-Reflective | Values high structured environments and views knowledge as fixed | Adherence to set norms and proven methods of instruction/coaching |
| Quasi-Reflective | Some tolerance for ambiguity with justifications that fit personal, established beliefs | Engages in imitation of instructional methods with some sensitivity to the needs of learners |
| Reflective | Critical evaluation of evidence as part of decision-making process | Able to "read and flex" with the needs of learners and consistently reevaluates instructional decisions |
| EGO DOMAIN | | |
| Pre-conventional | Has a need to minimize controversy and change with little openness to learner perspective | Impulsive and self-protective with minimal involvement with the perspective of others—controlling |
| Conventional | Feels responsible for learners and an obligation to prevent them from making mistakes | Predicated by need for acceptance and acceptability |
| Post-conventional | Recognizes need for learners to construct knowledge independently and views mistakes as part of the learning process | Provides more latitude in learning experiences and engages in mutual evaluation |

are related to underlying judgments (horizontal axis). For a complete matrix for each domain see Johnson (2004).

## DATA ANALYSIS

Pattern-matching investigates relationships between observed patterns with theoretical patterns (Campbell, 1975; Trochim, 1989). As well, it can compare mentors' judgment patterns with their action patterns. Its use greatly increases the validity of case study methodology (Yin, 2003). In this study, theoretical patterns were determined by administering quantitative assessments of judgment (DIT-2, SCT, and PCM). Although the authors were informed of the results of the DIT-2 for the participants in order to select study informants, they remained blind to the results of the SCT and PCM to prevent researcher bias. Observed patterns were examined qualitatively through interviews, artifact analysis such as reflective journaling and conference planning, and observations of conferences between the mentor and beginning teacher. The data were then coded according to the matrices described previously. A second rater, trained in theories of adult development as well as processes of mentoring, supervision, and effective teaching, coded a random sample of data from each domain, which resulted in an inter-rater reliability with the researcher of .73. Investigators then used pattern matching to examine the convergence between the predicted (quantitative) and observed (qualitative) patterns of mentor judgment. This was followed by an investigation into the congruence between teacher judgment patterns and teacher action patterns for each domain.

# Results

The following section presents results in terms of the three cognitive domains: moral/ethical, ego, and conceptual. Each section begins with an examination of how the theoretical patterns assessed by the quantitative measures converged with those that were observed. Trends in mentor action are then presented and analyzed according to the congruence with mentor judgment.

## MORAL/ETHICAL DOMAIN

### Convergence between Theoretical and Observed Patterns for Mentor Teachers

Convergence existed between the theoretical patterns and the observed patterns for all three mentor teachers. Logan, scoring above average at 58% postconventional reasoning, made judgments that were representative of her moral ideals such as the need to be "nonjudgmental and straightforward" and not make any "value judgments." She consistently recognized and considered her mentee's rights as a learner. Linda, scoring an average 46% postconventional reasoning, was able to show similar judgments such as considering the benefits and consequences of various school decisions, however, trends in her judgments were towards maintaining the norms of mentoring according to her school structure. "I am becoming aware of what an administrator looks for in an effective teacher and a classroom" (Linda, Self-Assessment #14). Thomas scored below average at 28% postconventional reasoning and tended to use the personal interest schema as a basis for his judgments. He was very concerned with "doing it right the first time." Thomas focused his concerns on his personal stake in being a mentor. "Overall if I had to give it a grade I would give it a B maybe a B+" (Thomas, Follow-Up Interview).

### Congruence of Judgments and Actions

Results from the GIAS were averaged across two pre- and post- mentor/beginning teacher conferences. For Logan, a ratio of 56% to 44% direct to indirect interaction was reported along with 62% to 38% mentor to mentee talk. This indicates that while Logan did over half of the talking during the conferences, about half of the time she was employing indirect strategies such as accepting beginning teacher feelings and ideas, reinforcing, or prompting inquiry. Linda had similar ratios of mentor/mentee talk (65% to 35%), although the ratio of direct interaction was higher, 63% to 37%. This is indicative of more time being spent by Linda providing her mentee with information or giving direction. Linda spent a great deal of time presenting her mentee with her own perspective on the lesson through both objective ("You asked questions like, 'Why do we paraphrase'") and subjective statements ("I was very impressed with your lesson"). Finally, results for Thomas showed a higher percentage of mentor talk at 69%. Direct interaction was also higher at 67%. Thomas talked for over two-thirds of the conference time with a majority of the verbal behavior being to provide information. His actions tended to be more congruent with the use of a personal interest schema focusing on goals he had for Susan versus using her perspective as indicated by the following interaction.

**Thomas:** "Do you want to do nonverbal cues? Do you want to do circulating around the room? Do you want to do a little bit of positive reinforcement with the kids?"

**Mentee:** "Um, I'm really looking for equity."

**Thomas:** [Later in the conference] "I'm going to give you some tactics today that I think will address that issue and help you out with that, but there's something else oh, moving around the room and reinforcement, verbal and nonverbal cues" (Thomas, Demonstration Pre-Conference).

During this exchange, it was obvious Susan wanted to work on equity; however, Thomas continued to stress the nonverbal behaviors he felt needed work.

Significant trends were apparent between these data gathered by the GIAS and the standard assessment of moral/ethical judgment. According to the DIT-2, Logan used 58% postconventional reasoning, Linda used 46%, and Thomas used 28%. Such findings indicate that those mentors who were more open to question and debate about established rules and norms (higher percentage of postconventional reasoning), engaged in more indirect behaviors such as accepting ideas and prompting inquiry versus providing information and direction. This, in turn, afforded the opportunity for the mentee to participate more actively in the conference by sharing self-analysis and reflection.


## EGO DOMAIN

### Convergence between Theoretical and Observed Patterns

**Convergence.** Thomas, assessed as late conventional by the SCT, acknowledged concerns his mentee had about balancing work and family, "I know she gets frustrated, she has kids of her own and she's concerned about that" (Thomas, Follow-Up Interview). Linda, assessed as postconventional, stressed the need to address behaviors on which her mentee wanted to focus, "We had discussed equity at one point, but he really wanted to focus in on some areas he wanted to fine tune . . . he wants to work on higher order questioning and he also wants to work on positive reinforcement so that's what we'll be doing" (Linda, Initial Interview). Finally, Logan (late conventional) made judgments that were evident of building self-awareness and being self-critical, typical of the late conventional ego. "I'm still nervous about making sure I do things right. . . . I felt a little unsure of myself like maybe I was making too many suggestions for change" (Logan, Follow-Up Interview). Linda and Thomas seemed to exhibit similar judgments of self-awareness such as being nervous about performing in front of peers for a demonstration lesson.

**Divergence.** Rarely do individuals make judgments that are consolidated within one level of ego. However, some judgments made by the participants were significantly uncharacteristic of their assessed judgment level. For example, Thomas based many judgments in conventional stereotypes. "New teachers are overwhelmed by their workload and need a good structure from day one" (Thomas, Self-Reflection #13). This indicated a lack of awareness of individual differences characteristic of an early conventional ego level. Linda also made judgments that were less complex than suggested by the SCT. In regards to providing her mentee with feedback, she focused on being nice and not appearing critical. "I'm good at giving praise, but I didn't want it to seem that I was being harsh or just out to get him by telling him, well you need to do this or try it this way, it might help" (Linda, Follow-Up Interview). Even in her written reflections, Linda was concerned about hurting her mentee's feelings or "discouraging him" by "appearing critical" (Linda, Self-Assessment #2). Data gathered on Logan seemed convergent with her state of ego. Since she was assessed as late conventional, it would be expected that judgments would be made characteristic of this stage (viewing self as responsible for mentee learning) as well as the proceeding postconventional stage (understanding challenges of multiple roles, teacher, mentor, friend, etc.).

### Congruence of Judgments and Actions

Inconsistency was found in patterns of interaction and amount of mentor talk when compared to the SCT data. Logan and Thomas were assessed at similar judgment levels, however a 10% difference existed in their interactions. Logan allowed more time for her mentee to give her perspective (mentee talk at 38%) and engaged in more indirect interactions (40%) such as accepting and using her mentee's ideas. During written reflections, Logan's expression of emotion was more specific, rich, diverse, and showed an ability to reconcile conflicting emotions.

> I have been apprehensive, excited, stressed, and relieved. Early on, I was wondering what I had gotten myself into and if I was going to be an effective mentor. I have been impressed by the research and demonstrations. I was excited to put them to work in my class and with my mentee. . . . I enjoyed the experience (Logan, Self-Reflection #11).

Thomas was more apt to present information to his mentee from his own perspective as shown by the 67% direct interaction, 69% mentor talk. He was able to express some emotion although it tended to be simple and often one-dimensional such as "I'm a little nervous about it" and "anxious to get it done to see how we did." Linda's actions were more congruent with the coding matrix than with the SCT. She averaged 65% mentor talk and 63% direct interaction with an overwhelming concern for being critical. This was displayed in actions such as reporting to her mentee, "I was really impressed with your lesson" or, "I really felt like they were excited about it."

Both convergence and divergence existed in the ego domain in terms of the theoretical/predicted patterns and judgments and actions. Where participants were assessed to be at similar levels of ego, their judgments and actions could not necessarily be consolidated within a single category.

## CONCEPTUAL DOMAIN

### Convergence between Theoretical and Observed Patterns

Data indicated minor differences existing in the standardized measure for conceptual judgment. Reported by the PCM, judgments made by Linda were considered quasi-reflective while Thomas and Logan's judgments were more reflective. It is important to note, however, that while Thomas and Logan were both considered reflective, Thomas' score of 2.3 indicates emerging reflective judgments and Logan's score of 2.5 represents more consolidation within the reflective level.

**Convergence.** All three participants were able to consider multiple sources of evidence when making decisions. Thomas acknowledged information important to his mentee could come from a variety of sources such as the head of her department. When making some judgments regarding teaching and mentoring, Linda, assessed as being quasi-reflective, maintained a sense of authority and expertise commenting, "I feel my opinion is better. I have the experience of what has worked and not worked" (Linda, Follow-Up Interview). Logan, considered reflective, was able to evaluate sources of evidence and acknowledged the subjectivity that came with collecting and interpreting data. "It seems like you can find research that supports what you want it to support and numbers and data to look the way you want it to look" (Logan, Follow-Up Interview).

**Divergence.** Some divergence existed between the theoretical predicted patterns of conceptual judgment and data presented by the coding matrix. Acknowledging that rarely are cognitive structures restricted to a single level, a noteworthy divergence emerged. The PCM assessed Thomas at an emerging reflective level signifying an increased tolerance for ambiguity and preferred low structure environment. However, the coding matrix indicated Thomas placed a high value in structure.

> [The conference guide is] something we've been working on in class and it's important obviously or else it wouldn't be on there. We have a tendency to get off track so I think it's important to keep that level of feedback so that we keep a good dialogue and keep it more

instructional-based instead of more personal-based (Thomas, Initial Interview).

This view of structure is more characteristic of the pre-reflective level.

### Congruence of Judgments and Actions

For Logan, an increasing level of conceptual judgment complexity resulted in decreased amounts of direct interaction (56%) and amount of mentor talk (62%). This signifies about half of Logan's interactions with her mentee being behaviors such as accepting and using perspective presented by her mentee, providing reinforcement, and prompting inquiry with questions such as, "How would you evaluate the learning outcome?" or "What changes do you think you would make to the climate?" In terms of making decisions in mentoring situations, Logan was able to use current evidence gathered objectively and consistently reevaluated. This aligns to patterns in her conceptual judgment as well as the ratios presented by the GIAS. Linda's percentage of direct interaction and mentor talk was slightly higher than Logan's, 63% and 65% respectively. Linda used similar questions to prompt her mentee to evaluate his teaching, "How did you feel about the outcome? Did you get the outcome you expected?" (Linda, Observation Post-Conference). Linda was not, however, able to recognize her mentee's need for more structured feedback in areas in which improvements could be made. She focused on providing evidence of positive events and even justified student behavior that concerned her mentee. This seemed frustrating for Linda's mentee who needed more specific feedback in terms of changes he needed to make. For Thomas, an increase in mentor talk (69%) and direct interaction (67%) was found, yet his conceptual level is actually more, not less complex than Linda's. According to the theory, during interactions with his mentee, Thomas would be interested in acknowledging and using her feelings and ideas as well as prompting evaluation and synthesis of evidence. Data gathered from the GIAS showed a significant portion of interactions with his mentee being mentor directed, affording his mentee only about 31% of the time to respond to questions and initiate talk. The majority of Thomas' interactions involved presenting his mentee with information that was rarely based in evidence. For example, Thomas tended to put himself in an authoritative position when talking with his mentee, "You did everything that I think you should have done, so that was a good thing" (Thomas, Observation Post-Conference). Conferences between Thomas and his mentee only lasted about seven minutes. This afforded little time for his mentee to engage in and share self-analysis and for Thomas to prompt deeper inquiry. Where this seemed to match the GIAS data, Thomas' actions were not congruent with the PCM.

In summary, the theoretical and observed patterns of conceptual judgment showed significant convergence for Logan and Linda. Thomas exhibited judgments and actions that were more congruent with a less complex conceptual level than that reported by the PCM.

# Conclusions

This study examined mentor disposition as professional judgment and action. Although the main questions of the research focused on the congruence between these two components and the influence on beginning teachers, other significant findings emerged. First, an overall convergence existed between the theoretical patterns predicted by the standard measures of judgment and observed patterns summarized through the application of a coding matrix. As Loevinger (1976) noted, rarely do individuals exist in one consolidated ego level. In cases where divergence occurred, it seemed consistent within a single participant. Thomas' ego (conventional) and conceptual judgment (emerging reflective) were reported significantly higher on the quantitative assessments than what was actually gathered through interviews, observations, and artifact analysis. He was not able to empathize with and respond to the emotional and instructional needs of his mentee as the theory suggested. For all participants, the three domains of judgment needed to be examined as separate but related entities of disposition. Where an individual may be able to reconcile conflicting emotions and accept various perspectives (ego), he or she may not make judgments based upon moral/ethical ideals and vice versa. In addition, standardized measures are reliable and valid in measuring psychological systems, however, the coding matrices played a significant role in assessing judgments within the specific context and complex new role of mentoring.

The main purpose of the research was to examine the congruence between mentor judgment and action. In reference to assessing professional actions, the GIAS proved reliable in assessing interactions during conferences between the mentor and beginning teacher. Application of the coding matrices supplied supporting evidence for the GIAS and provided significant data as to whether mentors were direct presenters of information or more facilitative in nature, prompting the beginning teacher to be more self-reflective and independent. When these data were compared to the mentor judgments, significant congruence was found, especially between the coding matrices and the GIAS. Where divergence existed in the standardized measure of judgment and the coding matrix, actions were congruent with the coding matrix. For example, Linda was assessed as being postconventional by the SCT, although the coding matrix assessed Linda's judgments as more conventional. Actions measured by the

GIAS and the coding matrices were congruent with this assessment. In reference to the moral/ethical domain, as the percentage of postconventional reasoning increased, mentors showed actions that adhered to moral ideals, were open to questions and debate, and were resolved to consider the rights of the beginning teacher when making decisions. The conceptual domain showed similar trends. Mentors displaying more reflective judgments were able to consider and evaluate different viewpoints and other sources of evidence. When engaging in conferences with the beginning teachers, their actions were more facilitative than directive (i.e., they spent more time prompting inquiry or accepting beginning teacher emotion and ideas than providing information or giving direction). Finally, the ego domain proved the most intricate of the three domains. Trends were difficult to identify although they hold significant impact on mentor action. Mentors whose judgments were assessed by the matrix to be more complex were able to identify and reconcile the conflicting emotions that often accompany a new role. They valued collaboration and viewed the beginning teacher with whom they worked as a colleague versus a subordinate. Conferences tended to have more of a balance of mentor and mentee talk considering the mentor valued the ideas and emotions of the mentee.

# Implications

Teacher differences reflect more than developmental factors. For example, an exhaustive review by Borko and Putnam (1996) illustrates that learning to teach, even when situated in cognitive psychology, must draw upon a rich and diverse body of evidence that illuminates the various aspects of teacher learning and development. Such areas include teacher socialization and career development. However, the current research follows a line of assumptions that an individual's psychological structures and the related mental representations of the world play a central role in thinking, acting, and learning. Results of this study have key implications for teacher education and professional growth programs interested in fostering cognitive growth.

Overall, convergence was found between the standardized measures of judgment and the coding matrices and congruence was apparent between judgment and action. This first implies the dispositions of emerging mentors can be assessed with three standardized measures. Using such assessments can provide trends across large samples of mentors. However, as findings show, the coding matrices proved more specific in providing descriptive indicators of individual mentor dispositions during certain events such as the cycles of assistance. Dispositions can be assessed with the matrices or the standardized measures before and after extensive developmental programming to address how dispositions may have changed over time. Assessing mentor disposition provides valuable information in terms of appropriate matches with beginning teachers. As research by Thies-Sprinthall (1980) suggests, such matches are crucial in the development of preservice and beginning teachers. The GIAS was significant in measuring mentor interactions during conference situations. It can be used to gather evidence on the interactions between mentors and beginning teachers during conferences. Are the mentors providing sufficient opportunity for the beginning teacher to engage in self-analysis and reflection? Are the mentors prompting inquiry and clarifying ideas presented by the beginning teacher to assist the teachers in becoming independent problem solvers? Again, using the GIAS to assess mentor action before, during, and after professional development programs will provide descriptive evidence on change in actions that may or may not be occurring.

While further research is necessary in the use of dispositions in teacher education and continued professional development, the first steps have been taken. Use of the coding matrices proved reliable in providing supportive evidence for quantitative measures (DIT-2, SCT, and DIT-2) and descriptive characteristics for each participant. The GIAS was effective in measuring action in conferencing situations. Using larger samples of mentors will provide more evidence on whether or not statistically significant correlations exist between the GIAS as a measure of the action and the PCM, SCT, and DIT-2 as measures of professional judgment. In addition, examining variations in certification programs and teaching areas (elementary, middle, high schools) of mentors is needed. Implementing the coding matrices and the standardized measures into existing mentoring programs will provide further information as to the applicability and practicality of the two assessment pieces. Through continued study, more refined programs of fostering and assessing mentor dispositions will emerge. These programs will see the development of mentors who are more capable of supporting the thousands of new teachers entering the profession and the need for new teachers may eventually decrease.

# References

Bebeau, M. J. (2002). The Defining Issues Test and the four component model: Contributions to professional education. *Journal of Moral Education, 31*(3), 271–295.

Borko, H., & Putnam, R. T. (1996). Learning to teach. In D. Berliner and R. Calfee (Eds.), *Handbook of educational psychology* (pp. 673–708). New York: Simon and Schuster.

Blasi, A. (1980). Bridging moral cognition and moral action: A critical review of the literature. *Psychological Bulletin, 88*(1), 1–45.

Campbell, D. T. (1975). Degrees of freedom and the case study. *Comparative Political Studies, 8,* 178–193.

Chang, F.-Y. (1994). School teachers' moral reasoning. In J. Rest & D. Narvaez (Eds.), *Moral development in the professions* (pp. 71–84). Hillsdale, NJ: Lawrence Erlbaum.

Cummings, A. L., & Murray, H. G. (1989). Ego development and its relation to teacher education. *Teaching and Teacher Education, 5*(1), 21–32.

Dewey, J. (1904). The relation of theory to practice in education. In *The third yearbook of the national society for the scientific study of education: Part I: The relation of theory to practice in the education of teachers* (pp. 9–30). Chicago: University of Chicago Press.

Flanders, N. A. (1967). Some relationships among teacher influence, pupil attitudes, and achievement. In E. J. Amidon & J. B. Hough (Eds.), *Interaction analysis: Theory, research and application* (pp. 103–116). Reading, MA: Addison-Wesley.

Hunt, D. E. (1975). Person-environment interaction: A challenge found wanting before it was tried. *Review of Educational Research, 45*(2), 209–230.

Hunt, D., Butler, L., Noy, J., & Rosser, M. (1977). *Assessing conceptual level by the Paragraph Completion Method.* Ontario Institute for Studies in Education.

Hy, L. X., & Loevinger, J. (1996). *Measuring ego development* (2nd ed.). Mahwah, NJ: Lawrence Erlbaum.

Johnson, L. E. (2003, February). *Discussing dispositions in teacher education.* Paper presented at the Southeastern Association of Educational Studies, Chapel Hill, NC.

Johnson, L. E. (2004). *Congruence between professional judgment and professional action as disposition: A case study of mentors and beginning teachers.* Unpublished doctoral dissertation. North Carolina State University, Raleigh, North Carolina.

Katz, L. G., & Raths, J. D. (1985). Dispositions as goals for teacher education. *Teaching and Teacher Education, 1*(4), 301–307.

King, P. M., & Kitchener, K. S. (1994). *Developing reflective judgment.* San Francisco: Jossey-Bass.

King, P. M, & Kitchener, K. S. (2001). The reflective judgment model: Twenty years of research on epistemic cognition. In Hofer, B. K., & Pintrich, P. R. (Eds.). *Personal epistemology: The psychology of beliefs about knowledge and knowing* (pp. 37–62). Mahwah, NJ: Lawrence Erlbaum.

Loevinger, J. (1976). *Ego development: Conceptions and theories.* San Francisco: Jossey-Bass.

Loevinger, J. (1998). *Technical foundations for measuring ego development.* Mahwah, N.J.: Lawrence Erlbaum.

MacCullum, J. A. (1993). Teacher reasoning and moral judgment in the context of student discipline situations. *Journal of Moral Education, 22*(1), 3–18.

Mentkowski, M., & Associates. (2000). *Learning that lasts.* San Francisco: Jossey-Bass.

Merriam, S. B. (1998). *Qualitative research and case study applications in education.* San Francisco: Jossey-Bass.

Miles, M., & Huberman, M. (1984). *Qualitative data analysis.* Beverly Hills, CA: Sage.

Miller, A. (1981). Conceptual matching models and interactional research in education. *Review of Educational Research, 51*(1), 33–84.

National Council for the Accreditation of Teacher Educators. (2002). *Professional standards for the accreditation of schools, colleges, and departments of education.* Washington, DC: Author.

Narvaez, D. (2002). *Moral judgment and theory*. Unpublished manuscript, University of Malaya, Kuala Lumpur.

Narvaez, D., & Bock, T. (2002). Moral schemas and tacit judgment of how the defining issues test is supported by cognitive science. *Journal of Moral Education, 31*(3), 297–314.

O'Keefe, P., & Johnston, M. (1989). Perspective taking and teacher effectiveness: A connecting thread through three developmental literatures. *Journal of Teacher Education, 40*(3), 20–26.

Oser, F., Dick, A., & Patry, J. (1994). Responsibility, effectiveness, and the domains of educational research. In F. Oser, A. Dick, & J. Patry (Eds.), *Effective and responsible teaching: The new synthesis* (pp. 3–13). San Francisco: Jossey-Bass.

Raths, J. (2001). Teachers' beliefs and teaching beliefs. *Early Childhood Research and Practice, 3*(1), 385–391.

Reiman, A. J. (1999). The evolution of social role taking and guided reflection framework in teacher education: Recent theory and quantitative synthesis of research. *Teaching and Teacher Education, 15*, 597–612.

Reiman, A., & Johnson, L. E. (2003). Promoting teacher professional judgment. *Journal of Research in Education, 13*(1), 4–14.

Reiman, A. J., & Thies-Sprinthall, L. (1998). *Mentoring and supervision for teacher development*. New York: Addison Wesley Longman.

Reiman, A. J., & Watson, B. (1999). Beginning teacher development: A cognitive-developmental approach. *Journal of Research in Education, 9*(1), 56–65.

Rest, J. R., & Narvaez, D. (1998). *Guide for the DIT-2*. Minneapolis, MN: Center for the Study of Ethical Development.

Rest, J., Narvaez, D., Bebeau, M. J., & Thoma, S. J. (1999). *Postconventional moral thinking: A Neo-Kohlbergian approach*. Mahwah, NJ: Lawrence Erlbaum.

Shulman, L. S. (1998). Theory, practice, and the education of professionals. *Elementary School Journal, 98*(5), 511–526.

Thies-Sprinthall, L. (1980). Supervision: An educative or mis-educative process? *Journal of Teacher Education, 31*(4), 17–20.

Trochim, W. M. (1989). Outcome pattern matching and program theory. *Evaluation and Program Planning, 12*, 355–366.

Yin, R. K. (2003). *Case study research: Design and methods*. Thousand Oaks, CA: Sage.

# CHAPTER 8

# Mentoring

## A SERENDIPITOUS PROFESSIONAL DEVELOPMENT OPPORTUNITY

*Lynn S. Kline*
University of Akron

*James Salzman*
Cleveland State University

Lynn S. Kline is an assistant professor of early childhood education at the University of Akron. She has professional and research interests in performance assessment and professional development of teachers, preservice through inservice. This research was completed with support from the Cleveland State University Doctoral Dissertation Research Expense Award Program.

Jim Salzman is an associate professor of literacy education at Cleveland State University and co-director of the *Reading First–Ohio Center for Professional Development and Technical Assistance for Effective Reading Instruction*. He has published articles on teacher induction, action research, and literacy, co-authored a textbook on teacher planning, and authored two manuals on teacher induction.

## ABSTRACT

Do legislated changes in Ohio's licensing procedures offer serendipitous professional development opportunities for veteran teachers who mentor beginning teachers through the performance-assessment process? Anecdotal information from mentors indicates that Pathwise Classroom Observations System training acts as a catalyst for veteran teachers' reflection on their own teaching. This study focused on K–8 mentor and non-mentor teaching practice. Data were collected from teaching artifacts, classroom observations and interviews. Quantitative and qualitative techniques were used to analyze the data. The quantitative analyses indicated no statistically significant difference in the practice. However, the qualitative analysis indicated group differences that reflect mentors' sense of collegiality and teaching efficacy. Both groups performed best in communicating clear goals and procedures and worst in using questions and discussion techniques.

Teacher mentoring programs have dramatically increased since the early 1980s as a vehicle to support and retain novice teachers. In addition, mentors reported that mentoring a novice teacher provided a catalyst for reflecting on their own classroom practices, increased their self-awareness of instructional techniques and fostered a sense of professional rejuvenation (Ford & Parsons, 2000; Pullman, Pullman, Newman, & Turner, 2002). In Ohio, every candidate seeking initial teaching licensure is required to successfully complete an Entry Year Program including formal mentoring support to foster professional growth and a classroom performance assessment (Teacher Education and Licensure Standards, 1996).

After review of several pilot performance assessment projects, the Ohio Department of Education adopted Praxis III of the Praxis Series: Professional Assessments for Beginning Teachers (1995) as the performance-based assessment system that is used to make initial teacher licensure decisions. The Pathwise Classroom Observation System (Pathwise COS) constituted the formative portion of the assessment model. Although Pathwise was not mandated by the state, over 21,000 teachers have participated in workshops to understand the language and observation protocol of the model as part of mentor training. There has been a lot of speculation about how these mandates influenced entry year teachers, teacher training institutions and school districts as a whole. However, few have speculated on how this process impacted the professional practice of veteran teacher mentors.

# Reported Benefits for Mentors

Mentoring programs are predicated on the belief that adults have the capacity for continued growth and learning, which can be enhanced or impeded by specific interventions (Levine, 1989). Effective mentoring relationships provided for high expressions of synergy. In fact, the most effective mentors admitted that they learned as much, if not more, from their protégés as the protégés learned from them (Farnsworth & Morris, 1996).

Little (1982) concluded that the potential to influence teachers' practice improved if the language shared by teachers was used to describe, analyze, interpret or evaluate teaching. Professional discourse embedded in organizational contexts provided informal and incidental learning outside the formally structured classroom-based professional development model. Structuring this discourse within a mentoring process provided both the entry-year teacher and the mentor opportunities to analyze and evaluate professional practice.

Furthermore, teachers learned best when they continuously engaged in inquiry about teaching and learning. Some mentoring programs accomplished this by forming ongoing discourse communities where teachers came together to discuss strategies, concepts and tools for teaching and learning (Ball & Cohen, 1999; Darling-Hammond, 1998). Foote and Walker (1998) found that although mentor teacher development and benefits were not intended outcomes of their work with pre-service teachers, they "surfaced and became of major significance to those examining what is really happening in the public schools . . ." (p. 5). Serendipitous to their research intentions, facilitators of mentoring programs have begun to recognize the substantial benefits of the mentoring experience for mentors as well as novice teachers (David, 2000; Holloway, 2001).

Unfortunately, research investigating the impact of mentoring on the mentor teacher was limited and most often derived from self-reported interviews, surveys or questionnaires. For instance, Huling and Resta (2001) reported that benefits of mentoring for the mentor included developed reflective practice, increased professional competency, renewed commitment to teaching, enhanced self-esteem, increased confidence in collegial interactions and developed capacity for teacher leadership. The authors used Huling and Resta's categories below to explore the literature related to these perceived benefits.

## REFLECTIVE PRACTICE

Mentors suggested that guiding their protégés through critical reflection compelled them to be more reflective. For example, in a study of student teachers and cooperating teachers, Tatel (1996) found that teachers credited the supervision process for stimulating reflection. They indicated that the daily presence of a student teacher served as a catalyst for them to improve their immediate teaching practices. Mentors also identified reflection and introspection about teaching, learning new ideas about content and pedagogy, and satisfaction in helping someone else as benefits of the mentoring experience (Ganser, 1996).

## PROFESSIONAL COMPETENCY

As mentors confronted elements of professional teaching practice, they were prompted to self-examination. Mentors experienced changes in their role which in turn influenced their own teaching and professional life. The most pronounced changes occurred when student teachers introduced veteran teachers to new content materials and pedagogical strategies. Mentors reported changes in their professional practice including increased enthusiasm for teaching, increased use of technology, new approaches to time planning and knowledge of subject matter (Ariav & Clinard, 1996; Tatel, 1996). The combination of mentors' and protégés' critical reflection on practice, application of cognitive coaching skills and exposure to new ideas in content and pedagogy stimulated professional growth on the part of the mentors (Grossman, 1994; Ganser 1996; Wollman-Bonilla, 1997).

## RENEWED COMMITMENT TO TEACHING

Mentors cited personal enjoyment, contributing to the profession, rejuvenation (Ganser, 1992; Pullman, Pullman, Turner, Pascale, & Newman, 2004), reflection and learning new ideas and techniques as the most valued benefits of mentoring. Clinard and Ariav (1997) reported that mentor teachers experienced changes in their role, which in turn influenced their own teaching. Mentors in this study identified increased enthusiasm for teaching, opportunities for collaboration with colleagues, increased knowledge of subject matter and reflection on practice as powerful consequences of mentoring.

## PSYCHOLOGICAL BENEFITS

Mentors' expression of personal satisfaction in seeing their protégés succeed (Bova & Phillips, 1981; Ganser, 1996) improved social interaction and communication skills, enhanced sense of individual pride, increased motivation to remain in the profession (Tatel, 1996) and enhanced self-esteem (Wollman-Bonilla, 1997) have been reported as additional benefits of mentoring.

## COLLEGIAL INTERACTIONS

Teachers, institutionally, have been isolated in their classrooms. In schools, however, where a strong mentoring program existed, mentors often described collaboration with their protégés (Ariav & Clinard, 1996; Ganser, 1996; Grossman, 1994; McGee, 1998; Tatel, 1996) and reduced isolation and learning from their protégé (Wollman-Bonilla, 1997) as additional benefits of mentoring that extend beyond some of those described earlier. Phillips and Glickman (1991) found that when teachers acted as peer coaches they assumed more complex roles as they came together in collegial groups to reflect on their work. These collegial interactions resulted in the peer coaches' heightened awareness of the complexities of teaching (Stanulis & Weaver, 1998).

## CAPACITY FOR LEADERSHIP

Finally, mentor training and experience also enabled mentors to move into leadership roles or participate in research projects. Freiberg, Zbikowski and Ganser (1996) found it was not uncommon for successful mentors to be offered unsolicited positions as a result of their experiences. As veteran teachers helped in the professional development of interns, they developed their own skills in the areas of leadership, reflection, collegiality, best practice, professional growth and respect for the profession (Foote & Walker, 1998; Pullman et al., 2004).

Many teachers commented on changes in their thinking about their own classroom practice as a result of the Pathwise training experience (Salzman, 1999, 2000). This supported the notion that the most powerful form of learning for teachers and the most sophisticated form of professional development came from teachers sharing what they know through reflection on their practice and articulation of their craft (Barth, 1990). Training teachers to observe classroom practice provided them with structured opportunities to dialogue with colleagues about teaching and learning using a shared definition of teaching excellence. Furthermore, analyzing teaching practice through the lens of the Praxis/Pathwise criteria became the crucible in which veteran mentor teachers reflected upon and adjusted their own teaching practices.

Systematic guided reflection, of the type in which mentors and protégés engaged as they used the Pathwise protocols, has been identified as a key component to promote mentor and novice teacher development (Reiman & Thies-Sprinthall, 1993). Data from the Eisenhower Professional Development Program (Porter, Garet, Desimone, Suk Yoon, & Birman, 2000) indicated that non-traditional types of professional development such as study groups, committee work and mentoring led teachers to self-reported changes in their practices. Systematic guided reflection is part and parcel of the training and mentoring regimen for participants in this program, and an end result is the expectation that novice teachers will improve their practices. The question that drove this study was: What is the impact of mentoring on the teaching practices of the mentors?

# Purpose of the Study

This study was designed to determine how the teaching practices of mentors were different from their non-mentoring colleagues. Unlike the self-reported research discussed in the literature, this study focused on observed and documented teaching behaviors as well as teachers' discourse about their practice. This study compared the teaching practice of K–8 mentors with that of their non-mentoring colleagues. All of the mentors had participated in two-day Pathwise COS training and used the language and protocol to guide the novice teachers' professional reflections.

Unfortunately, it was not possible to study mentor change over time in this study; rather a comparison was made between the practice of experienced teachers who mentor and those who do not. Therefore, the cause of any differences cannot validly be attributed to the Pathwise COS training and mentoring experience alone. However, this study is important; it is the only known examination of the documented professional practices of veteran teachers who are Pathwise COS trained mentors and their non-mentoring colleagues. In addition, it provided empirical evidence of potentially substantive benefits of mentoring for the mentor, as well as the novice.

## PRAXIS/PATHWISE AND FRAMEWORK FOR TEACHING

Together the Praxis/Pathwise criteria and *Enhancing Professional Practice: A Framework for Teaching* (Danielson, 1996) components presented a continuum of teaching behaviors within a shared definition of teaching excellence. Both viewed teaching through four domains—planning, classroom environment, instruction and professionalism. Grounded in empirical and theoretical research the descriptions of teaching (i.e., the rubrics) reflected a constructivist approach to learning in which the teacher guides the learning process, but students themselves must undertake and manage the construction of understanding. The rubrics in both systems rewarded teachers for designing activities, generating problems, and providing exercises that engaged students in constructing important knowledge, rather than making presentations, creating worksheet assignments or asking low-level questions. The Framework for Teaching was used because it was more appropriate in capturing and differentiating levels of performance of veteran teachers since Pathwise/Praxis rubrics are based on novice teacher performance only.

# Methods

## PARTICIPANTS

Participants for this study consisted of 15 matched pairs of veteran K–8 teachers. Data were collected using Pathwise Classroom Observation System protocol and forms. Mentors and their non-mentoring colleagues were recruited and blind-paired by school administrators. Mentor/non-mentor pairs were matched according to district, age and number of years of teaching experience. All but one of the participants was female. The age of participants ranged from 25 to 60. The number of years of teaching experience ranged from six to 31 years. Thirteen matched pairs were within three years of each other in age and experience. The additional two pairs contained participants who were about the same age but had a six-year and a four-year difference respectively in their teaching experience. Generally, the paired teachers were not assigned to the same grade level or content area; however, in 11 of the pairs, both the mentor and non-mentoring teacher were faculty members in the same school. The four remaining pairs of teachers were teaching in different buildings within the same school district. Participant pairs were drawn from large and small districts as well as urban, suburban and rural areas.

## DATA COLLECTION PROCEDURE

The research protocol followed the Pathwise Classroom Observation System sequence. This protocol included a review of planning artifacts, pre-observation interview, classroom observation and post-observation interview. Each participant was observed once by the same Praxis/Pathwise/Framework trained observer during a self-selected teaching episode. The teaching episodes averaged 40 minutes and were in a variety of content areas.

Evidence of teaching behaviors was documented from primary sources. Data were grouped by domain and component as described in Danielson (1996). Data collected and used for evidence were relevant to each of the components, representative of observed behaviors, and categorized within 72 hours after observation. Written artifacts, planning documents and teachers' discourse provided primary sources of evidence of teaching behaviors in planning for instruction (Domain 1) and professional responsibilities (Domain 4). The classroom observation provided the primary source of evidence for teachers' skills in establishing a classroom environment (Domain 2) and delivering instruction (Domain 3). In addition, the post-observation semi-structured interview provided an opportunity for the teachers to reflect on instruction to clarify any teaching behaviors.

Documented behaviors were compared to the level of performance descriptions for each component. Comparisons were done by the lead author, who is a trained Praxis III Assessor for the state of Ohio and a National Certified Pathwise Trainer. A level of performance score, from 1 to 4, was assigned to all participants in a component before behaviors in the next component were analyzed. Lower levels of performance were identified as levels 1 and 2. Level 1 indicated the teacher lacked understanding of the concepts underlying the component. Level 2 indicated that the teacher understood the component, attempted to implement its elements but was not entirely successful. Higher levels of performance were levels 3 and 4. Level 3 indicated the teacher clearly understood the component and successfully implemented its elements. At level 4, classrooms were characterized by learning communities of highly motivated and engaged students who assumed responsibility for their own learning.

## DATA ANALYSES

Quantitative and qualitative techniques were used to analyze data. Two non-parametric tests were used to establish significance. The Sign Test was used to calculate frequency of difference in levels of performance and the Wilcoxon Matched-Pairs Signed-Ranks Test was used to calculate the magnitude of difference in levels of performance. Categorizing and quantifying behaviors within each of the professional practice components did not tell the whole story, however. Teaching behavior in reality is multidimensional and fluid, not a single fixed phenomenon waiting to be discovered, observed and measured. Thus, qualitative analyses were also conducted. The Constant Comparison technique (Glaser & Strauss, 1967) was employed as a second mode of analysis to illuminate characteristics within and between mentors and non-mentors that defined and differentiated teaching practice. Bits of data were organized into component piles during the first level of analysis (Dye, Schatz, Rosenberg & Coleman, 2000). The researcher compared data bits within each pile, and identified similarities or differences within the data. Patterns or variations in data emerged when comparisons were made between the different component piles. Distinctions between data piles reflected some criterion or criteria that discriminated one bit of data from another (Dye et al.).

# Results

Although the non-parametric tests, as summarized in table 8.1, indicated no statistically significant differences in the professional practice of each mentor/non-mentor pair, the qualitative analysis illuminated similarities and differences as well as patterns of practice within and between the professional practice of mentors and their non-mentoring colleagues.

## DOMAIN 1: PLANNING AND PREPARATION

Data collected from the planning documents indicated how teachers used knowledge of students and content in making pedagogical decisions as they designed instruction. Levels of performance on all five of the planning components were similar for mentors and teachers. Most of the participants explicitly stated or implied that they used a variety of instructional strategies to accommodate learning needs. However, 27 out of the 30 participants selected teacher-directed pedagogy for the major part of the instruction that was observed. Also, 75% of the mentors and non-mentors demonstrated behaviors that were consistent with lower levels of performance descriptions in the following areas: demonstrating knowledge of students, selecting instructional goals and assessing student learning. Table 8.2 summarizes the similarities and differences in levels of performance as well as characteristics of mentor and non-mentor behaviors in each of the components of the planning domain (Domain 1).

## DOMAIN 2: CLASSROOM ENVIRONMENT

Components in this domain provided evidence of teachers' skills in creating a physically and psychologically safe learning environment. Data were collected from the classroom observation and supported by responses to prompts on the Class Profile. Although behaviors were similar in creating an environment of respect and rapport, the mentors displayed a wider range of behaviors from encouraging students to value each other to demonstrating insensitivity with sarcastic comments. In establishing a culture for learning, all participants except three non-mentors demonstrated behaviors that consistently supported a culture for learning. The mentors' behaviors, demonstrated in managing classroom procedures and managing student behavior, provided more opportunities for students to become involved in the development of class rules and procedures. Finally, mentors and non-mentors organized the physical space to support and

**Table 8.1   Summary of Sign Test and Wilcoxon Test**

| Component | Mentor score higher | Scores equal | Teacher score higher | Sign Test* | Wilcoxon Test* |
|---|---|---|---|---|---|
| Domain 1 (Planning and Preparation) | | | | | |
| (1a) Demonstrating knowledge of content and pedagogy | 4 | 11 | 0 | .12 | .12 |
| (1b) Demonstrating knowledge of students | 3 | 10 | 2 | 1 | 1 |
| (1c) Selecting instructional goals | 2 | 10 | 3 | 1 | .81 |
| (1d) Demonstrating knowledge of resources | 6 | 7 | 2 | .28 | .19 |
| (1e) Designing coherent instruction | 3 | 12 | 0 | .25 | .25 |
| (1f) Assessing student learning | 4 | 10 | 1 | .37 | .31 |
| Domain 2 (Classroom Environment) | | | | | |
| (2a) Creating an environment of respect & rapport | 4 | 7 | 4 | 1.27 | 1.05 |
| (2b) Establishing a culture for learning | 3 | 12 | 0 | .25 | .25 |
| (2c) Managing classroom procedures | 3 | 9 | 3 | 1.31 | 1 |
| (2d) Managing student behavior | 3 | 9 | 3 | 1.31 | 1 |
| (2e) Organizing physical space | 0 | 15 | 0 | 2 | 0 |
| Domain 3 (Instruction) | | | | | |
| (3a) Communicating clearly and accurately | 1 | 14 | 0 | 1 | 0 |
| (3b) Using questioning and discussion techniques | 3 | 1 | 1 | .62 | 0 |
| (3c) Engaging students in learning | 2 | 12 | 1 | .62 | 1 |
| (3d) Providing feedback to students | 5 | 8 | 2 | .45 | 0 |
| (3e) Demonstrating flexibility and responsiveness | 1 | 13 | 1 | 1.5 | 0 |
| Domain 4 (Professional Responsibilities) | | | | | |
| (4a) Reflecting on teaching | 5 | 9 | 1 | .21 | 0 |
| (4c) Communicating with families | 4 | 10 | 1 | .3 | 0 |
| (4d) Contributing to school and district | 4 | 10 | 1 | .37 | 0 |
| (4e) Growing and developing professionally | 3 | 12 | 0 | .5 | 0 |

*Note. None of the tests were statically significant at p = .05

**Table 8.2 Summary of Domain 1 (Planning and Preparation) Similarities and Differences in Practice**

| Level of Performance | Mentor | | | | Non-mentor | | | | Constant Comparative Analysis |
|---|---|---|---|---|---|---|---|---|---|
| | 1 | 2 | 3 | 4 | 1 | 2 | 3 | 4 | |
| (1a) Demonstrating knowledge of content and pedagogy | 0 | 0 | 13 | 2 | 0 | 2 | 13 | 0 | Most mentors said they included content because it fit into unit or discipline. Most non-mentors said they included content because it fit into graded course of study. All non-mentors and most of the mentors chose to use teacher-directed pedagogy. |
| (1b) Demonstrating knowledge of students | 0 | 11 | 4 | 0 | 0 | 12 | 2 | 1 | To learn about students, mentors talked to students, previous teachers and reviewed students' permanent folder while non-mentors used pretests, classroom observation and conversation with students. One non-mentor used information to differentiate instruction. |
| (1c) Selecting instructional goals | 5 | 10 | 0 | 0 | 4 | 11 | 0 | 0 | Although goals can represent different types of learning, both mentors and non-mentors tended to articulate learning goals as activities or a single goal such as factual knowledge, conceptual understanding or skill building. |
| (1d) Demonstrating knowledge of resources | 0 | 0 | 6 | 9 | 0 | 2 | 7 | 6 | Both mentors and non-mentors were aware of resources and sought assistance from support teams, other teachers, administrators and parents. |
| (1e) Designing coherent instruction | 0 | 0 | 12 | 3 | 0 | 0 | 15 | 0 | Most mentors and all non-mentors designed lessons that supported stated learning goals and engaged students in meaningful learning. Several mentors invited students to select materials, resources or learning groups. |
| (1f) Assessing student learning | 0 | 13 | 2 | 0 | 0 | 11 | 0 | 1 | Both groups aligned assessment to instruction, but did not articulate how information would be used to plan for individual students. |

enhance learning in many of the same ways. Table 8.3 summarizes the similarities and differences in levels of performance as well as characteristics of mentor and non-mentor behaviors in each of the components.

## DOMAIN 3: INSTRUCTION

The instruction planned for in Domain 1 was carried out in Domain 3. Through the presentation of content, use of questioning and discussion techniques, and feedback to students, teachers engaged students in learning. Evidence of teaching skill in this domain was collected during the observation and was augmented by the teachers' responses to the post-observation interview prompts. Although the mentor and non-mentor behaviors were similar, the levels of performance for mentors were collectively higher than their non-mentor counterparts in all of the components across the domain. The constant comparative analysis revealed patterns of behavior as well as differences as seen in table 8.4. Patterns were revealed at high and low levels. Both groups demonstrated the highest level of performance in communicating clearly and accurately to students. On the other hand, the quality of questions posed, as well as the discussion techniques used, aligned with low levels of performance for both groups. Furthermore, the quality of student feedback was inconsistent for both groups. Differences in behavior were seen in the ways in which mentors and non-mentors demonstrated flexibility and responsiveness to student needs.

## DOMAIN 4

Professionalism is an elusive concept that permeates all aspects of teachers' work. It begins with the teacher's ability to reflect accurately on classroom practice and to learn from that reflection to improve future practice. It is seen in a teacher's persistence to reach a challenging student, resolve a difficult problem or intercede with an alienated family. By understanding the consequences of instructional actions and by contemplating alternative courses of the action, teachers refine their practice. Many educators believed that this ability is the mark of a true professional (Danielson, 1996). Mentors and non-mentors demonstrated similar patterns of behavior. They articulated that they continually reflect on their instruction, but their discourse disclosed that their reflections were often very general. When talking about instruction, they were not inclined to articulate alternative strategies or cite specific evidence of student engagement. However, mentors more often than their non-mentoring counterparts displayed behaviors that addressed individual students and invited student contributions.

**Table 8.3  Summary of Domain 2 (Classroom Environment) Similarities and Differences in Practice**

| Component Level of Performance | Mentor | | | | Non-mentor | | | | Constant Comparative Analysis |
|---|---|---|---|---|---|---|---|---|---|
| | 1 | 2 | 3 | 4 | 1 | 2 | 3 | 4 | |
| (2a) Creating an environment of respect and rapport | 0 | 2 | 7 | 6 | 0 | 0 | 11 | 4 | Mentors and non-mentors had similar behaviors but mentors had a wider range of behaviors described in levels of performance. |
| (2b) Establishing a culture for learning | 0 | 0 | 15 | 0 | 0 | 3 | 12 | 0 | Neither mentors nor non-mentors provided opportunities for students to assume responsibility for maintaining culture for learning. |
| (2c) Managing classroom procedures | 0 | 0 | 9 | 6 | 0 | 0 | 9 | 6 | 40% of the mentors and non-mentors provided opportunities for students to assume responsibility for procedures. |
| (2d) Managing student behavior | 0 | 0 | 12 | 3 | 0 | 0 | 12 | 3 | Mentors and non-mentors generated rules at the beginning of the school year. A few mentors and non-mentors invited students to assist in creating a list. |
| (2e) Organizing physical space | 0 | 0 | 15 | 0 | 0 | 0 | 15 | 0 | Neither mentors nor non-mentors talked about students' contributions to the physical environment. |

**Table 8.4  Summary of Domain 3 (Instruction) Similarities and Differences in Practice**

| Level of Performance | Mentors | | | | Non-mentors | | | | Constant Comparative Analysis |
|---|---|---|---|---|---|---|---|---|---|
| | 1 | 2 | 3 | 4 | 1 | 2 | 3 | 4 | |
| (3a) Communicating clearly and accurately | 0 | 0 | 0 | 15 | 0 | 0 | 1 | 14 | Mentors' and non-mentors' highest level of performance. |
| (3b) Using questioning and discussion techniques | 8 | 5 | 2 | 0 | 10 | 4 | 1 | 0 | Mentors and non-mentors displayed poor use of questions and no real discussion. |
| (3c) Engaging students in learning | 0 | 8 | 5 | 2 | 0 | 9 | 5 | 1 | Hard to determine in teacher-directed lesson if students were intellectually engaged unless articulated by the teacher in the post-observation conference. Most mentors and non-mentors used appropriate materials, pacing, and activities. Students were on task most of the time. |
| (3d) Providing feedback to students | 0 | 0 | 11 | 4 | 0 | 5 | 6 | 4 | Researcher documented the oral feedback of the mentors and non-mentors while monitoring learning. The non-mentors' feedback was more inconsistent in quality. |
| (3e) Demonstrating flexibility and responsiveness | 0 | 2 | 13 | 0 | 0 | 2 | 13 | 0 | Mentors said they modified the pace and used a variety of teaching strategies to assist students. Non-mentors said they met with support staff, other teachers and modified lesson expectations. |

A summary of the findings from the four areas of the professional responsibilities domain is reported in table 8.5.

In addition to higher levels of performance, the mentors displayed some interesting differences in the area of professional responsibilities. Mentors' responses to post-observation interview prompts about students' learning revealed some differences in teacher self-efficacy. According to the Pathwise Orientation Guide (1995), teachers who displayed a high sense of teaching efficacy attribute students' success to factors within the classroom and their realm of influence. In addition, they demonstrated understanding of their role in learning, as they persisted in finding ways to help their students meet learning goals. When mentors were asked how they assisted students who were not meeting the learning goals, their responses focused on students as they articulated trying a variety of strategies to assist students. On the other hand, non-mentors articulated that students were successful because of their natural ability or intelligence. Reflecting a lower sense of teaching efficacy, non-mentors attributed student success or failure to conditions outside of classroom influence. In addition, when non-mentors were asked how they assisted students who were not meeting the learning goals, they most often responded with reference to conversations with support staff, other teachers or parents.

One possible explanation for the differences in discourse, especially the discourse that revolved around teaching efficacy, may be that as a result of the Pathwise training the mentors were savvier about how they should respond to these questions to reflect high levels of efficacy.

# Discussion

## DIFFERENCES IN PRACTICE

Differences in practice were reflected in three ways. First, the Sign Test indicated that mentors demonstrated higher levels of performance than their matched non-mentoring colleagues on 70% of the components. Second, mentors demonstrated, in total, more level 3 and level 4 behaviors (220) than their non-mentoring colleagues (202) and less level 1 and level 2 behaviors, 80 to 98 respectively. Third, the constant comparative revealed differences in mentor and non-mentor teaching efficacy and sense of collegiality.

While not statistically significant, the mentors demonstrated higher levels of performance in the mentor/non-mentor pairs on 14 components: (a) demonstrating knowledge of content and pedagogy, (b) demonstrating knowledge of students, (c) demonstrating knowledge of resources, (d) designing coherent in-

**Table 8.5  Summary of Domain 4 (Professional Responsibilities) Similarities and Differences in Practice**

| Level of Performance | Mentor | | | | Non-mentor | | | | Constant Comparative Analysis |
|---|---|---|---|---|---|---|---|---|---|
| | 1 | 2 | 3 | 4 | 1 | 2 | 3 | 4 | |
| (4a) Reflecting on teaching | 0 | 13 | 2 | 0 | 3 | 11 | 1 | 0 | Mentors and non-mentors reflect in general terms with little or no specific evidence of learning. |
| (4c) Communicating with families | 0 | 3 | 11 | 1 | 0 | 6 | 8 | 1 | Most mentors and non-mentors described frequent communication but did not invite students into process. Mentors and non-mentors used notes, parent conference and phone calls to communicate with families. One mentor/non-mentor pair from same school invited students into communication process. |
| (4d) Contributing to school and district | 0 | 0 | 11 | 4 | 0 | 0 | 14 | 1 | Several mentors assumed leadership roles and wrote grants that benefited all teachers. |
| (4e) Growing and developing professionally | 0 | 0 | 12 | 3 | 0 | 0 | 15 | 0 | Mentors chose collegial activities like workshops and graduate classes for professional development. Non-mentors chose to read professional literature most often for professional development. |

struction, (e) assessing student learning, (f) establishing a culture for learning, (g) communicating clearly and accurately, (h) using questioning and discussion techniques, (i) engaging students in learning, (j) providing feedback to students, (k) reflecting on teaching, (l) communicating with families, (m) contributing to school and district and (n) growing and developing professionally.

Other differences emerged in how mentors and non-mentors gained knowledge of their students and selected professional development activities. The mentors' sense of collaboration was reflected in their choices. Mentors more often than non-mentors chose conversations with their peers to find out about students' background knowledge, skills and individual learning needs. Furthermore, mentors more often chose professional development activities that put them into collegial settings such as workshops or college courses. This finding was supported by research done by Davies, Brady, Rodger, and Wall (1999) who found that mentors became more self-confident, self-reflective and collegial as a result of the mentoring experience.

The veteran non-mentoring teachers, on the other hand, made more solitary choices. They most often chose observation and pre-lesson assessment strategies to find out about their students' knowledge and skills. To develop their own content and pedagogical knowledge they most often chose to read professional literature.

One possible explanation for differences in practice may be that the mentors demonstrated these teaching behaviors before the mentoring. However, the collaborative nature of Pathwise training and mentoring provided a reform type of professional development described in the literature (Little, 1992; McLaughlin, 1990; Porter et al., 2000) that may have impacted the mentors as well as the beginning teachers (Clinard & Ariav, 1995; Foote & Walker, 1998; Grossman, 1994). Mentoring a beginning teacher using Pathwise protocol encouraged activities with some of the same characteristics, such as reflection, peer observation and collaborative analysis of teaching practices, that teachers' have identified as powerful enough to impact their practices (Garet, Porter, Desimone, & Herman, 1999; Porter et al., 2000).

Although the professional development serendipitously provided by Pathwise training and mentoring does not have all the components of effective professional development as described in the literature, it appeared to provide a type of professional development (Porter et al., 2000) that was systematically embedded in the natural day-to-day work of teachers (Little, 1992), reflected high standards that were linked to teacher licensure standards (Garet et al., 1999), recognized and honored the learning that took place in response to real life challenges (McLaughlin, 1990), valued collegiality and continuous improvement (Little, 1982), used flexible formats and was job-applicable (Askvig,

Coonts, & Haarstad, 1999) and supported accountability for teachers' impact on learning (Garet et al., 1999).

## PATTERNS OF PRACTICE

This study revealed most mentors and non-mentor veteran teachers operated at a level indicating a solid understanding and demonstration of component behaviors. Both groups demonstrated the highest level of performance in communicating clearly and accurately to the students. More interesting, the levels of performance for both groups were similarly low in demonstrating knowledge of students, selecting learning goals, assessing student learning, using questioning and discussion techniques, engaging students in learning and reflecting on teaching.

The instructional techniques used by both were similar. The participants tended to structure activity-based lessons, often with no clear learning priorities articulated in the lesson plan, to the students or in the assessment. Data collected in observations and interviews indicated that teachers focused on hands-on active learning rather than cognitively challenging minds-on instruction. Furthermore, participants rarely required their students to demonstrate that they understood the concepts or relationships at the core of the subject they were studying. Rather, they needed only to participate in the activity. The design of the lessons, in many cases, had very little depth; therefore, students did not need to extrapolate, synthesize, evaluate, or make judgments within the content or between content areas. Non-mentors often referred to the success of their instruction in terms of the number of students who completed the activity with little discussion of students' cognitive engagement. The Third International Math and Science Videotape Classroom Study (Stigler, Gonzales, Kawanaka, Kroll, & Serrano, 1999) found that American teachers tended to emphasize procedures and skill over understanding. Teaching strategies such as group work, use of technology, and manipulatives suggested by the National Council of Teachers of Mathematics' standards were adopted. However, teachers failed to clearly communicate underlying mathematical concepts or monitor students' understanding of them. Thus, students often engaged in hands-on activities without understanding the underlying concepts for which they were designed.

Not surprisingly, the patterns of low levels of performance in the planning and instruction domains reflected what Wiggins and McTighe (1998) call *learning by osmosis*. The non-mentor participants articulated learning goals in combination with activities or just as activities. The activities themselves became the focus of the instruction not the vehicle for learning. Students were not required to demonstrate the kind of understanding or ability necessary to think and act flexibly (Wiske, 1997); rather, they were most often encouraged to plug in a rote response.

The study revealed that although teachers articulated that they like to use a variety of instructional strategies, whole-group teacher-led questioning and discussion was the most often observed pedagogy at every grade level and in every content area. Research suggested that in an average classroom, about 40% of instructional time is spent in asking and responding to questions. Teachers asked between 300 and 400 questions a day (Leven & Long, 1981). Of these questions, only about 20% required the students to respond with more than factual recall (Gall, 1984). Only 1% of the classroom discussions invited students to give their own opinions and reasoning (Appalachian Regional Educational Laboratory). Furthermore, the majority of the suggestions in teacher's guides and student workbooks were devoted to factual recall of information (Goodlad, 1983). Particularly obvious in mathematics instruction, research indicated that although 90% of student working time in math was spent on practicing routine procedures, the lesson content was on the average one grade below international standards (Stigler et al., 1999).

The kinds of recitation-type discussions seen in this study were validated in the literature. Studies conducted at the State University of New York revealed that teachers found it difficult to engage students in guided discussions. In many cases, the discussions disintegrated to recitations, drills or lectures as the teacher attempted to cover the material. Most of the teacher-student interactions were fast-paced drill, review for tests with emphasis on low-level memory questions or lectures peppered with brief discussion questions. Few could have been classified as discussions. Students did not typically ask questions during the discussions nor were they encouraged to do so (Swift, Gooding, & Swift, 1996). Although research revealed the low-level drill and discussion that permeated classrooms was seldom the best tool for learning, teachers persisted in using it as their primary instructional strategy (Gall, 1984; Stigler et al., 1999).

Woven throughout low-level teacher performances was the tendency for low expectations of performance from students. Low expectations for students were demonstrated by shallow, misaligned or unarticulated learning goals, preponderance of teacher-centered pedagogy, lack of student assumption of responsibility for learning, low-level teacher-generated questions, and instructional strategies that neither required nor provided opportunities for students to demonstrate sophisticated knowledge of the content. Very few mentors practiced the kind of teacher-centered, conceptually oriented pedagogy called for by reformers (Cohen, McLaughlin & Talbert, 1993). Recognizing this common problem, the 1996 report by the National Commission on Teaching and America's Future articulated low expectation for student performance as one of the primary challenges to American schools and teachers.

This study revealed that mentors and their non-mentoring colleagues aligned assessment tools with learning goals and used the feedback to inform their teaching practice. Dorr-Bremme (1982) found that teachers spent up to a third of their time in assessment-related activities. However, teachers in this study tended to use information obtained in classroom assessments to plan for the whole class or general groups of learners, not individual students.

Most of the mentors and non-mentor teachers reflected on their instruction in general terms. However, they did not often cite specific evidence of student engagement to support their conclusions. Research indicated that when teachers were asked to justify their instruction they referred most often to surface features, such as use of manipulatives or cooperative groups (Stigler et al., 1999). The findings in this study supported the contention that, while reflection on teaching practice, defined as self-directed learning from experience in natural settings, was an important component of adult learning (Licklider, 1997), reflection alone was insufficient to transform practice (Gage, 1978; Sprinthall, Reimann, & Thies-Sprinthall, 1996).

# Implications

This study illuminates the need to consider how the mentors' low-level performance in critical areas of practice, such as planning assessments and engaging students through questioning and discussion, impacted the novice teachers with whom they worked. If mentors do not model the kinds of cognitive engagement that support student learning at the highest level, can novice teachers be expected to utilize the strategies in their everyday professional practice? Furthermore, this finding highlights the importance of the mentor selection process, training, and support systems (Pullman et al., 2004).

Research on effective practice over the last two decades indicates that effective teaching practice was linked to inquiry, reflection and continuous professional growth (Harris, 1998). As teachers analyze their practice through the lens of its impact on learning, most teachers will have to make momentous changes in their work and thinking about their role in teaching and learning. They need opportunities to think through what these role changes mean and how to best facilitate learning for everyone in the school community. Learning new roles and ways of teaching is a long-term developmental process. To do this, professional development must be part of the teacher's daily routine, not attached at the end of the day or a week in the summer. Teachers need time and structure to focus their attention on student learning as well as professional learning and sharing their expertise. Research indicates that if mentoring is to function as a strategy of reform, it must be tied to a shared vision of good teaching, guided by an understanding of teacher learning, and supported by a professional culture of collaboration and inquiry (Feiman-Nemser, 1996).

McFerrin (1999) found that often the unintended consequences of a learning situation are more important to the learner than the original objective. These findings suggest that a modification of the mentoring model might be beneficial for the professional practice of mentors. The most powerful learning for veteran teachers takes place in fine-tuning their practice in collegial settings where teachers share knowledge and solve problems (Darling-Hammond, 1997). Designing induction programs, which also provide professional development opportunities that transform mentor teachers' practice, is challenging. It stands to reason that when districts design induction programs, they consider allocating resources within the process to capitalize on the serendipitous professional development that occurs for mentors through the process. Such resources could create discourse communities in which mentors have sustained time to share knowledge, to build practice, to critique ideas, to polish lessons, to build curriculum, to create assessments and to review student work. All of these conditions provide the most powerful learning for the improvement of already skilled teachers (Sparks, 1997). When school districts create entry-year programs that are structured with growth-promoting experiences for mentors and protégés, they will realize dual benefits from their investment.

# References

Ariav, T., & Clinard, L. (1996). *Does coaching student teachers affect the professional development and teaching of cooperating teachers? A cross-cultural perspective.* Paper presented at the International Conference on Teacher Education, Netanya, Israel, June 30–July 4, 1996. (ERIC Document Reproduction Service No. ED409267)

Askvig, B. A., Coonts, T., & Haarstad, V. (1999, October). *Teacher performance follow-up from large group training: A pilot study.* (ERIC Document Reproduction Service No. SP038973)

Ball, D. L., & Cohen, D. K. (1999). Developing practice, developing practitioners: Toward a practice-based theory of professional education. In G. Sykes & L. Darling-Hammond (Eds.), *Teaching as the learning profession: Handbook of policy and practice* (pp. 3–32). San Francisco: Jossey Bass.

Barth, R. (1990). *Improving schools from within: Teachers, parents and principals can make a difference.* San Francisco, CA: Jossey -Bass.

Bova, B., & Phillips, R. (1981). *The mentor relationship: A study of mentors and protégés in business and academia.* University of New Mexico. (ERIC Document Reproduction Service No. ED208233)

Clinard, L., & Ariav, T. (1995, April). *Cooperating teachers reflect upon the impact of coaching on their own teaching and professional life.* Paper presented at American Education Research Association, San Francisco, CA. (ERIC Document Reproduction Service No. ED390843)

Clinard, L., & Ariav, T. (1997, March). *What mentoring does for mentors: A cross-cultural perspective.* Paper presented at American Education Research Association. Chicago, IL. (ERIC Document Reproduction Service No. ED 42229)

Cohen, D. K., McLaughlin, M. W., & Talbert, J. E. (Eds.). (1993). *Teaching for understanding: Challenges for policy and practice.* San Francisco, CA: Jossey-Bass.

Danielson, C. (1996). *Enhancing professional practice: A framework for teaching.* Alexandria, VA: Association for Supervision and Curriculum Development.

Darling-Hammond, L. (1998). Teacher learning that supports student learning [Electronic version]. *Educational Leadership 55*(5). Retrieved January 3, 2002, from http://www.ascd.org/readingroom/edlead/9802/darlinghammond.html

Darling-Hammond, L. (1997). *Doing what matters most: Investing in quality teaching.* National Commission on Teaching and America's Future. Retrieved June 2001, from http://www.tc.columbia.edu/nctaf/publications.

David, T. (2000). Programs in Practice: Teacher mentoring—benefits all around. *Kappa Delta Pi Record, 36*(3), 134–136.

Davies, M.A., Brady, M., Rodger, E., & Wall P. (1999). Mentor and school-based partnerships: Ingredients for professional growth. *Action in Teacher Education, 21*(1), 85–96.

Dorr-Bremme, D. (1982). *Assessing students: Teachers routine practices and reasoning* [CSE Report No. 194]. Los Angeles: Center for the Study of Evaluation.

Dye, J. F., Schatz, I. M., Rosenberg, B. A., & Coleman, S. T. (2000, January). Constant comparison method: A kaleidoscope of data [24 paragraphs]. *The Qualitative Report* [On-line serial], 4(1/2). Retrieved from http://www.nova.edu.sss/QR/QR-4/dye.html.

Farnsworth, C., & Morris, D. (1996). The seven habits of highly effective people: The key to effective educational mentoring. *Educational Horizons, 73*(2) 138–140.

Feiman-Nemser, S. (1996, July). *Teacher mentoring: A critical review.* (ERIC Digest No. ED397060). Retrieved November 11, 2001, from http://www.ed.gov.databases/ERIC_Digests/ed397060html.

Ford, D., & Parsons, J. (2000). *Teachers as mentors.* (ERIC Document Reproduction Service No. ED4487073)

Foote, M., & Walker, C. (1998, Spring). Mentor teacher: Professional development resulting from work with pre-service teacher. *Catalyst for change, 27*(3), 5–7.

Freiberg, M., Zbikowski, J., & Ganser, T. (1996, April). *Where do we go from here? Decisions and dilemmas of teacher mentors.* Paper presented at the American Educational Research Association, New York. (ERIC Document Reproduction Service No. ED395930)

Gage, N. (1978). *The scientific basis of the art of teaching.* New York: Teachers College Press.

Gall, M. (1984). Synthesis of research on teachers' questioning. *Educational Leadership, 42*(3), 40–47.

Ganser, T. (1992, February). *The benefits of mentoring as viewed by the beginning teachers and mentors in a state-mandated mentoring program.* Paper presented at the annual meeting of the Association of Teacher Educators, Orlando, FL. (ERIC Document Reproduction Service No. ED343870)

Ganser, T. (1996, Summer). What do mentors say about mentoring? *Journal of Staff Development, 17*(3), 36–39.

Garet, M. S., Porter, A. C., Desimone, L., & Herman, R. (with Suk Yoon, K.), (1999). *Designing effective professional development: Lessons from the Eisenhower Program.* Washington, DC: U.S. Department of Education.

Glaser, B., & Strauss, A. (1967). *The discovery of grounded theory: Strategies for qualitative research.* Chicago, IL: Aldine.

Goodlad, J. (1983). *A place called school.* New York: McGraw-Hill.

Grossman, P. L. (1994). Changing roles and relationships of teachers as learners and as leaders. In A. Lieberman (Ed.), *The changing contexts of teaching: Ninety-first yearbook of the national society for the study of education* (pp. 179–196). Chicago, IL: University of Chicago Press.

Harris, A. (1998). Effective teaching: A review of the literature. *School Leadership and Management, 18*(2), 169–183.

Holloway, J. (2001). The benefits of mentoring. *Educational Leadership, 58*(8), 85–86.

Huling, L., & Resta, V. (2001, November). *Teacher mentoring as professional development.* (ERIC Digest No. ED460125). Retrieved May 20, 2002, from http://www.ed.gov/databases/ERIC_Digests/ed460125.html.

Leven, T., & Long, R. (1981). *Effective instruction.* Washington, DC: Association for Supervision and Curriculum Development.

Levine, S. (1989). *Promoting adult growth in schools: The promise of professional development.* Boston: Allyn & Bacon.

Licklider, B. L. (1997). Breaking ranks: Changing the inservice institutions. *NASSP Bulletin, 81*, 9–22.

Little, J. W. (1982). Norms of collegiality and experimentation: Workplace conditions of school success. *American Education Research Journal, 19*(3), 325–340.

Little, J. W. (1992). Teacher development and educational policy. In M. Fullan & A. Hargreaves (Eds.), *Teacher development and educational change* (pp. 170–189). London, England: Falmer Press.

McFerrin, K. M. (1999). Incidental learning in a higher education asynchronous online distance education course. In *Site 99: Society for information technology and teacher educational international conference proceedings.* Charleston, VA: Association for the Advancement of Computing in Education. (ERIC Document Reproduction Service No. ED432288)

McGee, P.A. (1998). *Unintended professional development curriculum-based K–12 telementoring projects.* [On-line]. Abstract from Digital Dissertations Publication (AAT 9838045)

McLaughlin, M. W. (1990, December). The Rand change agent study revisited: Macro perspectives and micro realities. *Educational Researcher, 19*(9), 11–16.

*Pathwise orientation guide.* (1995). In the PATHWISE Observer Manual. Princeton, NJ: Educational Testing Service.

Phillips, M., & Glickman, C. (1991). Peer coaching: Developmental approach to enhancing teacher thinking. *Journal of Staff Development, 12*(2), 2–25.

Porter, A. C., Garet, M. S., Desimone, L., Suk Yoon, K., & Birman, B. F. (2000, October). *Does professional development change teaching practice? Results from a three-year study* (U.S. Department of Education Contract No. EA 970001001). [Online]. Retrieved January 5, 2001, from www.ed.gov/pubs/edpubs.htlm.

*Praxis III: Classroom performance assessments.* (1995). In the Praxis Series: Professional assessments for beginning teachers. Princeton, NJ: Educational Testing Service.

Pullman, H., Pullman, S., Newman, I., & Turner, S. (2002, June). *Examining mentor program practices that promote success for beginning teachers.* Paper presented at the Fifth Annual Framework for Teaching Conference, Minneapolis, MN.

Pullman, H., Pullman, S., Turner, S., Pascale, P., & Newman, I (2004, February). *National teacher education standards: Three-way impact in Ohio.* Paper presented at the Association of Teacher Educators Annual Meeting, Dallas, TX.

Reiman, A., & Thies-Sprinthall, L. (1993). Promoting the development of mentor teachers: Theory and research programs using guided reflection. *Journal of Research and Development in Education, 26*(3), 179–185.

Salzman, J. A. (1999). With a little help from my friends: A course designed for mentoring induction-year teachers. *Mid-Western Educational Researcher, 12*(4), 27–31.

Salzman, J. A. (2000). *Talking the same language: Training mentors to use the Pathwise Performance Assessment with induction-year colleagues.* (ERIC Document Reproduction Service No. ED442772)

Sparks, D. (1997). An interview with Linda Darling-Hammond. *Journal of Staff Development, 18*(1). Retrieved December 29, 2001, from http://www.nsdc.org/library/jsd/darling 181.html.

Sprinthall, N. A., Reiman, A. J., & Thies-Sprinthall, L. (1996). In J. Sikula, T. J. Buttery, & E. Guyton (Eds.) *Handbook of research on teacher education* (2nd ed.) (pp. 666–703). New York: Simon & Schuster, Macmillan.

Stanulis, R., & Weaver, D. (1998). Teacher as mentor, teacher as learner: Lessons from a middle school language arts teacher. *Teacher Educator, 34*(2), 134–143.

Stigler, J. W., Gonzales, P., Kawanaka, T., Kroll, S., & Serrano. (1999, February). *The TIMSS videotape classroom study: Methods and findings from an exploratory research project on eighth-grade mathematics instruction in Germany, Japan and the United States* (NCES 99–074). Retrieved January 2002, from http://nces.ed.gov/pus99/1999074.pdf.

Swift, J. N., Gooding, C. T., & Swift, P. R. (1996, October 23). Research matters to the science teacher. *National Association for Research in Science Teaching, 9601.* Retrieved February 2, 2002, from http://www.edus.sfu.ca/narstsite/research/discuss.html.

Tatel, E. S. (1996). Improving classroom practice: Ways experienced teachers change after supervising student teachers. In W. W. McLaughlin & I. Oberman (Eds.) *Teacher learning: New policies, new practices* (pp. 48–52). New York: Teachers College Press.

Teacher Education and Licensure Standards. (1996). Ohio Senate Bill 230 Administrative Code, Chapter 3301–24.

Wiggins, G., & McTighe, J. (1998). *Understanding by design.* Alexandria, VA: Association for Supervision and Curriculum Development.

Wiske, M. S. (1997). *Teaching for understanding: Linking research with practice.* San Francisco: Jossey Boss.

Wollman-Bonilla, J. E. (1997, Summer). Mentoring as a two-way street. *Journal of Staff Development, 18*(3) 50–52.

# Summary and Conclusions

*Virginia Resta*
Texas State University–San Marcos

The four chapters in this division of the *Yearbook* focus on influential dimensions of the mentoring experience. Yendol-Hoppey and Dana describe a yearlong case study in which they explore the problems and pitfalls resulting from difference in perceptions and expectations between a mentor and novice teacher. Their study demonstrates the importance of and provides suggestions for better matching of mentors and novices. Wang, Odell and Strong examine the interactions of three mentor-mentee pairs. Their findings raise questions about the effectiveness of lesson-based discussion as a means of supporting novice teachers' focus on standards-based teaching as envisioned by reformers. Johnson and Reiman in chapter 7 report on their study of the influence of mentor dispositions on mentor-mentee interactions and suggest tools for measuring mentor disposition that may be useful in mentor selection. In chapter 8, Kline and Salzman present the results of their study focused on serendipitous professional development for mentors through Pathwise Classroom Observation System training. These four studies taken together provide a more in-depth view of both the possibilities and pitfalls of the process of mentoring novice teachers. Each study examines the mentoring experience from a different perspective and set of lenses, and together provide a mosaic of important insights and factors related to effective mentoring processes.

## The Influence of Preconceptions and Proximity

Yendol-Hoppey and Dana's yearlong, in-depth case study examines one teacher's journey through her first year as a high school social studies teacher, focusing on her preconceptions about the mentoring experience and how those preconceptions influence the relationship that develops with her assigned mentor and with other teachers in close proximity to her in the building. This study supports previous research on the importance of mentor/mentee matching and mentor/mentee proximity. Matching mentors and mentees whose personalities are compatible increases the likelihood that mentoring will be successful. In Sara's case a clash of political views prevents her from developing a trusting relationship with her assigned mentor and therefore she neither sought nor benefited from advice that he shared or could have shared with her. In contrast, Sara did form relationships with teachers who were in closer proximity to her classroom and whose schedules were similar to her own. Sara interacted with these teachers more often and builds relationships with them and seeks their advice. Like many beginning teachers, Sara wants mentoring support on her own terms, desiring assistance with technical aspects of teaching and emotional support. She feels frustrated when she does not receive the support based on her preconceived expectations. Sara's preconception of how she thinks the mentor relationship would operate were at odds with her lived experience and caused her to feel that she did not get the help she needed from her mentor. Because a trusting relationship is not built in advance of her mentor's observation of her teaching, Sara finds it difficult to accept his suggestions. Had a trusting relationship been built between Sara and her mentor she would have been less likely to misinterpret his helpful comments as being challenges to her ability to handle potentially difficult students and situations. Sara establishes collegial relationships with those with whom she is closest in proximity and with those who share similar schedules to hers that she sees regularly in informal settings. As is evident in Sara's case, although a formal mentoring program is in operation in the building, it did not guarantee that effective mentoring took place. Sara's case illustrates why mentors need to be trained to be thoughtful and deliberate in building a foundation of trust early on and continuing throughout the year. Trusting relationships are most likely to develop when the mentors spend considerable amounts of time with their mentees learning about the novice's preconceived ideas about what types of services mentors provide and in helping their mentees develop clear and reasonable expectations for how the mentoring relationship will work. Failure to build clear and reasonable expectations or to build trust may jeopardize any potential benefits the mentoring program may offer. Implications from this study for mentor program coordinators include the need to:

- Provide professional development to assist beginning teachers to develop collaboration and communication skills with other teachers.
- Match mentees and mentors whose personalities fit together well.
- Place mentees in close proximity to their mentors.

- Give mentees similar schedules to their mentors.
- Help mentors understand the importance of building a trusting relationship early on so that a truly beneficial mentoring experience can result.

# The Influence of Lesson-Based Discussion

Wang, Odell and Strong analyze the content and focus of four audio-taped novice-mentor pre-lesson discussions by three randomly selected novice-mentor pairs, two pre-lesson discussions in the first year and two pre-lesson discussions in the second year of their induction program. The pre-lesson conversations are intended to review the novice's lesson plans, make suggestions based on the novice's questions/concerns and the state standards for teaching and to determine the focus of the subsequent lesson observation. Analysis of the pre-lesson conversations reveals that the mentors and novices discuss teaching strategies focusing on the novices' instruction and student activities about half the time on average. Teaching strategy discussions stress what the student needs to do (activity) rather than what the novice needs to do (instruction). Very little attention is paid to student understanding of concepts or content or to the individual student's feelings and needs. Similarly, in conversations about assessment of student performance, student needs and feelings are seldom addressed. There is little discussion of the curriculum or teaching standards encouraged by the induction program and school. Eighty percent of the total conversations are devoted to the present lesson, with the bulk of the remaining conversation referencing prior lessons and, to a lesser extent, future lessons. Questions originate most often from the mentor, not from the novice.

The mentors observed in the study infrequently offer direct advice or concrete suggestions to the novices. Where elaborated statements did occur, the vast majority involve concrete examples as opposed to elaborated reasons or analysis. These data suggest that lesson-based novice-mentor conversations are unlikely to be fully effective in supporting novice teachers' focus on standards-based teaching when the novice's needs and feelings are ignored or not attended to by the mentor. Implications from this study suggest the need to include in the mentor program:

- Substantial mentor preparation on how to address the developmental continuum of learning to teach.
- Substantial emphasis on how to promote the acquisition of flexible subject-matter knowledge and engender inquiry, problem solving, and contextualized reasoning by the novice.

# The Influence of Disposition

Johnson and Reiman explore congruency between mentor professional judgment and professional action using data drawn from three mentor/beginning teacher dyads. They suggest three standardized measures for assessing dispositions of emerging mentors:

- Defining Issues Test-2 (moral/ethical judgment) used to assess professional judgment
- Sentence Completion Test SCT (ego judgment) and Paragraph Completion Method PCM (conceptual judgment).
- GIAS (Guided Inquiry Analysis System) used to measure mentor/mentee interaction during conferences.

These assessments have a number of important uses in mentoring programs and for future research. For example, these measures have the potential for assisting decision-makers in making appropriate matches between mentors and mentees. The assessments also may be used to provide before and after measures for extensive developmental programming designed to address how mentor dispositions change over time. These assessments may be useful tools to researchers and program planners in identifying trends across large samples of mentors. The GIAS can be used to assess interactions between mentors and beginning teachers during conferences. Future directions for research using these instruments may include:

- Using larger samples of mentors to explore further the relationships between the GIAS as a measure of the action and the Paragraph Completion Method (PCM), Sentence Completion Test (SCT), and Defining Issues Test-2 (DIT-2) as measures of professional judgment.
- Continuing to conduct studies of mentor dispositions to develop deeper levels of understanding of strategies to foster mentor dispositions in mentoring programs.

# The Influence of Professional Development

Lastly, Kline and Salzman compare the teaching practice of K–8 mentors with those of their non-mentoring colleagues. All the mentors in the study participate in a two-day Pathwise Classroom Observation System training program and subsequently use the language and protocol to guide the novice teachers' professional reflections.

Mentors demonstrate higher levels of performance than their matched non-mentoring colleagues on 70% of the study components. For example, mentors demonstrate an increased frequency of higher level behaviors than did their non-mentoring colleagues and also manifested fewer low level behaviors. Differences are also revealed on measures of teaching efficacy and sense of collegiality. Mentors also demonstrate higher levels of performance in the mentor/non-mentor pairs on 14 components: demonstrating knowledge of content and pedagogy; demonstrating knowledge of students; demonstrating knowledge of resources; designing coherent instruction; assessing student learning; establishing a culture for learning; communicating clearly and accurately; using questioning and discussion techniques; engaging students in learning; providing feedback to students; reflecting on teaching; communicating with families; contributing to school and district; and growing and developing professionally. These findings provide supportive evidence of a serendipitous effect of professional development for mentors using the Pathwise COS.

The results of the study raise some concerns about mentors' and non-mentors' patterns of practice. Although mentors outperformed non-mentors on many dimensions, both groups are similarly low in demonstrating knowledge of students, selecting learning goals, assessing student learning, using questioning and discussion techniques, engaging students in learning and reflecting on teaching. Participants tend to structure activity-based lessons, often without clear learning priorities articulated in the lesson plan, for the students, or in the assessment. Teachers tend to focus on hands-on active learning rather than minds-on instruction. Participants rarely require their students to demonstrate understanding of concepts, and students did not need to extrapolate, synthesize, or evaluate their learning. The study also reveals that the instructional strategy most often used by mentors and teachers was whole-group teacher-led questioning and discussion. Both groups demonstrated a tendency toward low expectations of student performance. In addition, teachers tend to use classroom assessment data to plan for whole-class lessons, but not for individual students. It is clear that if mentors model less effective patterns of practice or fail to provide cognitive engagement that supports student learning, then the potential benefits of the mentoring experience will likely be seriously reduced.

Implications from this study suggest the need to include the following elements in the mentor program:

• Support for mentor training that helps mentors develop the necessary skill set to be able to model high quality, standards-based instruction for the benefit of students and beginning teachers.

• Careful monitoring of program implementation to ensure effective practices and growth-promoting experiences for mentors and protégés.

# Implications and Conclusions

The importance of the authors' work presented in this division of the *Yearbook* is that the findings not only validate previous research related to issues of mentor characteristics, selection, proximity, commitment, teaching skill, and communication skill, but underscore the continuing need for close examination of the mentoring process in context. These studies suggest that a gap continues to exist between what is hoped for by reform-minded teacher educators and policy makers, and what may actually transpire in contextualized mentoring experiences. Through the work of these authors, it can be seen that simply providing a mentor without the training and support suggested by the findings of these studies may not provide the type and level of assistance needed by beginning teachers who are challenged by the complex demands of teaching in the context of today's schools.

As is illustrated through these studies, mentoring is a highly complex process. Interpreting a novice teacher's conversations and actions and shaping interactions that are productive for the beginning teacher requires, on the mentor's part, knowledge of child and adolescent development, knowledge of how to support students' cognitive, social, physical, and emotional growth, and how to help the beginning teacher reflect on, analyze, and grow from their classroom experiences. Mentors must understand the developmental continuum of learning to teach. Mentoring in ways that connect with beginning teachers and ultimately benefit their students requires mentors to be able to inquire sensitively, listen carefully, and look thoughtfully at their classrooms at work. Motivating beginning teachers requires an understanding of what individual beginning teachers believe about themselves and what they care about.

The pay-off for successful mentoring is that all students benefit from better instruction and their academic gains will increase as a result of the mentoring beginning teachers experience. The key factor related to the success of the mentoring experience is the quality of the mentoring provided to the novice teacher. While the four studies in this division contribute significantly to our knowledge about the mentoring process in context and about the complexities of the mentoring endeavor, it is clear that, if novice teachers are to develop their capacities for continuous reflection, inquiry and assessment of their own practice, they must be paired with mentors who are skilled in those capacities themselves. The four studies underscore the need for mentors who are skilled in guiding the novice teacher in self-study and who also value and use these skills as tools for improvement of instruction of beginning teachers.

The challenge then becomes how to assist those responsible for mentoring programs to ensure that a pool of adequately prepared mentors exists within the school or district context to meet the induction needs of increasing numbers of beginning teachers. Difficult-to-staff schools may find that experienced teachers are in such short supply that all experienced teachers on a campus are called upon to mentor beginning teachers. In such instances, ongoing mentor training is critical if novice teachers are to receive high quality mentoring that assists them to rapidly improve their teaching skills in the dynamic and demanding contemporary classroom environment in order that they may, in turn, provide their students with high quality instruction that promotes student achievement.

# Recommendations

The following recommendations are offered related to the issues that surface from the studies of mentoring experiences.

- Develop a shared and clear understanding among university/district administrators, school personnel, and faculty about what constitutes good mentoring and what it will take from all stakeholders to develop, support, and sustain effective mentoring programs for beginning teachers.
- Design professional development for mentors to work with beginning teachers in ways that improve instruction for students and lead to better student performance.
- Develop a clear set of practice and performance standards for mentoring against which mentors' work is guided and assessed.
- Develop tools for data collection that provide for evidence-based decision-making regarding mentors' work in the context of mentoring.

# Possible Directions for Future Research

An important goal of future research in this area is to continue our efforts to more deeply understand the nature and impact of the mentoring experience on a variety of outcomes including teacher and student performance. Such research could embed inquiry into ongoing education programs in multi-institutional partnerships. These suggestions are offered as beginning points to stimulate future dialogue leading to research on mentoring in context. Hopefully, universities and school districts will form partnerships to accomplish the following:

- Develop better measures of mentor knowledge and performance.
- Develop research studies into the process of learning to mentor.
- Conduct research that connects mentoring efforts to student learning, not simply student achievement test scores.
- Develop strategic research partnerships connecting university and school districts for the purpose of designing, implementing, and studying mentoring in context.
- Develop multi-institutional studies pooling data across institutions using common research methods, instrumentation and outcome measures.
- Develop studies comparing approaches to mentoring traditionally prepared fully-certified teachers with mentoring of non-traditionally prepared teachers.
- Develop studies of mentoring programs provided by various entities: state sponsored, university sponsored, and district sponsored.

Those working in the field of mentoring and mentoring development have accomplished a great deal since the 1980s. They have made their voices heard and states, districts and universities have responded by designing and implementing mentoring programs that have, in many cases, impacted in positive ways the attrition rate of beginning teachers. Perhaps it is time now to move from an emphasis on retention to an emphasis on the quality of mentor experience for beginning teachers and to set student achievement as a mentoring goal.

# DESIGNING AND IMPLEMENTING QUALITY MENTORING PROGRAMS

# Overview and Framework

*Sandra J. Odell*
University of Nevada, Las Vegas

Sandra J. Odell is a professor of teacher education and coordinator of doctoral studies in the Department of Curriculum and Instruction at the University of Nevada, Las Vegas. Dr. Odell maintains career-long research interests in teacher development, teacher induction, and mentoring in the context of collaborative university/school district programs. She conceived and co-edited the first three ATE *Yearbooks* with Mary John O'Hair. Recent publications include articles in *Review of Educational Research*, the *Elementary School Journal, Teacher's College Record*, and *Journal of Research on Technology in Education*.

## Definitions of Mentoring and Teacher Induction

The terms *mentoring* and *teacher induction* have been defined variously in the literature. Mentoring is currently viewed as one component in a set of structured professional development experiences provided for novice teachers (Bartell, 2005; Wong, Britton, & Ganser, 2005). Mentoring is typically associated with having experienced teachers work with novice teachers to help ease the novices' transition from being a university student learning to teach to full-time teacher in the classroom. For the purposes of the current discussion, mentoring is conceptualized explicitly as a professional practice much as teaching is a practice. Like teaching, the professional practice of mentoring includes dispositions and beliefs, conceptual and theoretical understandings, as well as skills for implementing the practice. Also like teaching, mentoring requires specialized preparation for the mentor and a significant time commitment on the part of the mentor (Odell, 1990).

While mentoring is a professional practice, induction is viewed as a specific period of time, the first three years of teaching, on the teacher development continuum that moves from preservice teacher education to teacher induction to sustained inservice teaching to teacher renewal in the later years of teaching (Odell & Huling, 2000). Since mentoring is defined as a practice and preservice, induction, inservice, and renewal are defined as sequential periods of time, mentoring can be practiced throughout the teacher development continuum. Typically, however, formal teacher mentor programs have been designed, as in the chapters that make up this division of the book, for the preservice and induction periods.

# Dimensions of Quality Mentoring

There are many examples of preservice and induction mentoring programs across the United States. They clearly vary in how they are designed, organized, and implemented. Indeed, they are shaped by local contexts such as whether the novices are at the preservice and/or induction level, the size of the population being served, whether they are school/university partnerships or solely school based, and whether they are state mandated or voluntary.

The ATE National Commission on Professional Development and Support of Novice Teachers identified six dimensions for characterizing mentoring programs in their book *Quality Mentoring Programs* (Odell & Huling, 2000). These dimensions provide a framework for analyzing mentoring programs and will provide a convenient framework for discussing the four subsequent chapters of this division of the ATE *Yearbook*. The six dimensions of quality mentoring programs are:

- Program Purpose and Rationale
- Mentor Selection and Mentor/Novice Matching
- Mentor Teacher Preparation and Development
- Mentor Roles and Practices
- Program Administration, Implementation, and Evaluation
- School, District, and University Cultures and Responsibilities

## PROGRAM PURPOSE AND RATIONALE

Arguably, the most important dimension of quality mentoring programs is articulating the underlying purpose and rationale for the program. Programs have varying purposes that range from helping novices fit into the current school culture with a good understanding of information related to school and district policies and procedures, to retaining novices in the profession, to learning from experienced teachers, to learning particular content and ways of teaching. Actually, the purposes of mentoring programs have evolved over time. For example, Wang &

Odell (2002) recently make the case that the primary goal of mentoring programs should be to mentor novices toward standards-based teaching or clinical teaching that is intellectual, constructivist, and problem oriented. What follows is a brief overview of the evolution of the purpose of mentoring programs from mentoring for personal support into that of mentoring toward standards-based teaching.

If we consider the history of mentoring and teacher induction programs, a humanistic perspective provided the rationale for most mentor programs in the early 1980s. The humanistic perspective was considered to be important in helping teachers deal with the reality and personal problems of teaching and in countering the serious problem of beginning teacher attrition that has been estimated to be as high as 50% during the first five years of teaching (e.g., Ingersoll & Kralik, 2004). In humanistic mentoring, the mentor helped novices solve problems and feel less stressed about teaching. Interpersonal skills were key for the mentor; mentors needed to be empathic listeners and help novices build their self-esteem and confidence. The primary purpose of this approach, retaining teachers in the profession, is a goal that continues to be paramount in many mentoring programs today.

During the mid 1980s to mid 1990s, the mentoring and teacher induction literature emphasized the importance of moving beyond the humanistic perspective to a goal of having novices learn about teaching from their mentors. This essentially represented a shift to having mentors serve as educational companions (Feiman-Nemser & Parker, 1992). Mentors serving as educational companions meet the goal of having mentors help novices examine and reflect about their teaching and learn about effective instruction and student assessment. During this period there was also a movement by universities to encourage partnership programs that would allow preservice students to connect theoretical information learned through coursework with actual teaching with mentors in schools. Preservice teachers in many programs moved from being students with primarily textbook knowledge to being competent practitioners with substantial practical knowledge gleaned from work with experienced mentor teachers. Basically, this movement extended the practice of mentoring from the induction to the preservice period.

During the mid 1990s, the educational reform literature encouraged mentor programs to adopt the purpose of guiding novice teachers to teach in ways consistent with educational reform and teaching standards (Odell & Huling, 2000). Rather than guiding novices to teach in traditional ways, where the focus is on the transmission of knowledge from teacher to students, mentors serving as educational companions were encouraged to mentor toward standards-based teaching that focuses on students' active construction of knowledge through exploration, inquiry, orchestrated discourse, and connecting personal experiences to real-life contexts (Wang & Odell, 2002).

Bartell (2005) highlighted the importance of elucidating the purposes of a mentor program to all program stakeholders so as to foster communication and goal-relevant program activities, training and implementation. Beyond that, program goals need to be reviewed regularly and revised based upon current research.

## MENTOR SELECTION AND MENTOR/NOVICE MATCHING

The characteristics of the mentor are a major determinant of the outcomes of the mentoring program. This suggests that mentors should be identified as the result of a purposeful selection process and should exhibit characteristics appropriate to the stated purpose of the mentoring program. Fortunately, several mentor characteristics are identified in the literature as desirable for mentoring toward standards-based teaching (Odell, 1990; Odell & Huling, 2000). These include experience at modeling standards-based teaching, studying and developing their own teaching practice, working effectively with adults from diverse backgrounds, commitment to ethical practice, sensitivity to the viewpoint of others, and being informed about mentor responsibilities.

All too often mentor selection occurs simply by identifying which teachers are willing to work with novices or by assignment by the principal of a school without consideration of the mentor characteristics appropriate to the program's purpose (Bartell, 2005). Understandably, this happens sometimes in big-city school districts or preservice programs where there is a need for large numbers of mentors. However, it is clear that best practice would resist the selection of mentors based solely on convenience, the need for large numbers, or the desire of the mentor to have the in-classroom help that a co-teaching novice might provide.

The matching of mentors to novices is also a consideration. Placing novices with mentors using the same curriculum at the same grade level and in physical proximity to one another obviously gives more face validity to the mentoring relationship and allows for more relevant and frequent mentoring to occur. In preservice contexts, similar consideration needs to be given to matching novices with mentors who are teaching subjects and grade levels for which the novice is preparing to teach.

## MENTOR TEACHER PREPARATION AND DEVELOPMENT

As stated earlier, mentoring is a practice much as teaching is a practice. Accordingly, experienced teachers still need to prepare to be effective mentors. Indeed, it has become axiomatic that providing mentors with professional development as mentors is essential for realizing quality mentoring (Odell & Huling, 2000).

Mentors may find it provocative to learn about new educational ideas and practices. Some of the preparation sessions for mentors should occur prior to the time that they begin work as mentors. Ideally, this should be followed by ongoing and frequent professional development opportunities to explore topics such as studying their own teaching, communicating with novices, supporting and challenging novices as they are learning to teach, mentoring toward standards-based teaching, providing constructive feedback, developing strategies for mentoring, studying mentor roles and responsibilities, assessing instruction, working with novices as adult learners, and promoting mentoring program goals. It is also helpful to give mentors the opportunity to interact frequently with other mentors and to collaborate in analyzing mentoring through the use of real and fictional case studies (Shulman & Colbert, 1987).

The time necessary for mentor preparation is usually difficult to allocate because of the myriad of other responsibilities mentors typically have. Accordingly, it is important to provide mentors with incentives to justify their time commitment to becoming quality mentors. Honoraria, university course credit, and released time from teaching for professional development are examples of incentives that have been used successfully with mentors in the past.

## MENTOR ROLES AND PRACTICES

The Association of Teacher Educators (ATE) has established standards for teacher educators (ATE, 2005). In quality mentoring programs, it is important for mentors to view themselves as site-based teacher educators. Accordingly, it is appropriate to generalize the ATE standards for teacher educators to mentor teacher educators working with novices in schools. Mentors should also view themselves as role models for novices and model professional behaviors like self-reflection, solving problems, and working on the improvement of instruction. Quality mentors most often adopt the role of learner in seeking knowledge about mentoring and, ideally, strive to connect their own standards-based practice with research pertaining to effective teaching practice.

With respect to mentor practices, these are varied and numerous. At a minimum mentor practices include: regularly interacting with novices; observing novices and giving them feedback; providing novices empathy about the stresses of teaching; and deliberately focusing on standards-based teaching.

## PROGRAM ADMINISTRATION, IMPLEMENTATION, AND EVALUATION

This dimension of quality mentoring programs recognizes the importance of program leadership. This entails having a person whose designated job assignment is to be ultimately responsible for coordinating the program, to make certain that practices match the program goals, and who arranges for the professional development of mentors and novices. The program coordinator should also take responsibility for arranging incentives for mentors, selecting mentors, and matching mentors with novices.

Needless to say, program evaluation and research related to the program, mentors, and novices are necessary to provide data from which program decisions can be made. Moreover, such evaluation and research can provide the profession with information that will help support the overarching goal of developing quality mentoring programs and practices.

## SCHOOL, DISTRICT, AND UNIVERSITY CULTURES AND RESPONSIBILITIES

In the ideal situation, partnerships between school districts and universities can provide excellent contexts for mentoring programs. With the practical expertise of school personnel coupled with the theoretical expertise of university faculty, it is possible to develop strong mentoring programs during the preservice and induction periods. In keeping with a focus on standards-based teaching, school district and university officials can ensure that professional development opportunities are provided for mentors to learn about standards-based teaching practices in the various subjects taught. Importantly, they help policymakers understand that changes in school structures, like mentoring programs, take considerable time to impact student learning and that mentors and novices will need time built into their daily work for professional development.

District and university leaders can also influence policy so that novice teachers are given reasonable teaching assignments rather than the current practice of giving novices the most difficult assignments (Shanker, 1985; Ringstaff & Haymore Sandholtz, 2002). They can also recognize and compensate mentors for their work and can sanction the program and treat it as a priority.

# Impediments to Developing Quality Mentoring Programs

On reflection it seems that even though desirable practices for quality mentoring programs have been established, the implementation of these practices has been very limited across the country. This is a result of impediments that currently exist in school and university cultures. Time allocation to mentoring is a major factor that limits program developers, leaders, and participants. At the university level faculty are often not rewarded for work involved in collaborating with schools and, instead, are encouraged to spend their time in research and publication. The labor-intensive nature of adding mentoring responsibilities to excellent experienced teachers' already full plates is also a time problem. Another time-related issue is the fact that mentoring results are not immediate. The impact on the retention of teachers, changes in novices' teaching practice, and influences on student learning may take years to accomplish. In contrast, policymakers often want to see quick results. Yet another impediment related to time (and time is money) is that the time for systematic, ongoing mentor preparation is costly. While on the topic of money, it should be stated that in quality mentoring there is a need to provide incentives for mentors and program leadership.

Collaboration between schools and universities is complicated and has its own unique impediments. Often there are no monetary rewards for collaborative work. University faculty may have questionable views of school personnel and vice versa (university faculty view teachers as not having the most current information about research and teachers view university faculty as being out of touch with the reality of schools). Universities and schools have different cultures and university faculty may not have the skills to work effectively with teachers.

Still further, the culture of schools often works against the goals of mentoring programs (Little, 1990). The egalitarian nature of schools as well as the often-rejected notion of using differentiated staffing arrangements for mentor teachers work against having teacher leaders as mentors who are compensated for the additional responsibilities they have. In addition, the individualistic culture of schools where individual teachers have autonomy to make classroom-based decisions (Cohen & Spillane, 1992; Feiman-Nemser & Floden, 1986) can bias the collaboration that is necessary between mentor and novice teachers.

Another impediment to designing, developing, and implementing quality mentoring programs is the fact that most teaching is based on essentialist practice (Smith, 1996), which can be in direct conflict with the more reform-minded teaching expected in the standards movement and currently deemed appropriate for mentoring and induction (Odell & Huling, 2000; Sweeny & DeBolt, 2000).

Mentor programs that are attempting quality mentoring often are "boutique" in nature, that is, they have small numbers of preservice students or novice teachers involved in the program. Many university programs and school districts are very large in number. The challenge of "scaling up" the size of boutique programs is significant. This is particularly so because direct links between quality mentoring and student achievement are difficult to establish in large program contexts. Indeed, school district administrators may be reluctant to spend resources on mentoring programs, especially in the current educational environment where student achievement scores on standardized tests are driving many of the decisions in schools. Research that relies solely on self-report data is not sufficient to establish this linkage. Indeed, more research is needed to establish through direct observation the connections between mentoring and the novices' subsequent teaching practice in the classroom. From there, connections to student learning need to be directly established. Obviously, such research has been limited by methodological considerations, although some preliminary case studies attempt to elucidate the direct effects of mentoring on teaching and learning and show promise (Achinstein & Barrett, 2003; Wang, Strong, & Odell, 2004). See also Chapter 6 by Wang, Odell, and Strong.

## The Chapters

What follows next are four chapters that focus on effective mentoring. Chapter 9 by Hayes describes a mentoring program and its effects on teacher performance, novice teacher efficacy, and the retention of novices in the profession after the first and second years of the program. In chapter 10 McIntyre, Smith, Gilbert, and Hillkirk describe a graduate teaching fellows program where graduate students concomitantly pursue a Master's degree while teaching under the direction of a mentor teacher in the mentor's classroom. In chapter 11 author Hughes provides a description of the practices and features of a statewide effort to implement mentor teacher programs in Virginia. In the final chapter 12 in this division, Zeek and Walker describe a mentoring program that is part of an established professional development school.

Each of the programs described in these four chapters include some elements of quality mentoring and each has encountered various impediments. The reader is encouraged to keep in mind the framework of quality mentoring presented above while considering each of these mentoring programs. It might be helpful in gaining an appreciation of the chapters to probe each mentor program by asking questions. The framework for quality mentoring might lead the reader, for example, to ask: What is the stated purpose of the mentoring program? How were mentor teachers selected and prepared for mentoring? What are the incentives and impediments for implementing the program? A consideration of these and related matters will be presented in the response and discussion section that follows the chapters.

## References

Achinstein, B., & Barrett, A. (2003, April). *(Re)Framing classroom contexts: How new teachers and mentors understand and are influenced by diverse learners.* Paper presented at the Annual Meeting of American Educational Research Association, Chicago, IL.

Association of Teacher Educators. (2005). *Standards for teacher educators*. Retrieved May 15, 2005, from http://www.ate1.org/pubs/Standards_for_Teac.cfm.

Bartell, C.A. (2005). *Cultivating high-quality teaching through induction and mentoring*. Thousand Oaks, CA: Corwin Press.

Cohen, D. K., & Spillane, J. P. (1992). Policy and practice: The relations between governance and instruction. *Review of Research in Education, 18*, 3–49.

Feiman-Nemser, S., & Floden, R. (1986). The culture of teaching. In M. C. Wittrock (Ed.), *Handbook of research on teaching*, (3rd ed., pp. 505–526). New York: Macmillan.

Feiman-Nemser, S., & Parker, M. B. (1992). *Los Angeles mentors: Local guides of educational companions?* East Lansing, MI: National Center for Research on Teacher Learning, Michigan State University.

Ingersoll, R., & Kralik, J. M. (2004). The impact of mentoring on teacher retention: What the research says. *ECS Research Review*, Denver, CO: Educational Commission of the States. Retrieved May 15, 2005, from http://www.ecs.org/clearinghouse/50/36/5036.htm.

Little, J. W. (1990). The mentoring phenomenon and the social organization of teaching. In C. B. Cazden (Ed.), *Review of research in education, 16*, 279–252.

Odell, S. J. (1990). *Mentor teacher programs*. Washington, DC: National Education Association.

Odell, S. J., & Huling, L. (Eds.). (2000). *Quality mentoring for novice teachers*. Indianapolis, IN: Kappa Delta Pi.

Ringstaff, C., & Haymore Sandholtz, J. (2002). Out-of-field assignments: Case studies of two beginning teachers. *Teachers College Record, 104*(4), 812–841.

Shanker, A. (1985, October 27). Education's "dirty little secret." *New York Times*, section 4, p. E9.

Shulman, J. H., & Colbert, J. A. (1987). *The mentor teacher casebook*. San Francisco: Far West Laboratory for Educational Research and Development and ERIC Clearinghouse on Educational Management.

Smith, J. P., III (1996). Efficacy and teaching mathematics by telling: A challenge for reform. *Journal for Research in Mathematics Education, 27*(4), 387–402.

Sweeny, B., & DeBolt, G. (2000). A survey of the 50 states: Mandated teacher induction programs. In S. Odell & L. Huling (Eds.), *Quality mentoring for novice teachers*. Indianapolis, IN: Kappa Delta Pi.

Wang J., & Odell, S. J. (2002). Mentored learning to teach and standards-based teaching reform: A critical review. *Review of Educational Research, 7*(3), 481–586.

Wang, J., Strong, M., & Odell S. J. (2004). Mentor-novice conversations about teaching: A comparison of two U.S. and two Chinese cases. *Teachers College Record, 106*(4), 775–813.

Wong H., Britton T., & Ganser T. (2005). What the world can teach us about new teacher induction. *Phi Delta Kappan, 86*(5), 379–384.

CHAPTER 9

# A Longitudinal Study of the Effects of a Mentoring Program on Teacher Performance, Efficacy and Retention

*Judith L. Hayes*
Wichita State University

Judith L. Hayes is a faculty member in the Department of Curriculum and Instruction, College of Education, at Wichita State University (WSU). In addition to her teaching responsibilities she is the director of the Transition to Teaching Program and of the Raytheon Teaching Fellows Program. Her research interests include alternative certification, adult education, mentoring and professional development through learning communities.

## ABSTRACT

Realizing that teacher retention is impacted through quality induction, the Raytheon Teaching Fellows Program at Wichita State University includes a mentoring component which began with the undergraduate pre-service education student and continued through the first three years in the teaching profession. The purpose of this study is to research the effects of the Raytheon Teaching Fellows mentoring program, over a three-year period of time, comparing teachers' performance, feelings of efficacy and rates of retention. Four patterns were used throughout the program. The effect of the patterns that were utilized in the program and the resulting outcomes are discussed.

Chords of *Pomp and Circumstance* still echo through our minds as we celebrate the graduation of this year's class of undergraduate teacher education students.

Several of these individuals, now novice teachers, hold recently signed teaching contracts, while others anxiously anticipate the job offers to come. As surrounding school districts scout prospective employees from this latest group of undergraduates, their real concerns are not just directed towards the recruitment effort, but on the retention of these newly hired teachers.

Unlike many other professions, the education environment typically places the novice teacher in a performance-based arena working in isolation from other professional practitioners. Some extraordinary individuals surmount the obstacles of novice teaching. However, many novice teachers flounder, alone and frustrated, receiving elaborate performance critiques from a variety of audiences (school administrators, department reviewers, peer teachers, students, parents, and general public) and minimal support in actual performance improvement from their education colleagues. Without the aid of an effective mentoring program, many of these starry-eyed, capable novice teachers become disillusioned and exit the profession within their first three years of teaching.

This awareness has led to an increase in mentoring and induction programs over the past two decades, as support for new teachers has become the norm in many states (Fideler & Haseldorn, 1999). Research on these programs clearly indicates that the content, duration and delivery of mentoring and induction programs are varied, and the empirical support so limited, that it is difficult to establish conclusions on the overall impact to the teaching profession (Ingersoll & Kralik, 2004).

Confusion also exists between the terms *mentoring* and *induction*. Harry Wong distinguishes induction as a system of "comprehensive, coherent, and sustained professional development" (Wong, 2004, p. 2) offered by a school district. Mentoring is limited to "what mentors do" (Wong, 2004, p. 2) and is a component of the induction process. However, in Ingersoll & Kralik's (2004) study of mentoring and induction, this is not clearly distinguishable, as some mentoring programs may be elaborate enough to incorporate the professional development components typically left to the school districts.

# Objectives

The objectives of this research are to study the effects of one mentoring program, over a three-year period, examining novice teachers' performance, feelings of efficacy and rates of retention. The novice teachers and the mentor teachers have all participated in a mentoring program that utilized a variety of patterns in the induction process. The research questions are:

1. What effect did the mentoring program structure and patterns have on novice teacher candidates' teaching performance?

2. What effect did the mentoring program structure and patterns have on novice teacher candidates' feelings of efficacy?
3. What effect did the mentoring program structure and patterns have on novice teacher candidates' retention in the teaching profession?

# Literature Review

In the coming year, thousands of college graduates will enter the nation's classrooms to begin their teaching careers. Most of these teachers will have received high grades in their teaching methods courses and student teaching experiences. Most will have a genuine affection for young people and will be committed to making a difference in the lives of their students. Despite the good intentions and high expectations of these beginners, 40 to 50 percent of them will drop out of teaching within the first seven years (Ganser, 1999; Thomas & Kiley, 1994), most within the first two years (Schlechty & Vance, 1983). Of those who survive, many will have such negative initial experiences that they may never reach their full potential as educators (Huling-Austin, 1992; Romatowski, Dorminey, & Voorhees, 1989).

Districts have come to realize that retention of qualified teachers may be costly, but less than the constant recruitment and training of new personnel. The fiscal effect on education systems of teachers leaving the profession amounts to approximately 20 percent of each exiting teacher's salary with hiring and training costs considered (Benner, 2000). However, true turnover costs are more complex than simply figuring out the average cost of replacement. Unwanted turnover represents costs that are greater than simple replacement costs.

It is not surprising that an analysis of national data has shown that widely publicized school staffing problems are not the result of too few teachers being recruited and trained; instead, the data indicate that school staffing problems are to a significant extent, a result of large numbers of teachers departing the profession long before retirement (Ingersoll, 2001).

In a recent summary of research on mentoring and teacher retention, researchers address the question of "Why teachers quit" (Strong & Pultorak, 2004). Their conclusions suggest differentiating the data on teacher retention and attrition between those individuals that "leave" the profession and those that "move" to other positions in education or to other locations that cannot be tracked.

The inverse question is, "Why do teachers stay?" Numerous follow-up studies (Charles A. Dana Center, 2002; Fuller, 2003; Odell & Ferraro, 1992; Smith & Ingersoll, 2004), tracking cohorts of beginning teachers, have determined that there was a statistically significant effect on teacher retention when there is an effective mentoring or induction program available. In retrospect, teachers that participate in a mentoring program valued the emotional support and collaboration they receive from their mentors.

Well-designed mentoring programs lower the attrition rates of new teachers (National Association of State Boards of Education, 1998). According to a study of new teachers in New Jersey, the first-year attrition rates of teachers traditionally trained in an undergraduate teacher education program without mentoring is 18 percent, while those novice teachers whose induction program included mentoring is only 5 percent (Gold, 1999).

Effective mentoring programs provide training to the mentor, share a common focus, and have an established structure and accountability. Establishing a relationship between a newly hired teacher and a mentor teacher has become a fairly common practice in many school districts. However, definitions of a mentor teacher, the selection and training process, as well as parameters of responsibility vary from district to district. In a well-designed mentoring program, expectations are placed on the mentor teachers that move beyond the support of the novice teacher to the establishment of individual professional goals. Charlotte Danielson (1999) finds that mentoring not only helps the novice teacher make the transition into the profession, but also fosters the professional development of the veteran teacher.

With this research in mind, the Raytheon Teaching Fellows mentoring program is designed to reduce attrition rates, to enhance feelings of support and self-efficacy, and to positively impact teaching performance. The pre-service undergraduate teacher education fellow, the novice teacher fellow through the first three years of teaching, and the mentor teacher are all impacted through the mentoring interactions.

# Methodology

## DESCRIPTION OF PROGRAM

Wichita State University (WSU), with the Raytheon Aircraft Corporation, implemented a program that allowed for the growth and enhancement of qualified mathematics and science teachers. The Raytheon Teaching Fellows Program was established to encourage more talented people to enter the field of education and obtain the content knowledge and learning strategies necessary to become effective educators in the areas of mathematics and science.

An essential element of the Raytheon Teaching Fellows Program was the mentoring process available to pre-service education students and to novice teachers as they entered the profession. The data reported here were collected from the candidates participating in the Raytheon Teaching Fellows (RTF) Program.

## RESEARCH POPULATION

The research population included pre-service teacher education candidates from both the traditional undergraduate program (elementary and secondary education) and from the alternative licensure program (secondary education). Candidates were identified from the fields of mathematics and science using a rigorous selection process. The selection process began with an application which included three essays, copies of transcripts and three letters of recommendation (figure 9.1). Using a rubric and multiple-raters, an analysis of essay responses, grades, experiences, and letters of recommendation were completed. Candidates with the highest scores were then invited to meet with a selection committee (figure 9.2). In addition to an interview, these candidates were asked to prepare a microteaching lesson from a topic in their discipline. The selection panel was composed of faculty from the College of Liberal Arts and Sciences, the College of Education, and RTF Advisory Council members. They assessed and scored the interview and microteaching presentation according to a rubric (figure 9.3). Scores for all candidates were tallied and selections were made by the Advisory Council according to the top-scoring individuals.

Candidates were notified of the selection and invited to attend a Welcome-Orientation session. Details and grant limitations were outlined, scholarship stipends were explained, and RTF teacher candidates were asked to sign a contract agreeing to these conditions. A level of expectation was established with this initial contact.

New candidates were accepted each year of the program following this process. The numbers of candidates are displayed in table 9.1, with those entering the profession each year indicated in the far right column.

Mentors for the program were utilized in several ways. The mentors were recruited from local school districts. Letters were sent to the principals and to the science/mathematics department chairs briefly outlining the program and asking for mentor nominations. These individuals were asked to complete a form (figure 9.4) indicating the strengths the nominee possessed in the following categories: (1) Attitude & Character, (2) Communication Skills, (3) Professional Competence & Experience, and (4) Interpersonal Skills. Letters were then sent to the nominees along with a Teacher Mentor Application (figure 9.5) inviting them to apply to become a mentor in the RTF Program. Based on the responses from the application, mentor nominees were then invited to attend an informa-

## Figure 9.1    Application Form: Raytheon Teaching Fellows Program

Thank you for your interest in applying to the Raytheon Teaching Fellows Program. In addition to completing this form, you will also need to submit transcripts of all your college-level work. If you are an entering college student, or have fewer than 10 credit hours, submit your high school transcript and ACT scores. You will also need to arrange to have three letters of reference sent to: Raytheon Teaching Fellows Program, C/O Judie Hayes, Campus Box 28, Wichita State University, Wichita, KS 67260–0028. The letters of reference should be from individuals that can speak to your ability to teach, or to work with children. *If you have questions, call 316–978–6950 or e-mail* judith.hayes@wichita.edu.

Name: _____  Date: _____

Address: _____
                      City                        State            Zip

Phone: _____  Social Security number: _____

E-mail: _____  Application is for: _____Fall        _____Spring

Current educational level:                      Educational goal:
_____ Entering college student        _____ Undergraduate degree
_____ Undergraduate student          _____ Graduate degree
_____ Student with a degree           _____ Certification only: ___Alternative ___Traditional

Certification sought:

Level: **(Check One)** ___Secondary    ___Elementary with middle school endorsement

Content: **(Check All That Apply)** ___Mathematics___Physical science___Biological science

Undergraduate major: _____  Schools attended: _____

Have you been accepted into a College of Education teacher preparation program? _____

If so, where? _____  Describe your status. _____

Do you presently hold a teaching certificate? _____ In? _____
                                                                    Level              Subject

**Answer the following questions and submit attachment with your application.**

Write a short narrative explaining why you want to be a mathematics or science teacher.

Describe any experience you have had teaching or working with children and youth.

We realize that you may not be a teacher now, but describe what your classroom would be like if you were a teacher and what would be happening in your ideal mathematics or science classroom.

**Figure 9.2    Selection Criteria Rubric**

Name of Candidate _____

Semester _____ Education Objective _____

| *Points* | | *1* | *2* | *3* | *TOTAL* |
|---|---|---|---|---|---|
| Academic preparation & exposure | Overall GPA | 2.50–2.99 | 3.00–3.49 | 3.50–4.00 | |
| | Math/science strength & experience | Subject GPA 2.0: Subject exposure does not meet minimum program requirements | Subject GPA 2.5–3.0: Subject exposure meets minimum program requirements | Subject GPA 3.0: Subject exposure & requirements exceed expectations | |
| Communication | Written | Written response incomplete & poorly stated | Written response partially complete & adequately stated | Written response thorough, well-written & clear | |
| | Oral (interview) | Brief, disconnected responses | Some direction & connection in responses | Complete, direct, connected responses | |
| Teaching motivation | | Motivation is weak/unclear | Motivation is fairly clear & well-defined | Motivation is strong, directed & well-defined | |
| Teaching experience | | Experience is very limited (parent, SS) | Experience is limited & non-specific | Experience is extensive & diverse (coop/substitute) | |
| Teaching philosophy | | Philosophy is didactic | Philosophy shows some interaction | Philosophy is constructivist | |
| Letters of recommendation | | Letters are non-specific; address character only | Letters address character & general teaching qualities | Letters address character & specific teaching qualities | |
| Mini-Teach (Score transferred from Teaching Rubric) | | 14 points or lower | 15–19 points | 20–25 points | |
| | | | | | TOTAL |

Comments:


Signed _____

Names of Selection Committee participating in interview process:

1. _____

2. _____

## Figure 9.3   Micro Teach Rubric

Name of Candidate _____

Semester _____ Lesson Subject _____

*Please rank the candidate in the following areas by placing a check in the appropriate box, with 1 being low and 5 being high.*

| Description | 1 | 2 | 3 | 4 | 5 |
|---|---|---|---|---|---|
| Appearance, poise, and confidence | | | | | |
| Speech quality and control (rate, volume, enunciation) | | | | | |
| Preparation (approaches, materials & resources, thoroughness, timing, etc.) | | | | | |
| Knowledge of subject (information, concepts, skills) | | | | | |
| Instructional procedures (motivational techniques, variety of strategies, clarity of instruction, sequencing, questioning, etc.) | | | | | |
| | Total | Total | Total | Total | Total |

GRAND TOTAL _____

Comments:

## Table 9.1   Raytheon Teaching Fellow Candidates

| Year | Mathematics | Sciences | #Accepted In-Process | # Complete Entering Profession |
|---|---|---|---|---|
| 2001 | 8 | 6 | 56 | 14 |
| 2002 | 23 | 24 | 55 | 47 |
| 2003 | 37 | 25 | 35 | 62 |
| 2004 | 13 | 10 | 12 | 23 |
| 2005 | 7 | 5 | 0 | 12 |

## Figure 9.4   Teacher Mentor Nomination

Principal's Name: ——————————————— School: ———————————————
Please Print

Suggested **Mentor**: ———————————————————————————
Please Print

Subjects taught: ————————————————— Length of time teaching: —————

Please check the strengths this teacher demonstrates that would make them an effective mentor:
(**Check as many as apply.**)

### Attitude & Character

- Demonstrates patience & willingness to be a role model and improve skills
- Is eager to share new information & ideas
- Is resilient, flexible, persistent, & open-minded
- Exhibits good humor & resourcefulness
- Enjoys new challenges & solving problems
- Is reflective & able to learn from mistakes

### Professional Competence & Experience

- Has an excellent knowledge of pedagogy & subject matter
- Demonstrates excellent classroom management & organizational skills
- Understands the policies & procedures of the school, district, and teachers' association
- Collaborates well with other teachers & administration

### Communication Skills

- Is able to articulate effective instructional
- strategies
- Listens attentively
- Offers critiques in positive & productive ways
- Is discreet & maintained confidentiality

### Interpersonal Skills

- Is able to maintain a trusting relationship
- Is approachable; easily establishes rapport with others
- Is able to maintain a trusting relationship

Other Comments:

Please return this form to:
Raytheon Teaching Fellows Program
C/O Judie Hayes, Box 28
Wichita State University
1845 Fairmount
Wichita, KS 67260–0028

*Please feel free to duplicate this form for additional nomination*

**Figure 9.5    Teacher Mentor Application**

# WICHITA STATE UNIVERSITY
## Raytheon Teaching Fellows Program

### Teacher Mentor Application

Teacher's Name _____   Position: _____
                        Please Print

Name of School: _____

School Address: _____

_____ Phone: _____/_____
                                              School Year      Summer

Teacher's E-Mail Address: _____/_____
                                  School Year                Summer Access

Subject Area: _____   Number of Years Teaching: _____

**Please attach your responses to the questions below.**

✎ What were some of the struggles you encountered in your first years of teaching? How could they have been alleviated?

✎ What are some practical things that have helped you become a better teacher?

✎ What are some organizational "tricks" that have made you more efficient as a teacher?

✎ Describe a recent experience in your classroom where you felt like you really made a difference in a student's understanding  of a concept or motivation to explore (pursue) an academic investigation.

✎ The biggest obstacle to teaching today is . . .

✎ I've learned to overcome this obstacle by . . .

**Please return this form by July 11th to:**    Raytheon Teaching Fellows Program
                                                C/O Judie Hayes, Box 28
                                                Wichita State University
                                                1845 Fairmount
                                                Wichita, KS 67260-0028
                                                FAX: (316) 978-6935

Judie Hayes, Raytheon Teaching Fellows, Box 28, Wichita State University, 1845 Fairmount, Wichita, KS 67260-0028, 316-978-6950, judith.hayes@wichita.edu tional meeting outlining the expectations if they agreed to participate. The informational meeting was followed with a Mentor Training Workshop offered during the summer session at WSU. Participants could receive three hours of credit for attending the course, or they could receive the equivalent of tuition in the form of a stipend. ALL mentors were required to attend the workshop and maintain an established level of participation in the program throughout the school year. Additional mentors were recruited and trained each year of the program with the mentors that were not paired with a novice teacher entering the profession participating as part of a Mentor Team.

Mentors were selected from 16 districts and the Catholic Diocese. Table 9.2 lists the number of mentor teachers (MT) and their position of participation: (a) paired with a Novice Teacher, NTs (fellows who have entered the teaching profession) or (b) working as part of a Mentor Team, MTT (composed of undergraduate pre-service education fellows Pre-STs during their senior year).

Mentors not initially paired with a novice teacher participated as part of a Mentor Team. The Mentor Team worked with the undergraduate pre-service education fellows during their senior year. The Mentor Team interactions began with the second group of fellows. The Mentor Team was responsible for facilitating four workshops per semester during the school year. As field experiences intensified and the relationship continued, the mentor teacher and the undergraduate pre-service fellow worked together to clarify expectations and refine goals. Specific topics relevant to the fellows' student teaching experiences were investigated and understanding of school or district policies were enhanced. Although these workshops were informative, the intent of the workshops was to begin structuring the interactions between the mentor and the pre-service teacher. Collaboration, reflection, and research were important elements in these interactions, thereby establishing a foundation for the mentor-novice teacher relationship that was soon to come.

## RESEARCH DURATION

The Raytheon Teaching Fellows Program began in 2000 with the first cohort of graduates in May 2001. The mentoring program began with that cohort as they

**Table 9.2  Raytheon Teaching Fellow Mentors**

| Year | Trained | Paired w/Novice | Mentor Team |
|------|---------|-----------------|-------------|
| 2001 | 25 | 14 | 11 |
| 2002 | 25 + 40 | 39 (8 Triads) | 12 |
| 2003 | 25 + 40 + 30 | 34 (28 Triads) | 8 |
| 2004 | 25 + 40 + 30 | 8 (15 Triads) | 0 |

entered the teaching profession. During the fall of 2001, the Mentor Team began meeting with the pre-service undergraduate teaching fellows. Grant funding was terminated in 2003 and no new fellows were admitted to the program. Scholarship monies and mentoring continued for the fellows in the program with some mentor relationships continuing to date.

## RESEARCH METHODS

Research methods included several measurement tools and a variety of patterns in the mentoring program. The 14 novice teachers in the first year of the program were the only group that did not experience interactions with the Mentor Team. Mentors were recruited during the spring and trained during the summer with mentor pairing occurring just before the school year began. This group was representative of most mentor arrangements, with the novice teacher frequently meeting their mentor the first day of the new school year. Feedback from the novice teachers indicated that pairing earlier would have been desirable. Of the 14 novice teachers in the first year, 8 of them combined with another novice teacher during their second year of teaching to form a triad. As the numbers of fellows increased, more triads were formed.

### Research Tools

There were four primary measurement tools used in this research. Supplemental data were available through Administrator Evaluations, Novice Teacher Reflections, e-mails, and group interactions.

The Mentor Connections Log was used by the novice teacher and the mentor teacher to track the number of interactions, record the focus of the interaction, the time spent, and the participant who initiated the contact. These data presented a profile of self-initiated and scheduled meetings, development of focus topics, and time spent. Data were disaggregated and compared according to the pattern(s) administered in the mentoring program.

A Teacher Needs Assessment (author unknown) was completed by novice teacher fellows each year in the program. It enabled individuals to identify areas of teaching needs in relationship to their desire to satisfy those needs with quantifiable indicators. These data presented a profile of changing needs over time, and the urgency to satisfy those needs. The data also were disaggregated and compared according to the pattern(s) administered in the mentoring program. This assessment was composed of 49 statements concerning various components of teaching such as Instructional Variation, Professional Responsibilities, Questioning, Classroom Management, Pacing, Motivation, and Dispositions. For each statement the novice teacher was asked to rate the statement using a 5-point Likert scale according to three categories:

1. To what extent is the activity **important** in your teaching?
2. To what extent do you feel you can **accomplish** the activity?
3. To what extent do you have an interest to **improve** on this activity?

The need/interest score was computed by using the formula $(A - B + C)$. If a novice teacher thought it was important, didn't do it well, and wanted to improve, the score would be high. This targeted areas for the mentor/novice teacher to work on.

Focus Group Responses were also collected from all participants at the end of the program. Several focus group sessions were scheduled enabling mentors and novice teachers to respond to the same set of prompts. Responses were recorded and grouped providing qualitative insights into teacher feelings of efficacy and growth as reflective practitioners.

Finally, the Danielson Survey of Mentor and Self-Analysis of Performance (1996) was used as an indicator of teaching performance and to discern communication validity between the mentor and the novice teacher. Teaching performance was self-assessed and mentor assessed each year using a measurement rubric to assess four domains of teaching: (a) Planning & Preparation, (b) Classroom Environment, (c) Instruction, and (d) Professional Responsibilities (Danielson, 1996). This tool was administered for each year of novice teaching. Data were disaggregated and compared according to the pattern administered in the mentoring program.

### Research Patterns

Throughout the duration of the mentoring program a variety of patterns were employed with the participants. A pattern is a method for grouping participants within the mentor continuum. Because these various patterns are complex, figure 9.6 will provide visual assistance to this narrative. Trite symbols and false names have also been utilized to clarify the progression of the patterns. All mentors have been assigned names that begin with an "M" (Michael, Melissa, Miguel, Mary) and fellows have been assigned names that begin with an "A" for candidates entering teaching the first year of the program, "B" for the second year, and "C" for the third year. The symbol that is assigned to a particular participant remains the same throughout the three-year design. For example, Year 1, Pattern 1 displays a multi-armed icon for mentor teacher (MT) Michael. This symbol represents Michael in Year 2, Pattern 3, and in Year 3, Pattern 2. MT-Michael's movement can be tracked among the various patterns throughout his three years in the program.

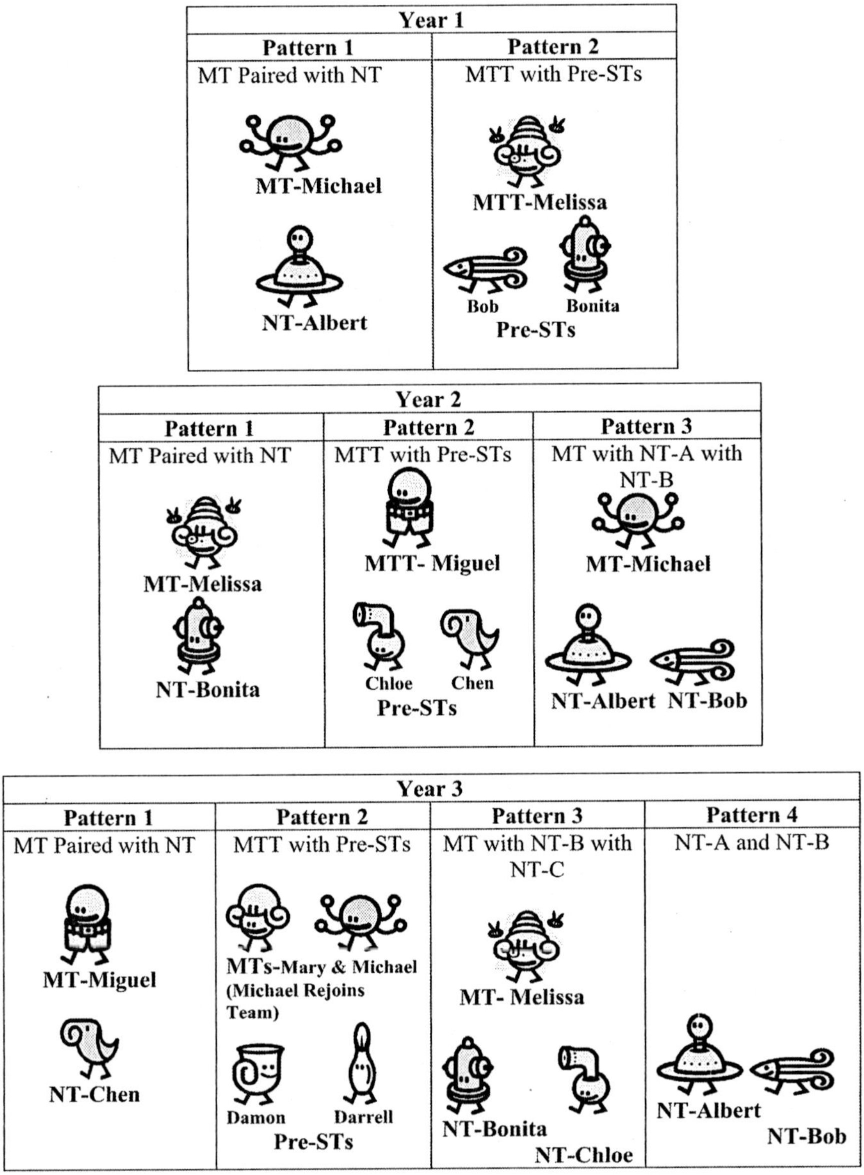

Figure 9.6   Mentoring Pyramid (MT = Mentor Teacher, NT = Novice Teacher, and MTT = Mentor Team)

In spring of 2001, the first group of Raytheon Teaching Fellows received contracts and entered the teaching profession. A group of mentors were trained and prepared to work with the fellows. From that group, based on content discipline and school location, pairs were established with the first cohort of novice teachers (NT). Pattern 1, a mentor teacher and a novice teacher forming a pair, is commonly seen in many mentoring programs. Pattern 2 consisted of the mentors from Year 1 that were not paired with a novice teacher who became part of a Mentor Team (MTT) and began working with the pre-service under-graduate teaching fellows (pre-ST's) during their student teaching year.

A new cadre of mentors was recruited and trained and the second group of RTF's (these individuals have been assigned names that begin with a "B") were ready to enter the teaching profession in the spring of 2002. Year 2, Pattern 1 is repeated with a pair formed between a mentor teacher (MT-Melissa) and a novice teacher (NT-Bonita). Unlike the first year however, Melissa and Bonita have worked together on the Mentor Team during Bonita's student teaching year. Year 2, Pattern 2 shows MT-Michael, from the new cadre of trained mentors, working with Chloe and Chen (Pre-STs) as part of the Mentor Team. Year 2, Pattern 3 continued with the established pair of MT-Michael and NT-Albert, but a novice teacher from the second cohort was added, NT-Bob, to now form a triad. The triad has a novice first year teacher, Bob, a novice second year teacher, Albert, and a mentor, Michael. Second year teacher Albert assisted first year teacher Bob as he transitioned into his first year of teaching.

As more fellows were accepted into the RTF program, additional mentors were recruited and trained. Year 3, Pattern 1 duplicated the prior years with the pairing of a MT-Mentor Teacher and a NT-Novice Teacher. MT-Miguel moved from the Mentor Team to form a pair with NT-Chen. Year 3, Pattern 2 repeated with the addition of the newly recruited mentors becoming part of the Mentor Team that works with the fellows who are now in the student teaching year. Year 3, Pattern 3 showed the Year 2 mentor pair, of MT-Melissa and NT-Bonita, now creating a triad with the addition of NT-Chloe. It is in Year 3, with Pattern 4 that the cycle is completed. Mentor Teacher Michael, who began in Year 1 paired with Novice Teacher Albert, and in Year 2 formed a triad with the additional Novice Teacher Bob, now returns to the Mentor Team, while Novice Teachers Albert and Bob continue as a pair. (See figure 9.7.)

### Pre-Service Teachers (Pre-STs)

Comparisons were made among groups that participated in the Mentor Team before becoming a Mentor Pair and between groups that participated as a mentor pair or as a mentor triad. Retention data are cited for the entire group. The Patterns used throughout the program are referred to later in the Results. Table

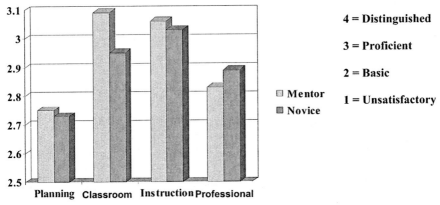

Figure 9.7   Mentor Assessment and Self-Assessment

9.3 summarizes these patterns. Data management was organized through the Raytheon Teaching Fellows Office with analysis of these data completed by two external grant assessment personnel and by the Raytheon Teaching Fellows Director.

# Results

This research yielded data that could be instrumental in the design of a mentoring program. Although there were no significant differences in novice teacher performance among the various patterns used with the fellows, there were nota-

### Table 9.3   Summary of Patterns

| | |
|---|---|
| Pattern 1 | A Mentor Teacher (MT) is paired with a Novice Teacher (NT) |
| Pattern 2 | A group of Mentor Teachers (MTT) work as a Mentor Team, interacting with a group of pre-service undergraduate fellows (Pre-ST) during their student teaching year |
| Pattern 3 | A triad is formed with the addition of a Novice Teacher (NT) to a pre-existing pair of Mentor Teacher (MT) and Novice Teacher (NT) from a prior year |
| Pattern 4 | A triad changes to a pair composed of a second year Novice Teacher (NT) and a third year Novice Teacher (NT) with the Mentor Teacher MT returning to the Mentor Team and acting as a consultant for the pair as needed. |

ble differences in mentor communications and in responses indicative of self-efficacy. In terms of the retention, it is still early to comment since the greatest numbers of new teachers leave the profession within their first five years, and the final group of fellows will be entering the classroom in fall 2005. However, to date, 99.9% of the fellows are still in the teaching profession with many having been recognized as leaders in their districts. Following is a discussion of the results from the four measurement tools that were employed, beginning with the Mentor Connections Log.

The frequency of communication between the novice teacher and the mentor teacher was recorded in a Mentor Connections Log. These data were averaged for each year (see table 9.4). During the 2001–2002 school year the only pattern utilized for novice teachers entering the profession was pairing them, as they entered the classroom, with the teacher of record. They had no experience interacting with a mentor team or practicing the skills required to participate in a collaborative professional community.

School years 2002–2003 and 2003–2004 showed an increase in total number of communications and an increase in novice teacher–initiated communications. Novice teachers initiated three times more communications in the 2003–2004 school year than were seen with the initial group of fellows. This may be a result of the comfort levels gained in establishing the mentor relationship and skills learned through the pre-service undergraduate involvement with the Mentor Team.

Another item of note collected from the Mentor Connections Log was the communication that occurred between the novice teachers who were interacting as part of a triad. The first year novice teacher would frequently contact the second year novice teacher rather than the mentor teacher for support and advice. These contacts and responses seemed to enhance the confidence levels of the second year novice teachers who participated in a triad as compared with the second year novice teachers who only interacted as a pair.

A Teacher Needs Assessment Questionnaire (see figure 9.8) was also given to the fellows each year. This assessment indicated the novice teachers' feelings, across a range of teaching components including instruction, management, pro-

**Table 9.4    Mentor/Novice Communications**

| School Year | MT Initiated Average # of Contacts | NT Initiated Average # of Contacts | Scheduled Contacts |
|---|---|---|---|
| 2001–2002 | 22 | 10 | 20 |
| 2002–2003 | 25 | 24 | 20 |
| 2003–2004 | 30 | 35 | 20 |

## Figure 9.8   Teacher Needs Assessment Questionnaire

Directions

On the following pages, 49 statements will be made concerning various teaching activities and role characteristics associated with your duties as a teacher. For each statement you will be asked to give three ratings:

- A. To what extent is the activity **important** in your teaching?
- B. To what extent do you feel you can **accomplish** the activity?
- C. To what extent do you have an interest to **improve** on this activity?

For each of these three areas please respond using a number 1–5. Low numbers represent low extents and high numbers represent high extents. For example, the following scales for each question could be used to mark responses:

| **Question A: Important** | **Question B: Accomplish** | **Question C: Improve** |
|---|---|---|
| 1 = None | 1 = Hardly Ever | 1 = Not Interested |
| 2 = Very Little | 2 = Seldom | 2 = Very Little |
| 3 = Somewhat | 3 = Sometimes | 3 = Somewhat |
| 4 = Highly | 4 = Often | 4 = Would Like To |
| 5 = Definitely | 5 = Almost Always | 5 = Definitely |

You will be asked to mark your responses on the provided answer sheet. **For each question** use column A for its **extent of importance**, B for **extent of accomplishment**, and C for your **interest to improve**. The need/interest score is computed in the final column by the formula $(A - B + C)$. By ranking these **Need/Interest** scores, you should be able to prioritize your professional needs. If you thought it was important, you didn't do it well, and you wanted to improve, the score will be high.

### EXAMPLE

**Questionnaire:**
- A. Extent Importance?              (min)  1  2  3  4  5  (max)
- B. Extent of Accomplishment?   (min)  1  2  3  4  5  (max)
- C. Desire to Improve?              (min)  1  2  3  4  5  (max)

**As a professional educator I typically:**
3. Develop long and short-term lesson plans which are sequential and based on the district's objectives for my subject area.

| Answer Sheet: | | A | B | C | $(A - B + C)$ |
|---|---|---|---|---|---|
| 1. | 1. | | | | |
| 2. | 2. | | | | |
| 3. Objective Usage | 3. | | | | |

## Figure 9.8    (Continued)

### As a Professional Educator, I Typically:

1. Believe that all my students can learn the intended curriculum and accept the responsibility for the quality of education delivered to each of my students.

2. Understand and share in the general responsibilities and duties associated with teaching such as hall duty, record keeping, etc.

3. Develop long- and short-term lesson plans that are sequential and based on the district's objectives for my subject area.

4. Write individual lesson plans that have objectives and use various activities, materials, and evaluation techniques to teach those objectives.

5. Use alternative instructional material and teaching strategies to make provisions for students who work at different rates with different learning styles and attention spans.

6. Conduct class every day with enthusiasm, consistently looking for ways to stimulate students.

7. Use voice, movement, and nonverbal communication to motivate and hold all students' attention during lesions.

8. Use few, if any, vocal segregates (un, ok, you, know, etc.) and grammar mistakes.

9. Have all materials organized before class and distribute material effectively to avoid loss of instruction time.

10. Begin most lessons with a motivational set that communicates the instructional objectives and purpose of the learning activity.

11. Review previous material in each lesson to provide continuity and sequence.

12. Know the elements and consistently use a direct instruction model in my teaching.

13. Know the elements of and use different cooperative learning strategies in my teaching.

14. Provide illustrations, examples, and applications of material during each lesson.

15. Try to mix literal, interpretive, and applied questions in an effort to develop higher order thinking skills.

16. Often use students' names after a question is asked and then provide adequate wait time for a response.

17. Use questioning techniques such as rephrasing, giving clues, or probing to obtain correct response when a student does not correctly answer.

18. Provide corrections and positive feedback to student answers.

**Figure 9.8 (Continued)**

**As a Professional Educator, I Typically:**

19. Try to achieve an equal distribution of questions so all students participate during each class period.

20. Use transitions between teaching points to focus student attention on important points.

21. Use a number of different techniques to check the students' understanding of material as it is taught.

22. Check to see if each student can successfully complete the homework assignment before they begin work on their own.

23. Provide an opportunity for all students to apply or practice knowledge and skills being learned through independent practice.

24. Achieve a closure or summary at the end of the lesson to focus student attention on important points.

25. Know what audio-visual material is available and try to use a variety of audio-visual teaching aids to reinforce instruction.

26. Give clear verbal and written directions to students by saying it, writing it, and checking to see if they understood it.

27. Keep all students busy during the entire class period by organizing and pacing instructional activity.

28. Use daily "sponge" activities to keep students thinking during non-instructional times such as roll taking.

29. Am aware of present learning environment research and use classroom space, furniture, and general layout to foster the maximum learning cycle.

30. Have a written set of classroom rules or expectations that all students are taught.

31. Use a discipline hierarchy for rule infractions that consistently corrects inappropriate behavior with appropriate consequences.

32. Have a positive reward system that strives to develop self-management skills in students.

33. Monitor all student behavior and redirect off-task students in the least disruptive manner to maximize student time on task.

34. Exercise care for students' physical safety and know how to effectively respond to emergency situations.

35. Develop and communicate to students a fair evaluation system that uses various methods of evaluating and assessing student performance.

## Figure 9.8   (Continued)

### As a Professional Educator, I Typically:

37. Daily monitor student progress and provide corrective action for students not achieving so that all my students succeed.

38. Develop and maintain a system of keeping students and parents aware of individual progress.

39. Try to establish rapport with students by showing patience, empathy, warmth, and respect.

40. Maintain a consistently pleasant disposition to all students in and out of class.

41. Consistently communicate high expectations for each student through my daily interactions.

42. Make use of all available sources (student records, counselors, resource specialists, test results, etc.) to assess the learning needs and capabilities of individual students.

43. Model effective human relation skills in an attempt to promote wholesome interpersonal student relationships that stress a consideration of the rights, feelings, and ideas of others.

44. Have knowledge of the school's referral process and can use specialized services as student needs arise.

45. Strive to work with and seek advice from the staff in my building.

46. Know all administrative staff in my district and try to keep them informed on appropriate school-related matters.

47. Establish two-way communication with parents through letters, telephone calls, and conferences.

48. Use effective interpersonal skills such as listening, attending, and responding in conducting effective parent-teacher conferences.

49. Have a working knowledge of current Effective Schools research and work within my school to implement the practices.

## Figure 9.8    (Continued)

### Teacher Needs Assessment Questionnaire
### Early Career Teacher Program

**Name:** _____  **Date:** _____

**School Type:** Elem   Middle   High        **School Location:** Rural   Suburban   City

**Gender:** Male   Female        **Number of Years Taught:** _____Years

| Statement Responses: | Your | A | B | C | (A − B + C) | Rank |
|---|---|---|---|---|---|---|
| 1. Professional Reasonability | 1. | | | | | |
| 2. School Responsibility | 2. | | | | | |
| 3. Objective Usage | 3. | | | | | |
| 4. Lesson Plan Construction | 4. | | | | | |
| 5. Instructional Variation | 5. | | | | | |
| 6. Enthusiasm | 6. | | | | | |
| 7. Motivation | 7. | | | | | |
| 8. Verbal Clarity | 8. | | | | | |
| 9. Material Organization | 9. | | | | | |
| 10. Motivational Set | 10. | | | | | |
| 11. Daily Review | 11. | | | | | |
| 12. Direct Instruction | 12. | | | | | |
| 13. Cooperative Learning | 13. | | | | | |
| 14. Adequate Illustration | 14. | | | | | |
| 15. Question Level Variation | 15. | | | | | |
| 16. Question Wait Time | 16. | | | | | |
| 17. Question Techniques | 17. | | | | | |
| 18. Question Correctives | 18. | | | | | |
| 19. Question Distribution | 19. | | | | | |
| 20. Transitions | 20. | | | | | |
| 21. Checks for Understanding | 21 | | | | | |
| 22. Guided Practice | 22. | | | | | |
| 23. Independent Practice | 23. | | | | | |
| 24. Closure | 24. | | | | | |
| 25. Teaching Aids | 25. | | | | | |
| 26. Clear Directions | 26. | | | | | |
| 27. High Time on Task | 27. | | | | | |

**Figure 9.8    (Continued)**

| Statement Responses: | Your | A | B | C | (A − B + C) | Rank |
|---|---|---|---|---|---|---|
| 28. Sponge Activities | 28. | | | | | |
| 29. Room Layout | 29. | | | | | |
| 30. Rules | 30. | | | | | |
| 31. Discipline Hierarchy | 31. | | | | | |
| 32. Positive Reward System | 32. | | | | | |
| 33. Monitoring | 33. | | | | | |
| 34. Physical Safety | 34. | | | | | |
| 35. Established Evaluation System | 35. | | | | | |
| 36. Assignment Feedback | 36. | | | | | |
| 37. Monitoring and Correctives | 37. | | | | | |
| 38. Student/Parent Communication | 38. | | | | | |
| 39. Empathy, Warmth, and Respect | 39. | | | | | |
| 40. Consistent Disposition | 40. | | | | | |
| 41. High Expectation | 41. | | | | | |
| 42. Knowledge of Students | 42. | | | | | |
| 43. Effective Role Model | 43. | | | | | |
| 44. Specialized Services | 44. | | | | | |
| 45. Staff Collegiality | 45. | | | | | |
| 46. Administration Relations | 46. | | | | | |
| 47. Parent relationships | 47. | | | | | |
| 48. Conference Skills | 48. | | | | | |
| 49. Effective Schools Implementation | 49. | | | | | |
| **Means:** | | | | | | |

fessional development, and planning, using a 5-point Likert scale. The formula (A − B + C) provided a need interest score. If a novice teacher thought it was important, didn't do it well, and wanted to improve, the score would be high.

Scores from the fellows on the Mentor Team, during their undergraduate student teaching year were high (3.75–4.8) on an average of 38 of the 49 indicators. They wanted to do well in everything and felt a need to improve in a variety of areas. These scores dropped at the end of the novice teachers' first year of teaching. The average range for these fellows was (3.47–4.25) on an average of 25 of the indicators. As the fellows from the same year were followed, how-ever, those novice teachers that became part of a mentor triad (Year 2, Pattern 3) with responsibility for helping a first year novice teacher transition into the profession showed some differences. As these novice teachers finished the cycle by becoming a pair (Year 3, Pattern 4) with the mentor moving to the position of consultant, they became more focused and self-sufficient. The average range for the novice teachers that were part of a triad was 2.75–3.8, with a mean of 10 indicators listed as focus areas. They demonstrated increased confidence in their teaching, in their ability to find solutions, and in working within profes-sional communities.

For this study, self-efficacy was defined as one's belief in their ability to organize and manage behaviors necessary to produce specific performance (Bandura, 1997). The Teacher Needs Assessment Questionnaire, the Mentor Interactions Log, and the Focus Group Sessions all yielded data to support enhanced feelings of self-efficacy for the novice teachers that participated as part of a triad and were able to assist a new teacher in the transition process.

A third measurement tool that was helpful in structuring the mentoring program design was the Focus Group Sessions. Undergraduate fellows, novice teachers, and mentor teachers were asked to respond to the same set of ques-tions, and data from their responses are summarized below.

*Briefly describe the activities that you have been involved in while participating in the Raytheon Teaching Fellows Program.*

Participants primarily listed the activities that they had attended throughout their involvement in the program. The more "meaningful" activities were con-sistently listed, while others were presumably forgotten. Those individuals that had the highest levels of participation also indicated high levels of value from their interaction in the program. (This became apparent through responses to some of the following prompts.)

*How meaningful do you feel these activities were in contributing to your growth as an effective teacher? Please explain.*

These responses centered around two themes: growth through social inter-actions and collegiality, and growth through enhancing pedagogical skills. All responses, from undergraduate pre-service teachers, novice teachers, and mentor teachers were favorable. Several mentor teachers spoke from both the perspective of what the novice teacher was gaining, as well as from the benefits they were receiving, i.e., "These activities reawakened the need to think about what I am doing in the classroom and why." An additional comment that was seen in the majority of the mentor responses was a reflective statement indicating how help-ful this type of program would have been for them as they entered the profession x-number of years ago.

*How meaningful do you feel these activities were in contributing to your understanding of science or mathematics content? Please explain.*

A summary of the comments in this area indicated very little additional content knowledge was added through the activities and interactions. Content was given meaning and relevance to life enabling fellows to transfer these applications of knowledge to their learning environment. Novice teachers commented that they preferred working with their individual mentor teacher rather than with large group activities to refine skills and understanding of content specific methods.

*What benefits have you experienced from the mentoring program?*

Most of these comments centered around intrinsic values; such as, new friends, support, encouragement, sound advice, a shoulder to cry on, guidance, affirmation of decision to teach, refined reflection, and sharing of resources.

*What elements would you like to see added to enhance the mentoring process?*

All responses were favorable with most indicating that they liked things the way they were. A few participants (from Year 1, Pattern 1) indicated that it would be more helpful to get to know their mentor teacher before the school year began.

*What needs do you have that could be satisfied through resources from this program?*

Most responses were indicative of the following: continuation of training, interactions with others, networking, and additional resources.

*What other comments can you make to enhance the program development?*

A novice teacher's response summarized the thoughts, "The most important part of being a RTF, for me, is that it has validated my desire to become a teacher. It is important to me that my mentor and others in the program believe I can succeed."

The final measurement tool was a rubric developed through Danielson's *Enhancing Professional Practice* (1996) which investigated four levels of performance in the areas of Planning and Preparation, The Classroom Environment, Instruction, and Professional Development. Performance was self-assessed by the novice teacher and also assessed by the mentor teacher. When these data were averaged and compared, there was no statistically significant difference in the self-perceptions of the novice teacher and the perceived perceptions of the mentor teacher. However, the data did indicate that the novice teachers were performing above "Basic" levels in all areas that were measured with higher scores in Classroom Management and Instruction than in Planning and Professional Development (see figure 9.2).

Through the sustained interactions that began as an undergraduate teacher education candidate, the results of these performance assessments indicate that the communication levels between the novice teacher and the mentor teacher were reliable. In summary, the primary findings from this research include the following:

- Frequency of mentor communication varied depending on the program pattern followed by novice teachers.
- The number of novice teacher–initiated communications varied depending on the program pattern followed by novice teachers.
- Teacher Needs Assessment scores varied depending on the program pattern followed by novice teachers.
- Novice teachers participating as part of a mentor triad displayed Teacher Needs Assessment scores that indicated less need in fewer areas when compared with novice teacher mentor pairs.
- Novice teachers participating as part of a mentor triad indicated enhanced feelings of self-efficacy in their teaching abilities.
- Focus group responses indicated the program was meaningful and provided a support system satisfying needs for all participants.
- Performance evaluation scores of novice teachers as assessed by self and by mentor showed statistically no significant differences but indicated that teachers were being successful, performing above "basic" levels of proficiency.
- Retention rates, although still early to indicate conclusive evidence, indicated 100% of the Raytheon Teaching Fellows were still employed in the teaching profession.

## Limitations of the Study

The findings reflect the outcomes for one select, specialized group of science and mathematics students. Without the substantial funding provided through grants, which supported the participants through scholarship and programming, this model may be difficult to replicate. The grants facilitated enriched program opportunities, research possibilities, and focused integrated training in the content disciplines (science and mathematics). These additional resources, coupled with surrounding district needs, strengthened partnerships between the local school district and the university, contributing to the success of the mentoring program.

## Implications and Conclusions

Adding the preliminary mentoring component to the student teaching experience provided opportunities for the student teacher to collaborate with other professionals and engage in shared learning. This moves the primary concern of the student teacher from the dimension of evaluation and performance into the dispositions necessary for a reflective practitioner.

Pairing experienced teachers as mentors for novice teachers can enhance professional development for both the veteran teacher and the novice teacher. But, beginning this relationship with the pre-service teacher candidate proves to be even more valuable. It is the responsibility of the teacher education institution to teach educational theory, model effective instruction, and refine content knowledge. The practicing teacher assigned as the preliminary mentor, however, is able to speak from the trenches regarding the day-to-day challenges teachers confront. Practicing teachers can validate decisions made by the undergraduate teacher candidate in lesson design or classroom management. When the "how" questions are posed by pre-service education students, they can illuminate the theoretical framework as well as model the process of a reflective practitioner.

At professional entry, most novice teachers are not ready to acknowledge their need for a mentor teacher. Many do not have a collaborative, reflective process in place for even utilizing the expertise of a mentor teacher. By establishing the preliminary mentoring relationship as an undergraduate teacher education student, the newly hired novice teacher has already experienced such a process for collaborative interactions with other professionals.

When this relationship is expanded through participation in a triad, or combining triads into learning communities, the support for the novice teacher is increased, multiple perspectives are provided, and feelings of isolation are diminished. Working with a cohort of professionals can increase feelings of satisfaction and validate the use of action research to effectively impact the individual classroom, the school, and the district. This is beneficial to mentor teachers and novice teachers.

When typical novice teachers begin their second year of teaching, they generally have moved from a stage of Survival toward a stage of Proficiency or even Mastery (Wong & Wong, 1998). The mentoring goals now move from the tyranny of the urgent toward refinement of skills and impact on student learning. Collaboration moves beyond the mentor, to other members of the professional community (or learning communities), and extends to other practitioners within the school or the district.

Although the second year novice teacher has successfully moved from the stage of Survival, the first year experiences are still keen, providing an authentic foundation for relating to both the undergraduate teacher candidate and the beginning first year teacher. When a mentor triad is formed with the newly hired first year teacher, and the established mentor pair (composed of the now second year teacher and the mentor teacher), the impact on the second year teacher is significant. The second year teacher is aware of the challenges that the new teacher is confronting, having recently been in that same position and can easily share from their framework of expertise.

As the second year teacher begins taking responsibility for the transition process of the first year novice teacher, the professional growth of the second year teacher is enhanced. The mentor teacher facilitates this development as the self-sufficiency of the second year teacher becomes evident through the mentoring process of the first year novice teacher. Second year teachers working in a triad show increased self-sufficiency earlier in their career when compared to second year teachers who remain in a paired setting as measured by a Teacher Needs Assessment instrument administered to each participant through the various levels of the induction process.

The final stage of this cycle begins when the triad "breaks" and the third year teacher moves into the position of Practicing Mentor Teacher paired with the second year teacher as a mentor pair. The original mentor moves to a position of "consultant" and interacts with the pair through the Mentor Team. The original mentor is now available to begin working with a new undergraduate teacher education candidate.

Enhanced communication, collaboration, and professional development focused on specific needs can encourage retention and empower teacher educators to impact their learning environments. The continuum of growth and development can be seen across multiple levels; (a) as partnerships are encouraged between professionals, the teacher moves from feelings of isolation and hopelessness, to being a change agent who makes teaching meaningful and student learning a measurable by-product, and (b) professionals work together on common needs and positively impact their individual learning environments.

# References

Author Unknown. *Teacher Needs Assessment Questionnaire.*

Bandura, A. (1997). *Self efficacy: The exercise of control.* New York, NY: W. H. Freeman.

Benner, A. D. (2000). *The cost of teacher turnover.* Austin, TX: Texas Center for Educational Research. Retrieved August, 2003, from http://www.sbec.state.tx.us/SBECOnline/txbess/turnoverrpt.pdf.

Charles A. Dana Center. (2002). *Texas beginning educator support system: Report for year three, 2001–02.* Austin, TX: University of Texas. Retrieved February, 2004, from http://www.sbec.state.tx.us/SBECOnline/txbess/evalrpt.asp.

Danielson, C. (1996). *Enhancing professional practice: A framework for teaching.* Alexandria, VA: Association for Supervision and Curriculum Development.

Danielson, C. (1999). Mentoring beginning teachers: The case for mentoring. *Teaching and Change, 6*(3), 251–257.

Fideler, E., & Haseldorn, D. (1999). *Learning the ropes: Urban teacher induction programs and practices in the United States.* Belmont, MA: Recruiting New Teachers.

Fuller, C. (2003). *Beginning teacher retention rates for TxBESS and non-TxBESS teachers.* Report. Austin, TX: State Board for Educator Certification.

Ganser, T. (1999). Joining forces: Mentors help new teachers adjust to school life. *Schools in the Middle, 8*(7), 28–31.

Gold, Y. (1999). Beginning teacher support. In J. Sikula, T. Buttery, & E. Guyton (Eds.), *Handbook of research in teacher education* (2nd ed., pp. 548–594). New York: Macmillan.

Huling-Austin, L. (1992). Research on learning to teach: Implications for teacher induction and mentoring programs. *Journal of Teacher Education, 43*(3), 173–180.

Ingersoll R. M. (2001). Teacher turnover and teacher shortages: An organized analysis. *American Educational Research Journal, 38*(3), 499–534.

Ingersoll, R. M., & Kralik, J. M. (2004). The impact of mentoring on teacher retention: What the research says. *ECS Research Review,* Denver, CO: Education Commission of the States. Retrieved February, 2005 from http://www.ecs.org/clearinghouse/50/36/5036.htm.

National Association of State Boards of Education. (1998). *The numbers game.* Alexandria, VA.

Odell, S. J., & Ferraro, D. P. (1992). Teacher mentoring and teacher retention. *Journal of Teacher Education, 43*(3), 200–204.

Romatowski, J., Dorminey, J., & Voorhees, B. (1989). *Teacher induction programs.* (ERIC Document Reproduction Service No. ED 316 525)

Schlechty, P. C., & Vance, V. (1983). Recruitment, selection and retention: The shape of the teaching force. *Elementary School Journal, 83*(4), 469–487.

Smith, T. M., & Ingersoll, R. M. (2004). What are the effects of induction and mentoring on beginning teacher turnover? *American Educational Research Journal, 41*(3), 681–714.

Strong, M., & Pultorak, E. (2004). *Induction, mentoring and teacher retention: A summary of the research.* Paper presentation at the Association of Teacher Educators of Europe, October, 2004, Agigento, Italy.

Thomas, B., and Kiley, M. A. (1994). *Concerns of beginning middle and secondary school teachers.* (ERIC Document Reproduction Service No. ED 373 033)

Wong, H., & Wong, R. (1998). *How to be an effective teacher: The first days of school.* Mountainview, CA: Harry K. Wong.

Wong, H. (2004) Induction programs that keep new teachers teaching and improving. *NASSP Bulletin, 87*(638), 5–27. Retrieved February, 2005, from http://www.principals.org/publications/bulletin/bltn_0304_wong.cfm.

# CHAPTER 10

# The Perceived Effectiveness of a Graduate Teaching Fellows Program

*D. John McIntyre*
Southern Illinois University–Carbondale

*Lynn C. Smith*
Southern Illinois University–Carbondale

*Sharon L. Gilbert*
Southern Illinois University–Carbondale

*R. Keith Hillkirk*
Pennsylvania State University–Schuylkill

D. John McIntyre is a professor in the Department of Curriculum and Instruction at Southern Illinois University–Carbondale. Major research interests include school partnerships, instructional supervision and teacher education policy.

Lynn C. Smith is an associate professor in the Department of Curriculum and Instruction at Southern Illinois University–Carbondale and the coordinator of the Teaching Fellows Program. Dr. Smith's research interests focus on reading and language studies.

Sharon L. Gilbert is an associate professor in the Department of Curriculum and Instruction at Southern Illinois University–Carbondale and the instructor of the action research component of the Teaching Fellows Program. Her areas of research are in teacher education and second language acquisition.

R. Keith Hillkirk is formerly dean of the College of Education and Human Services at Southern Illinois University–Carbondale and currently chancellor, Pennsylvania State University–Schuylkill.

# ABSTRACT

The Southern Illinois University School Partnership was formally established in 1999 as a key component of the partnership's admission to the Holmes Partnership. Southern Illinois University–Carbondale (SIUC), however, had established its first professional development schools (PDS) with two school districts in 1998. A key component of the PDS is the Teaching Fellows Program that was established as an induction program that would place newly certified elementary teachers as co-teachers in classrooms with trained mentor teachers. The Teaching Fellows taught full-time in the schools for four days a week while pursuing a master's degree from the Department of Curriculum and Instruction. At the early stages of the program, Teaching Fellows focused on literacy through the Reading and Language Arts specialty area. Recently, students have majored in a variety of disciplines. The Teaching Fellows were awarded graduate assistantships in order to provide a stipend and tuition waiver. Since inquiry was a key component of this program, the Teaching Fellows enroll in an Action Research course in the fall and then conduct an action research project in the spring. Data collected from current and former Teaching Fellows as well as from mentor teachers and school administrators revealed perceptions from each of the groups of a highly effective induction program.

Southern Illinois University–Carbondale's Teaching Fellows Program was conceptualized in December of 1998, with the aim of encouraging self-directed professional development among novice and practicing teachers so as to enhance learning opportunities for the large population of at-risk children in one of our local elementary school districts. Within a short period of time, four additional school districts joined the PDS in establishing the Teaching Fellows Program.

The decision to implement the Teaching Fellows Program—a graduate induction program—within our system of Professional Development Schools was based on a number of factors. First, PDSs allowed for a pooling of resources between university faculty, teachers and university teacher candidates all aimed at attaining a common goal (Levine, 2002; Schwartz, 1999). Second, research indicated that the PDS format was more effective in preparing teacher candidates to maintain classroom discipline, use technology effectively and reflect on their teaching than traditional student teaching sites (Neubert, 1998). The Teaching Fellows Program continued the collaborative relationship and simultaneous renewal of an institution of higher education and a local school district(s) that had come to highlight successful partnerships (Bullough, 1998; Darling-Hammond, 1994).

In 1996, Edward and Mary Ducharme argued for research on the value of yearlong internships. To date, very little data exist to shed light on yearlong internships, in general, or Teaching Fellows programs, specifically. Giles, Cramer and Hwang (2001) reported on a study that interviewed graduate Teaching Fellows over a five-year period regarding their greatest concerns as first year teachers. The researchers posited that the Teaching Fellows moved quickly from a self-benefiting concern to one more mature than normal first year teachers. They speculated that one reason for this finding was that the Teaching Fellows were a select group that was screened and selected through a rigorous application process.

The majority of research on yearlong internships focused on the undergraduate level rather than on graduate Teaching Fellows programs. Unfortunately, the data in this area is also sparse. Fischetti, Garrett, Gilbert, Johnson, Larson, Kenealy, Mitchell, Schneider, and Streible (2000) reported that yearlong student teachers believed they became more comfortable with their classroom, became knowledgeable about their teacher's planning and responsibilities, and developed meaningful relationships with their students as a result of being in the classroom for an entire school year. Many cooperating teachers also believed that they benefited from having a yearlong intern in the classroom because of the assistance an additional teacher can provide to the students.

Koehnecke (2001) reported that university faculty and public school teachers and administrators perceived that graduates from yearlong internships were better prepared for teaching and more advanced in their understanding and delivery of integrated educational practices than their peers from the traditional program. In addition, Conaway and Mitchell (2004) reported that yearlong interns in their program were rated more positive than their peers in traditional programs in the areas of instructional responsibilities, behavior management, problem solving, and perceptions of professional support.

On the other hand, Ridley, Hurwitz, Hackett and Miller (2005) reported that although PDS-prepared interns consistently trended toward higher scores than their campus-based counterparts, no significant differences were found in the areas of lesson planning, teaching effectiveness, post-lesson reflection and content retention of professional teaching knowledge. However, during their first year of teaching, PDS-prepared teachers scored significantly higher than campus-prepared teachers on teaching effectiveness. This lack of research regarding the effectiveness of yearlong internships supports the need for additional studies in this area.

# The Teaching Fellows Program

The Teaching Fellows Program provided newly certified teachers with a one- or two-year co-teaching opportunity while taking coursework toward a master's degree. Each year, a select number of highly recommended teacher preparation graduates who had received their initial teaching certification were admitted. After completing an initial screening process, they were interviewed by representatives of our PDS schools (usually principals or curriculum directors, though some teachers are also involved in the process). The goal of the interview was to match the Fellows with particular veteran teachers who had applied to participate and who, generally, had participated in one of a variety of mentoring programs/workshops. The matching process was informal but considered such variables as grade level, content interest and skill, personality, etc. The Fellows were placed with a co-teacher, Mentor Teacher (MT), in one of the five partnership school districts, thus creating a classroom with two certified teachers, one highly qualified and experienced and the other an inductee. The Teaching Fellows (TF) were paid a stipend to co-teach four days per week, and they received tuition waivers enabling them to begin their Master's degree programs. Mentor Teachers also received transferable tuition waivers enabling them or colleagues in their schools to continue or advance their own university studies. These costs were shared by SIUC's College of Education and Human Services (COEHS) and by the PDS partners, each supporting one or more Teaching Fellows.

The relationship between the Teaching Fellow and the Mentor Teacher was crucial for producing a beneficial learning environment in the classroom for all concerned. That relationship had been enhanced at an early stage in the program by the districts' willingness to support a half-day co-planning session for each dyad every two weeks. Rather than forcing the co-teachers to snatch planning time before and after school or during their lunch periods, a structured co-planning session allowed the two to plan ahead, to share concerns about students and the curriculum, and to help each other grow professionally in the process. This was also a time when the Mentor Teacher could acclimate the Fellow to the culture of schools and schooling from "the other side of the desk." The Fellows, Mentors, and administrators, alike, have deemed the co-planning sessions to be invaluable.

## PROGRAM GOALS

Early in the program's development, those involved in setting its goals viewed this as an opportunity to integrate benefits for several different constituents of the education process: pupils in our public schools, recent graduates who are newly certified teachers seeking induction into the teaching profession, and veteran teachers desiring to further their own professional development through a mentoring program. While all those in leadership positions agreed that the bottom line needed to be the beneficial nature of the program for the public school pupils, some felt particular responsibility, especially for the development of the Fellows and, to some degree, for that of their Mentors. The goals of the Holmes Group (1986, 1990) were of particular usefulness to the planning team.

Goals for the Teaching Fellows Program were differentiated among the Fellows, the Mentor Teachers, and the pupils in their classrooms. The goals for each group included:

*Teaching Fellows: enhance the preparation of novice teachers by* (a) obtaining effective mentoring and continued practice in classroom instruction, classroom management, planning, professional interactions both within and without the school; (b) obtaining facility in co-teaching and collaborating with another education professional; (c) learning about and engaging in inquiry through action research; and (d) earning a Master's degree. *Mentor Teachers: enhance the instructional skills of mentor teachers by* (a) mentoring a novice teacher; (b) enhancing their own professional development; and (c) viewing their classroom through a second and different professional lens. *Pupils: enhance P–12 student learning by* (a) engaging in enhanced learning with two certified teachers in the classroom; (b) receiving more immediate assistance when problems arise; and (c) receiving more personalized attention from teachers.

## PROGRAM CURRICULUM

The core curriculum for this program included at least one literacy course, a two-semester practicum, and an action research class. The remainder of the Fellow's coursework depended on the particular graduate program in which they were enrolled. While the first two years of the program saw participants completing one year of co-teaching and then leaving the program for either full-time positions in education or leaving the area and/or the profession entirely, the third full year found two of the Fellows entering their second year in the program. During the fourth year, eight out of seventeen Fellows were in their second year. This year, two returning Fellows were hired for full-time classroom positions by one of the districts, thus preventing their completing a two-year stint, while five others are back for a second year. Those second-year Fellows will complete the Master's degree in either May or August.

## PRACTICUM

Each semester of the first year, Fellows engaged in a multi-purpose practicum experience. Because the Fellows' stipend technically covered only 20 hours per week and because four school days involved a minimum of 32 hours, the practicum contributed a few clock hours to the first-year Fellows' week. Additionally, the Fellows sent the program coordinator a focused weekly reflection, which was read and responded to by the coordinator. Every other week, the Fellows met with the program coordinator in a practicum seminar to share joys and problems, to troubleshoot and vent, or to address particular issues of concern from the previous weeks' experiences. The seminars served, too, as an opportunity to share the delightful discoveries novice teachers made when they learned more about themselves as teachers and about their students as learners.

Both the coordinator and the action research instructor made school visits to monitor the progress of participating dyads and to offer facilitation if needed. Either the Fellow or the Mentor may request those visits, or they may simply involve a routine visit from the two lead instructors in the program. Twice a semester during the second year Fellows joined their newer comrades in a joint seminar. This was one aspect of the program that allowed the second year Fellows to project their leadership stance. Additionally, the Mentor Teachers met together twice a semester to share common concerns and positive experiences. This was especially useful when there were Mentors new to the program who appreciated hearing the veterans' experiences and suggestions.

In order to be chosen as a mentor, teachers must participate in at least one mentor training workshop that lasts for 2–3 days during the summer. These workshops focused on the skills necessary for becoming a competent mentor teacher. These included observation, data collection and conferencing skills, and problem solving strategies as well as knowledge of resources available to novice teachers. The workshop was conducted by Southern Illinois University faculty as well as experienced mentor teachers from the program.

## ACTION RESEARCH

Since the SIUC conceptual framework is based on developing reflective educators, one of the key components of the Teaching Fellows program was an explicit focus on teacher inquiry. Teacher inquiry, in the form of teacher action research, has the potential to develop high reflectivity, substantiate professional development, improve the quality of both teaching and learning, and support professional accountability (Dana & Yendol-Silva, 2003). The action research course helped facilitate one of the goals for fellows: to learn about and engage in inquiry while in the classroom. Other teacher educators have supported the partnership approach of PDSs as being successful in producing reflective, inquiry-oriented teachers (Dana, Gimbert, & Silva, 1999; Dana & Silva, 2001; Koehnecke, 2001).

First year Teaching Fellows attended an inquiry seminar—taught by SIUC faculty—which met approximately every other week during the fall and spring semesters. The focus in the fall was on understanding the theoretical foundations of teacher inquiry, developing researcher's tools, and demonstrating the relationship between reflective teaching and inquiry. Mentor Teachers and second year Teaching Fellows from the various school districts contributed to the seminar through discussions and panel presentations.

During the fall semester Fellows were encouraged to systematically observe themselves, their classrooms, and their students, in order to develop awareness of important meaningful questions about their own professional practices. By the end of the fall semester most Fellows had developed an action research plan that was approved by the Mentor Teacher, the appropriate school district's administration, and SIUC's Institutional Review Board. In the spring semester, Fellows met in a university faculty–led inquiry seminar to discuss difficulties that arose related to implementing the action research plan developed during the fall. They also received assistance with data reduction and analysis.

Inquiries were focused among several domains: *personal improvement,* such as instructional concerns with lesson organization or classroom management issues; *particular classroom concerns,* such as equitable inclusion strategies or attending to English Language Learners; *or curriculum questions revolving around student achievement,* for example, differentiating subject matter instruction. The Teaching Fellows presented their inquiries at an annual Action Research Symposium attended by SIUC faculty, school district Mentor Teachers, SIUC and school district administrators, former and future teaching fellows, and groups of students in other campus courses who were attempting similar inquiry efforts. Several Fellows have presented their research and results at both state and national conferences.

# Methods/Procedures

The Teaching Fellows Program has been evaluated on a yearly basis since its inception in 1999. However, during the first four years of the program, the assessment system was informal and anecdotal data gathered at annual spring retreats was utilized to assess its perceived effectiveness. At the conclusion of each academic year, the Southern Illinois School University Partnership sponsored a retreat that included SIUC faculty and public school partner administrators and mentor teachers. The purpose of the retreat was to jointly examine and assess partnership activities with a special focus on the Teaching Fellows Program.

Remarks made during the first four years of the Teaching Fellows Program were positive. Mentor teachers commented that there were definite advantages of having two certified teachers co-teaching and co-planning in a classroom. One kindergarten teacher stated, "With two of us in the classroom, I no longer have discipline problems. As a result, my students are more focused and I am certain my students' reading scores are improving." Teachers also supported the importance of the mentoring workshops as a vehicle for preparing them to work with a teaching fellow.

Program revisions were also the result of these retreats. For example, it was decided to permit a Teaching Fellow to return for a second year if they chose to do so. In addition, candidate interviews were changed to the end of the spring semester rather than during the summer to enable earlier decisions about who to admit and to facilitate a better mentor-teaching fellow match.

During the program's fifth year, the PDS Advisory Council determined that it was important to begin collecting quantifiable data in order to assess the effectiveness of the Teaching Fellows Program. The purpose of this study, which was to examine the perceived effect of a graduate teaching fellows program on K–8 students as well as novice and experienced teachers, evolved from this decision. The Advisory Council was interested in learning if the academic achievement of these students was enhanced as a result of the Teaching Fellows Program. The Council also was interested in whether or not the program had helped to improve the instructional skills of both teaching fellows and mentor teachers.

The members of the advisory council jointly developed four different questionnaires that were specific to the groups being assessed. These groups were current Teaching Fellows, former Teaching Fellows, mentor teachers and school administrators. The goals of the PDS and the Teaching Fellows Program were the focal points for the design of the questionnaires. Each questionnaire went through several modifications until approved by the PDS Advisory Council. Subjects were asked to respond to a statement utilizing a Likert Scale with 5 representing "strongly agree" and 1 representing "strongly disagree." In addition, a section for comments also was included on each questionnaire.

Questionnaires were mailed to current and former teaching fellows, mentor teachers and school administrators. Twelve of the sixteen current Teaching Fellows responded to the survey. All twelve of the administrators who received questionnaires returned them to the researchers. Sixteen of the 24 current or former mentor teachers participated in this study. Unfortunately only six former Teaching Fellows returned questionnaires. Finding current addresses of those who moved out of the area proved difficult. The research questions that were posed for this study were:

1. What are the perceptions of mentor teachers and school administrators regarding the effect of the Teaching Fellows Program on K–12 student learning?
2. What are the perceptions of current and former Teaching Fellows regarding the ability of the Teaching Fellows Program to improve their preparation as a teacher?
3. What are the perceptions of mentor teachers regarding the ability of the Teaching Fellows Program to improve their instructional skills?
4. What are the perceptions of current and former Teaching Fellows regarding the ability of the Teaching Fellows Program to enhance their practice of inquiry?

Mean scores were used to analyze the ratings of each question as it pertained to the goals of the program. Respondents could respond to questions using a five-point scale with "5" being the highest rating for any question.

There were limitations to the study, however. Although the questionnaire was piloted with the Advisory Council, reliability and validity measures were not determined. In addition, the small sample size, especially among former teaching fellows, makes it more difficult to generalize to other settings. However, the strength of the ratings combined with the participants' comments as well as the researchers' five-year experience with the Teaching Fellows Program contributes to our confidence in the study's findings.

# Findings

The following section reports data collected from the questionnaires. The data are reported for each of the four research questions and include pertinent comments from the questionnaires.

## RESEARCH QUESTION 1

What are the perceptions of mentor teachers and school administrators regarding the effect of the Teaching Fellows Program on K–12 student learning? The data in table 10.1 indicate that mentor teachers (4.75/5.00) and school adminis-trators (4.58/5.00) perceived that the inclusion of Teaching Fellows in the class-room enhanced student learning. In addition, the respondents believed that the K–12 students receive more individual attention through the Teaching Fellows Program. Mentor teachers rated this at 4.81 while school administrators rated this at 4.50. One of the building administrators perhaps summed it up best when stating, "This program supports so many of the needs of our students; needs that likely would be unmet if not for the Teaching Fellows Program. Our teachers grow in a way similar to the growth experienced by the teaching fellow. We are very well pleased."

Discussions with mentor teachers and school administrators made it clear to the researchers that there was a strong belief that student achievement—especially in the area of reading—was enhanced with the addition of a teaching fellow to the classroom. Unfortunately, quantifiable data do not yet exist that would support or not support this assumption. Research is currently being con-ducted to address this question.

## RESEARCH QUESTION 2

What are the perceptions of current and former Teaching Fellows regarding the ability of the Teaching Fellows Program to improve their preparation as a teacher? Table 10.2 indicates that both current and former Teaching Fellows believe that participation in the program has not only helped them to become better teachers but also provided them with more confidence to begin their teaching career than when they completed their certification program. Current teaching fellows responded to the statement regarding their teaching abilities at

**Table 10.1  Perception of Effect of Teaching Fellows Program on Student Learning**

|  | MT N= 16 Mean | ADM N= 12 Mean |
|---|---|---|
| I believe having a Teaching Fellow in the classroom has enhanced student learning. | 4.75 | 4.58 |
| I believe my classroom/our school has benefited from having a Teaching Fellow in the classroom | 4.81 | 4.50 |
| My/Our students received more individual attention as a result of having Teaching Fellows in my/the classroom. | 4.81 | 4.67 |

Note: MT = mentor teachers; ADM = administrators

**Table 10.2    Perception of Effect of Teaching Fellows Program on Novice Teachers**

|  | CTF N= 16 Mean | FTF N= 6 Mean |
|---|---|---|
| The Teaching Fellows Program has helped me become a better teacher. | 4.58 | 4.83 |
| I feel more confident in my abilities to begin my career as a result of the Teaching Fellows Program. | 4.50 | 4.33 |

Note: CTF = current teaching fellows; FTF = former teaching fellows

4.58 while former teaching fellows were at 4.83. In the area of becoming more confident as a result of being in the teaching fellows program, current teaching fellows responded with a mean score of 4.50 while former teaching fellows were at 4.33.

Some of the current Teaching Fellows offered the following comments. One of the students stated, "I love this program, and I think this should be a requirement before one is given his/her own classroom. If offered a job next fall, I would probably still opt to stay in the program." Another student replied, "I truly believe this program will benefit all. If it were required to participate in this program before getting your first job, all teachers would be much better prepared for the teaching world. Everyone should do whatever they can to save and continue this program." Finally, a Teaching Fellow commented that, "Overall, I feel this program is helping me become a better teacher. It offers me the experience of a classroom with the expertise of a mentor teacher. I feel that all students should have the experience of being in the classroom all day for a year."

A former Teaching Fellow stated, "I was confident in my abilities prior to the PDS program; however, I did gain more confidence during my fellowship. I feel very fortunate to have participated in the PDS program." Another commented, "This was a wonderful program. I was not prepared to teach after receiving my certificate. After the TF program I was more confident about myself and teaching."

As a result of these data, it is clear that both current and former teaching fellows perceive that participation in the Teaching Fellows program helped them become better teachers and that their confidence in their ability as teachers was enhanced by the additional experiences they received during the Teaching Fellows Program.

## RESEARCH QUESTION 3

What are the perceptions of mentor teachers regarding the ability of the Teaching Fellows Program to improve their instructional skills? Table 3 indicates that mentor teachers believe that participation in the Teaching Fellows Program has improved their instructional skills. A score of 4.50 indicates that mentor teachers attempt new instructional methods and/or strategies as a result of having participated in the program. Presumably, mentor teachers were being exposed to new ideas and instructional strategies by having a Teaching Fellow as a co-teacher. In addition, they stated that they had grown professionally by participating in the program (4.56). Mentor teachers met periodically to discuss issues and ideas and were also given opportunities to attend national conferences such as the Holmes Partnership and the Association of Teacher Educators.

Some of the mentor teachers contributed the following comments regarding the effect of participating in the Teaching Fellows Program on their instructional skills and professionalism. One mentor teacher stated, "Thank you for the opportunity. Special education can sometimes be overlooked in some projects. Having a teaching fellow not only benefited instruction within the pull-out environment, but it also enabled us to try some inclusion strategies that were not possible with just one teacher." A second teacher stated, "Having a teaching fellow allowed me time to reflect on my own teaching style and gave me someone to bounce ideas off of or to determine how they felt about them." A third mentor teacher replied, "Besides the above (referring to the questionnaire), the teaching fellow helped me (a) organize and integrate information, (b) get involved with action research, (c) use technology more, (d) improve classroom behavior (individual monitoring of behavior), (e) engage in professional development that improves teaching, (f) discuss relevant research and (g) analyze ourselves as teachers." Finally, perhaps this mentor teacher summed it up best, "Having a teaching fellow has put the excitement back into teaching!"

One of the goals of the Teaching Fellows Program was that the mentor

**Table 10.3   Perceptions of Mentor Teachers on the Effect of the Teaching Fellows Program on their Instructional Skills**

|  | Mean N= 16 |
|---|---|
| I have grown professionally as a result of having participated in the Teaching Fellows Program | 4.56/5.00 |
| I have attempted new teaching methods/strategies in the classroom as a result of having a Teaching Fellow in the classroom. | 4.50/5.00 |

teachers would also benefit professionally and instructionally through their participation with the Teaching Fellows. The data and comments do indicate that the mentor teachers believe that they also reap the benefits from the Teaching Fellows Program.

## RESEARCH QUESTION 4

What are the perceptions of current and former Teaching Fellows regarding the ability of the Teaching Fellows Program to enhance their practice of inquiry? Both Teaching Fellows (4.25) and Former Teaching Fellows (4.33) reported that the Teaching Fellows Program helped them learn how to reflect upon their teaching (table 10.4). Other data regarding inquiry were related to the effect of the action research course and project. Although the results were positive they were not as positive as the data concerning the teaching/learning process. On a scale of 5.00, the Teaching Fellows responded with a mean score of 4.08 to the statement "Through the Action Research course, I have learned/am learning how to use inquiry to improve my classroom practice," Former Teaching Fellows responded with a mean score of 3.33 to, "I continue to use inquiry to improve my classroom practice." One former Teaching Fellow commented, "I was confident in my abilities prior to the PDS program; however, I did gain more confidence during my fellowship. I learned the importance of reflection during my course work. I feel very fortunate to have participated in the PDS program."

Teaching Fellows respond to, "The Action Research project has helped me

**Table 10.4    Perceptions of Effect of Teaching Fellows Program to Facilitate Teacher Inquiry**

|  | CTF<br>N= 16<br>Mean | FTF<br>N= 6<br>Mean |
|---|---|---|
| The Teaching Fellows Program, has helped me learn how to reflect upon my own teaching. | 4.33 | 4.25 |
| The Action Research course has helped learn to use inquiry to improve my classroom practice. | 4.08 | 4.00 |
| The Action Research project has helped me to analyze classroom behavior and student learning in new ways. | 3.92 | 3.33 |

Note: CTE = current teaching fellows; FTF = former teaching fellows to analyze classroom behavior and student learning in new ways," with a mean of 3.92/5.00. On the other hand, the former Teaching Fellows responded to the same statement with a mean of 4.00/5/00. Of the six former Teaching Fellows who responded, 50% (3/6) continue to utilize action research in their classrooms. We believe that these lower responses are the result of action research being tied to a course and not—at least in the minds of the Teaching Fellows—as directly related to the teaching/learning process of the classroom. Although the number of responding former Teaching Fellows is small, it is important that 3 of the 6 respondents continue to conduct action research in their classrooms.

# Implications and Conclusions

Since the majority of Teaching Fellows programs—or similar type programs—are at the undergraduate level (Dana & Silva, 2001; Giles, Cramer, & Hwang, 2001; Koehnecke, 2001; Neubert, 1998), the Southern Illinois School University Partnership's Teaching Fellows Program has great potential for serving as a model for similar induction programs at the graduate level. The research emerging from the program will assist other programs in gaining insights for how collaborative partnerships can produce positive effects on novice and experienced teachers as well as P–12 students.

More specifically, this model has the potential for providing the profession with valuable information as to how to effectively induct novice teachers into the realm of teaching. Future research needs to examine the teaching effectiveness of Teaching Fellows that participated in a one or two-year induction program as a Fellow compared to teachers who did not have a similar opportunity. The data also can provide information on the effectiveness of trained mentors on the induction of newly certified teachers.

In addition, the program's emphasis on inquiry and its impact on novice teachers seem to play a positive role in the development of the Teaching Fellows' classroom disposition and approach to instruction. Both current and former Teaching Fellows indicate that they have learned how to reflect upon their teaching, learned how to use inquiry to improve classroom practice, and learned how to analyze classroom behavior and student learning in new ways. Much of this, of course, is due to their involvement in the action research component of the program. However, inquiry also permeates the students' journals as well as the regular meeting with program coordinators and mentors. Given the emphasis on inquiry during this induction phase, it would be useful to gather data that would ascertain whether or not these Teaching Fellows develop classroom environments that are conducive to an inquiry-oriented approach and if they continue to use action research beyond this program.

It is clear that all involved in the Teaching Fellows Program hold it in high esteem and are convinced of its merits for improving P–12 student learning as well as improving the teaching effectiveness of new and experienced teachers. Perhaps a former Teaching Fellow sums it up best.

> It seems to me that this program's success is rooted in a successful "fit" of the mentor and fellow. There are many variables that must be considered such as work ethic, styles, and philosophies. This experience provided NOTHING but positives for me and I share that often. It was more than teaching; it was team building! I spent a great deal of my energy on my working relationship w/my mentor. That experience paid off for me because everything I've done since then has always involved collaboration and team planning w/my peers. Having that year was a great asset! Thanks to that fellowship year, I had 22 hours completed toward my masters. Under regular circumstances, that would not have been feasible at all and my MS was done in 3 years. Thank you for that marvelous opportunity to serve as a teaching fellow; hopefully it will allow me to serve as a mentor soon.

Future research will examine student test scores and will make comparisons to control groups in an attempt to find statistically significant differences. In addition, it is important to note that an undergraduate version of the Teaching Fellows program is currently being piloted with elementary education majors in the final two semesters of their education program. However, all initial data indicate that the Teaching Fellows Program is an effective program that meets or exceeds its original goals.

# References

Bullough, S. (1998). Professional development schools: Catalysts for collaboration and change. *Clearing House, 72*(1), 47–50.

Conaway, B. J., & Mitchell, M. W. (2004). A comparison of the experiences of yearlong interns in a professional development school and one-semester student teachers in a non-PDS location. *Action in Teacher Education, 26*(3), 21–28.

Dana, N. F., Gimbert, B., & Silva, D. Y. (1999). Teacher inquiry: Staff development for the 21st century. *Pennsylvania Educational Leadership, 18*(2), 6–12.

Dana, N. F., & Silva, D. Y. (2001). Building an inquiry oriented PDS: The journey toward making inquiry a central part of mentor teacher work. In I. Guadarrama, J. Nath, & J. Ramsey (Eds.), *Research in Professional Development Schools.* Greenwich, CT: Information Age.

Dana, N., & Yendol-Silva, D. (2003). *The reflective educator's guide to classroom research: Learning to teach and teaching to learn through practitioner inquiry.* Thousand Oaks, CA: Corwin Press.

Darling-Hammond, L. (1994). *Professional development schools: Schools for developing a profession*. New York: Teachers College Press.

Ducharme, E. R., & Ducharme, M. K. (1996). Needed research in teacher education. In J. Sikula (Ed). *Handbook of research in teacher education*. (2nd ed., pp. 1030–1046). New York, NY: Macmillan.

Fischetti, J., Garrett, L., Gilbert, J., Johnson, S., Larson, A., Kenealy, A., Mitchell, B., Schneider, E., & Streible, J. (2000). This just makes sense: Yearlong experience in a high school professional development school. *Peabody Journal of Education, 73*(3&4), 310–318.

Giles, C., Cramer, M. M., & Hwang, S. K. (2001). Beginning teacher perceptions of concerns: A longitudinal look at teacher development. *Action in Teacher Education, 23*(3), 89–98.

Holmes Group. (1986). *Tomorrow's teachers: A report of the Holmes Group*. East Lansing, MI: Author.

Holmes Group. (1990). *Tomorrow's schools: Principles for the design of professional development schools*. East Lansing, MI: Author.

Koehnecke, D. (2001). Professional development schools provide effective theory and practice. *Education, 121*(3), 589–91.

Levine, M. (2002). Why invest in professional development schools? *Educational Leadership, 59*(6), 65–68.

Neubert, G. (1998). Professional development schools—the proof is in the performance. *Educational Leadership, 55*(5), 44–46.

Ridley, D. S., Hurwitz, S., Hackett, M. R. D., & Miller, K. K. (2005). Comparing PDS and campus-based preservice teacher preparation: Is PDS-based preparation really better? *Journal of Teacher Education, 56*(1), 46–56.

Schwartz, F. (1999). Milestone or millstone. *Education Week, 18*(40), 41–42.

Chapter 11

# Selecting and Training Mentors
## PRACTICES AND FEATURES IN MENTOR TRAINING PROGRAMS ACROSS VIRGINIA

*Michelle Hughes*
James Madison University

Michelle Hughes, Ph.D., is an assistant professor in early childhood/elementary education at James Madison University, Harrisonburg, Virginia. She spent 14 years in the classroom and six years as a staff developer before earning her doctorate in curriculum and instruction. She continues to seek ways to support and mentor beginning teachers.

## ABSTRACT

This study determined the extent to which research-based practices were evident in the mandated mentor teacher programs across Virginia. A survey was developed that incorporated common features and practices advocated in previous research and identified in the Virginia *Guidelines for Mentor Teacher Programs for Beginning and Experienced Teachers*. The survey return rate was 90 percent. In addition, school officials from a small sample of school divisions were interviewed to identify implementation procedures, obstacles, and solutions to those obstacles. Data were analyzed using descriptive statistics with the interview data offering narrative support. Selection of mentors was based primarily on informal criteria across the Commonwealth; discrepancies between school division practices and research-based best practice were found. Inconsistencies emerged between the training mentors received and the duties to which they were assigned. Implications are drawn and suggestions given for refining mentor selection and mentor training.

Mentoring is by no means a new concept in the teaching profession. How to support beginning teachers has been discussed since Frances Fuller's conclusion

259

that beginning teachers have particular needs different from veteran teachers (1969). Mentoring has often been touted as a way to provide that support. In a mentor teacher program, an experienced teacher is assigned to a new teacher. Some define mentoring as "a formalized relationship between a beginning teacher and a master teacher (mentor) that provides support and assesses teaching skills" (Education Commission of the States, 1999). The roles and responsibilities undertaken by the mentor vary from program to program. In all cases, however, it is the mentors who can play an essential role in helping the beginning teacher make the transition to the profession. It would seem important, then, that selection and training of mentors receive appropriate attention within a school division.

This mentor teacher study is designed to gather data pertaining to mentor teacher programs across Virginia. The Commonwealth of Virginia has mandated such programs and the study captures what school divisions are doing that mirror research-based best practice and the Commonwealth's mandates. The purpose of this article is to report a portion of the findings from a state-wide study of mentor teacher program features and practices across the Commonwealth of Virginia. The alignment of school divisions' mentor teacher programs with the Virginia regulations and research-based best practices will be presented along with discrepancies between the divisions' reported practice and the research and state regulations. Implications relative to mentor selection and training will be discussed.

# Background

The Commonwealth of Virginia has a rich history of assisting beginning teachers. Starting with their Beginning Teacher Assistance Program in 1985, it was recognized that novice teachers needed additional support if they were to be successful in the classroom. Soon state-funded pilot mentor teacher programs tried to identify the mechanisms that would be most effective in supporting novice teachers as they developed their professional skills. Pilot programs continued until 1998 when the Commonwealth determined they had enough data to champion change.

In 1999 the Commonwealth of Virginia legislated mentoring. Each beginning teacher would be assigned a mentor. These individuals were to be "specially trained public school teachers" who would provide "assistance and professional support" (Virginia Legislature, 1999). The legislation identified the qualifications for the mentors. Mentors had to "be classroom teachers who had achieved continuing contract status and who worked in the same building as the teachers they were assisting or be instructional personnel who were assigned solely as mentors . . ." (Virginia Legislature, 1999). In addition, the legislation required that the Board [of Education] establish criteria for "training of mentor teachers" (Virginia Legislature, 1999).

The *Guidelines for Mentor Teacher Programs for Beginning and Experienced Teachers* was adopted by the Virginia Board of Education on June 22, 2000, to meet the legislative requirement (Virginia Department of Education, 2000). This document outlined the features and practices that should be present in mentor teacher programs. School divisions had latitude in interpreting some features and practices; however, many were mandated. The content of the required mentor training was one area well defined by the *Guidelines*. Four specific training areas were identified. Training was to include the Virginia *Guidelines for Uniform Performance Standards and Evaluation Criteria for Teachers, Administrators, and Superintendents*, formative assessment, developing personal professional development plans, and providing individualized assistance. The structure and format of the training was left to the discretion of the local school divisions; however, suggestions for the length of training and its scheduling were given. Many of the decisions affecting the Virginia mandates were founded on previous mentoring research. Mentor selection and training required in the *Guidelines* were two components that were well supported by previous research.

# Previous Research

## MENTOR SELECTION

Careful selection of veteran teachers to act as mentors is suggested in a number of studies (DeBolt, 1989; Feiman-Nemser & Parker, 1992; Houston, 1990; Huffman & Leak, 1986; Tillman, 2000). Moir (2003) cited interpersonal skills, professional skills, and excellent communication skills as necessary for success as a mentor. As researchers were attempting to identify features and practices of effective mentor teacher programs, they often turned to the perceptions of new teachers who had worked with mentors. Certain interactions between beginning teachers and their mentors and their mentors' personal characteristics seemed to influence feelings of satisfaction.

Feiman-Nemser and Parker (1992) used a system of classification to label the roles teachers assumed as they worked as mentors. *Local guides* defined mentors who supported beginning teachers as they learned the policies and procedures of the school. Mentors helped the beginning teachers learn how the school division and their building operated. Beginning teachers reported specific ways in which their mentors helped. New teachers stated that mentors who shared ideas and materials, provided information about policies and procedures, and helped them gain an understanding of the school and its staff, were effective in their roles (DeBolt, 1989; Feiman-Nemser & Parker; Houston, 1990; Huffman & Leak, 1986).

Additionally, beginning teachers reported that mentors who moved the conversations from procedural issues to conversations about teaching and learning were helpful (DeBolt, 1989; Feiman-Nemser & Parker, 1992; Houston, 1990; Huffman & Leak, 1986; Wildman, Magliaro, Niles, & Niles, 1992). This type of mentoring, an *educational companion*, helped new teachers reflect on their performance and decisions so that improved student learning was the outcome (Feiman-Nemser & Parker). As educational companions, the mentors asked questions, guided the development of teaching strategies, observed the beginning teachers, and offered feedback to them. Again, mentors exhibiting these behaviors were deemed helpful by beginning teachers.

While the role the mentors played was important, the mentors' personal characteristics contributed to the beginning teachers' feeling of success. Several studies concluded that emotional support, willingness to participate, sincerity, confidentiality, approachability, and being a good listener were essential personal characteristics that mentors should possess (DeBolt, 1989; Feiman-Nemser & Parker, 1992; Ganser, 1999; Houston, 1990; Huffman & Leak, 1986; Odell, 1986; Wildman et al., 1992).

## MENTOR TRAINING

Just as important as the selection of quality mentors was the issue of training veteran teachers to be mentors. Working with adults was different from working with children; mentors needed to be trained in the new responsibilities they would be asked to assume. Conclusions from several studies supported the need for training mentors. Teachers who received formal mentor training seemed to help beginning teachers develop classroom routines, manage instruction better, and gain a higher level of student cooperation (Evertson & Smithey, 2000). One longitudinal study from the National Center for Research on Teacher Learning concluded that "Mentors need time to mentor and opportunities to learn to mentor" (2001, p. 8). Furthermore, mentors needed to exhibit skills not necessarily used when working with children: identifying effective instructional practices, subject-matter discussions, and providing feedback on instruction (Andrews & Martin, 2003; Ganser, 1999, 2001; Houston, 1990; Huling-Austin, 1992; Odell, 1986; Odell & Ferraro, 1992; Southwest Educational Development Laboratory, 2002). Being skilled in these areas enhanced the mentors' effectiveness.

Recognizing that school divisions across Virginia were designing and implementing mentor teacher programs, how were mentors being selected? What training were they receiving? A state-wide study was designed to ascertain the answers to these and other questions about the features and practices of mentor teacher programs across Virginia.

# Methods and Technique

The study, conducted in 2002, was composed of two parts: a survey and a small number of interviews. Surveys were sent to 131 of the 132 public school divisions in the Commonwealth of Virginia; one division participated in a pilot survey and was excluded from the final survey. Interviews with personnel from six school divisions that represented the school size variation within the Commonwealth were conducted. The survey was designed to elicit general information about the features and practices of the school divisions' mentor teacher programs. The interviews were intended to shed more light on how the divisions designed and implemented their mentor teacher programs.

Using characteristics and features identified in previous research on mentor teacher programs and those required in the *Guidelines for Mentor Teacher Programs for Beginning and Experienced Teachers*, the principal researcher developed a survey to send to the Virginia school divisions. A modified pilot process suggested by Dillman (1978) when working with small populations was followed. Categories within the survey included mentor teacher program goals, design features, mentor selection and training/responsibilities, and program evaluation. Respondents indicated the presence and absence of features and practices within these categories. Individuals who completed the survey were identified by their central office personnel as having responsibility for the mentor teacher program. Respondents indicated their position on the last question on the survey; they chose superintendent, assistant superintendent, building level principal, assistant principal, professional development, administrator in charge of the mentoring program, teacher, or other. The surveys were sent via the U.S. Postal system and self-addressed stamped envelopes were included for the return of the surveys. Responses were anonymous. The return rate was 90 percent; 118 completed surveys were returned.

The interview questions were designed to elicit a rich description of the methods employed to design and implement the mentor teacher programs, the obstacles encountered, and the challenges yet to overcome. Twenty guiding questions were developed to probe how school divisions structured their programs, supported their mentors, involved administrators in the program, dealt with challenges, and evaluated their programs. Interview participants were identified from a pool of school divisions that had participated in the earlier mentor teacher pilot programs sponsored by the Virginia Department of Education. Six divisions were chosen to represent the size diversity across Virginia: two small, two medium, and two large school divisions. In each case, the person interviewed was a central-office administrator who had direct responsibility for the mentor teacher program; no one was a building-level administrator. The interviews were slated to last no more than one hour; all but one interview ended within the timeframe. The interviews were audio-taped and later transcribed for analysis.

Quantitative data were reduced by coding responses and entering them into a statistical software program. Data were reported as percentages of school divisions' personnel responding to particular items. At the time of the survey, Virginia school divisions were assigned to eight regional education centers. Data were analyzed twice: as a whole to determine the overall presence or absence of features and by regional centers to determine if differences among centers existed.

The information gathered from the interviews was transcribed and then grouped into categories representing the questions asked: design development, mentor selection and training, evaluation, obstacles and challenges, solutions, and advice for other divisions. Quotes from the interview data were used to support and illustrate features and practices identified in the survey data. In addition, frequencies of responses and patterns related to size were reported. From interview data, common design and implementation methods, obstacles, and solutions were noted.

# Results/Conclusions

## MENTOR SELECTION

Based on previous studies that identified particular characteristics and the Virginia requirements for mentors, survey respondents were asked to identify selection criteria that were used in their school divisions to make choices in deciding which teachers were selected as mentors. They checked one of three selection options: formal criteria, informal criteria, or not a consideration. Formal criteria were defined as selection criteria that were written and shared with teachers interested in becoming mentors. Formal criteria were characteristics made public that would be used to select candidates. Informal criteria were those criteria that the selection committee or person used to distinguish between candidates, but were not written and were not a matter of public record. The final way in which respondents identified criteria was to leave an item blank to indicate that the criterion was not considered when selecting mentors (table 11.1).

It was interesting to note that, except in the cases of principal recommendation and number of years of experience, informal criteria were used more frequently than formal criteria. Mentor selection seemed to be based on criteria not publicly known to those wishing to be mentors. One could speculate about the consistent application of "informal" selection criteria across mentor candidates.

The principal's role in selecting the mentors was evident also in the interviews conducted with the six school divisions. As one school official said during the interview, "It's at the discretion of the principal to decide who the mentor will be." Another school official explained that "we send a memo out to principals and we say, 'Okay, these are the qualities you will need to be looking for in certain teachers that would make good mentors or whatever.' But really . . . they [the principals] know the teachers better than we do." Principals carry the authority to make decisions about who is a mentor in 98 percent of the school divisions responding to the survey.

Of further interest was the percentage of respondents who indicated that "at least three years of teaching experience" was not a consideration in selecting

Table 11.1   Percentage of Respondents Identifying Type of Mentor Selection Criteria Used

| Criterion | Formal | Informal | No consideration |
|---|---|---|---|
| Proficient or outstanding performance as a teacher | 42 | 48 | 2 |
| Recognition by peers as one who maintains positive relationships | 18 | 56 | 20 |
| Recommendation of the principal | 59 | 34 | 1 |
| At least three years teaching experience | 59 | 21 | 14 |
| Knowledge of beginning teacher development | 15 | 46 | 33 |
| Willingness to participate | 37 | 51 | 6 |
| Knowledge of formative evaluations | 19 | 38 | 37 |
| Ability to communicate effectively | 31 | 57 | 7 |
| Willingness to share ideas and materials | 30 | 56 | 9 |
| Ability to collaborate effectively | 23 | 59 | 13 |
| Commitment to one's own professional growth | 32 | 49 | 13 |

Note: Seven surveys indicated that this question was not answered; these missing data account for the sums not equal to 100%.

mentors. This was in light of the Virginia Department of Education require-ment that mentors be teachers "who have achieved continuing contract status" (*Guidelines*, 2000, p. 5); this status was granted after three years of successful classroom teaching. Over one-third of the school divisions indicated that they used "years of experience" only informally or not at all.

Two criteria had rather high marks for "not a consideration" when selecting mentors in Virginia. Twenty percent of the respondents indicated that "peer recognition for having positive relationships" was not a factor in choosing men-tors. Research, however, supported the concept of a positive mentor-new teacher dyad enhancing a successful relationship (Southwest Educational Development Laboratory, 2002). In addition, "ability to collaborate effectively" was a neces-sary characteristic if the mentor was to assist the new teacher in instructional matters. This criterion was not used in selecting mentors in 13 percent of the school divisions. Furthermore, while not a high percentage (6%), it was surpris-ing that "willingness to participate" was not a consideration for selecting men-tors in some school divisions. Determining the teacher's interest in being a mentor was a research-based criterion for selection.

## TRAINING AND RESPONSIBILITIES

> I think the training part is essential . . . you just can't say, "Oh,
> you're going to be a mentor" and hand them the notebook and say,
> "Go do it." You have to have some grounding; you have to have
> some basis for what you're doing and the philosophy has to be there.
> They [the mentors] have to know the objectives of the whole pro-
> gram and why they're doing what they're doing. That's extremely
> important . . . (School official from a small, rural division)

The Virginia legislation articulating the parameters of mentor teacher programs stated that such programs use "specially trained public school teachers as men-tors" (*Guidelines*, 2000, p. 5). According to the responses to the survey regarding the training of mentors, less than three-quarters of the school divisions required teachers to be trained as mentors. Furthermore, mentor training occurred prior to mentors assuming their responsibilities in only 70 percent of the school divi-sions for which surveys were returned. For the remaining school divisions that trained their mentors, mentors received their training after their relationships with the beginning teachers had started.

The content of the mentor training was diverse across the school divisions as well. When asked about the topics in which mentors were trained, several clusters emerged. These topics were grouped by: knowledge of the responsibilities assigned to participants and system's information (figure 11.1), personal needs and establishing relationships (figure 11.2), and required Virginia Department of Education material (figure 11.3). Overall, the most reported training issues focused on understanding new teachers and expectations of school divisions as mentors assisted the new teachers in the transition to the profession. The survey design did not allow respondents to explain specific objectives within the broad survey training topics, nor to indicate the instructional methods used in training the mentors. The *Guidelines* suggested that training last for one-half day to two days. The least number of training topics identified by any one school division that provided training was 11; the most number of topics was 23. Given the training time suggested in the *Guidelines*, it seemed plausible to conclude that, for many school divisions, the most widely used instructional strategy for training mentors was primarily lecture.

The "needs of beginning teachers" was a topic that many (72 percent) school personnel identified as a component of their training for mentors. Information on how adults learn was included in training in fewer than 38% of the school divisions. While mentors learned what new teachers need, they learned infrequently how best to teach them—as adult learners. Teachers who work effectively with children do not necessarily teach adults well. Many of the skills for teaching adults are different from those needed for teaching children (Cave, LaMaster, & White, 1997; Kelly, n.d.; Online Learning, 2000). In Virginia,

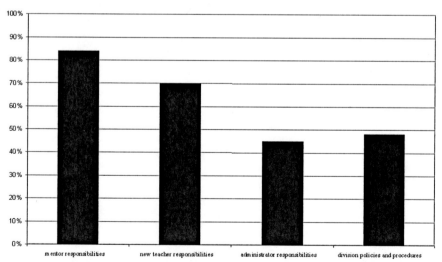

**Figure 11.1   Percentage of Respondents Indicating Training in Responsibilities and Systems Information**

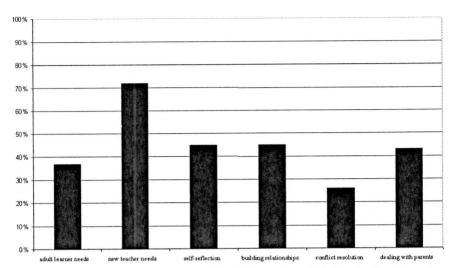

**Figure 11.2   Percentage of Respondents Indicating Training in New Teacher Needs and Establishing Relationships**

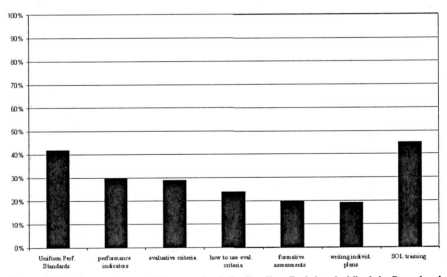

**Figure 11.3   Percentage of Respondents Indicating Training in Virginia Required Topics**

deliberate attempts to teach mentors how to teach adults was not evident in the training provided to mentors; it was, however, recognized by some school officials as critical.

> Just because you're an experienced teacher does not mean that you are automatically a good mentor. An experienced teacher could be a novice mentor and a lot of research also indicates that there's a set of skills for mentoring . . .

> I'm a big believer that you just can't throw a veteran in and say, "You're a mentor" because of some of the heartaches we've experienced . . . not all mentors know how to work with adults and that adult learning piece that we provide in the mentor training . . . is essential.

A final observation regarding the training topic data in general was that almost 70 percent of the respondents indicated that mentors were trained in providing feedback. The complementary training component of observation skills was presented in less than 50 percent of the training programs. This was a curious discrepancy given that feedback is usually given after observing some event.

Indeed, mentors received training on a number of topics. Arguments could be made for and against the inclusion of these topics. A telling way to review the data on training was in comparison to the reported responsibilities mentors fulfilled while working with new teachers. The survey had one-to-one correspondence between some training topics and mentor responsibilities: division policies and procedures, observation, feedback, formative evaluations, and individualized professional development plans. While not exactly the same, some items could be considered correlates. These included instructional strategies (training topic) and collaborating on lesson and unit planning (mentor responsibility). At times, mentors received training in areas in which they had no duties; at other times their duties were performed without formal training (figure 11.4).

What was unknown was whether the skills necessary to perform the duties were prerequisites to being chosen as a mentor. For example, do the 110 school divisions that ask mentors to inform new teachers about policies and procedures assume the mentors possess accurate information about these topics? This question is raised because only 36% of the school divisions trained their mentors on this information. In addition, at times, training time was spent teaching a skill or body of knowledge that the mentors would not be called upon to use in fulfilling their responsibilities. For example, in one area of the Commonwealth, 88% of the school divisions trained their mentors in giving feedback. Less than 60% of the school divisions, however, had mentors provide feedback on a teaching episode to their new teachers.

Some glaring omissions from mentor training existed in the data. The

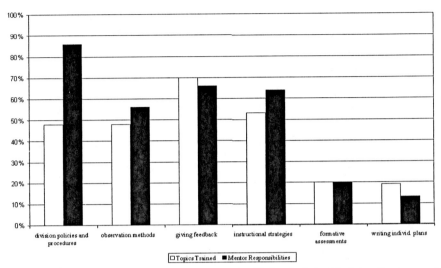

**Figure 11.4    Percentage of Respondents Identifying Related Training Topics and Mentor Responsibilities**

*Guidelines* charged school divisions with training their mentors in the categories incorporated in the *Guidelines for Uniform Performance Standards and Evaluation Criteria for Teachers, Administrators, and Superintendents* (Virginia Department of Education, 2002). Included as part of this training was information about the *Standards'* performance indicators, evaluative criteria, and how to use the criteria. These elements of training were the lowest for all training components reported by school personnel completing the survey. Also, the *Guidelines* stated that mentors know how to assess beginning teachers' performance as a teacher. These were formative evaluations. Again, formative evaluation as a training topic was relatively low (23%). A final component of mentor training required in the *Guidelines* was the development and use of individualized plans for professional growth, based on the formative evaluations. Instruction to mentors on how to write individual plans was a component of training in less than one-quarter of school divisions.

Mentors were assigned numerous and varied responsibilities. Using the categories of *local guide* and *educational companion*, it was easy to see that many school divisions used their mentors as local guides (table 11.2). The mentors' primary responsibilities were to shepherd the new teachers through the logistical workings of the school divisions. Few responsibilities required mentors to stretch the new teachers in the arenas of effective instruction and improved student performance. Except for providing feedback (67%) and planning collaboratively

**Table 11.2    Percentage of School Divisions Indicating Responsibilities Assigned to Mentors**

| Responsibility | Frequency |
|---|---|
| *Orient new teachers to physical layout* | *97* |
| *Inform new teachers of policies & procedures* | *86* |
| *Introduce new teachers to faculty* | *65* |
| Provide feedback to new teachers | 67 |
| Collaboratively plan with new teachers | 64 |
| Conduct observations of new teachers | 57 |
| Conduct formative assessments of new teachers | 20 |
| Implement professional development for new teachers | 20 |
| Design professional development opportunities for new teachers | 19 |
| Write individual professional plans with new teachers | 14 |

Note: Italics indicates responsibilities associated with mentors acting as *local guides*.

(64%), responsibilities which could be considered those of an *educational companion* were much less frequently given to mentors.

One section of the survey asked respondents to identify the top three difficulties associated with implementing their mentor teacher program. Training mentors and finding quality mentors were two of the choices. Over 30% of the school divisions ranked training mentors as a top three difficulty; almost one in four school divisions reported finding quality mentors as one of their three difficulties. It was from interview data that the information about these difficulties became more compelling. During their interviews, four of the six school officials focused their concerns on mentor training and mentor quality when asked about the hardest part of their mentor teacher program. These school officials struggled with two issues. First, the most capable potential mentors were those most often involved in a myriad of other school functions. The school officials made these remarks about finding qualified mentors:

> The hardest thing for me has been to try to get the people that [I] really would like to see as mentors, people that are strong instructional leaders; [these people] typically are aced out. It's hard to get them to do this as well. (School Official A)

> We have found that principals will tend to recommend their teacher leaders, the ones who are into everything and doing everything. . . . Those are not always the best mentors because they don't have the time to devote. (School Official B)

> Our biggest thing is that our teachers are extremely involved, not only from 9:00 a.m. to 3:40 p.m. in elementary school, but in working with children after school and that kind of thing and just the

> feeling of being overburdened with those. It's difficult to carve out
> time . . . (School Official C)

Furthermore, once mentors were selected and trained, the issue of division-wide consistency and quality interactions between mentor-new teacher dyads arose. Some mentors fulfilled or surpassed the expectations of the school division in relation to their responsibilities within the mentor teacher program; some mentors did not. The frustrations experienced by the school officials could be seen in their comments.

> The hardest thing is when we get a survey back that says, "How often has your mentor visited or helped you on a scale of 0 to 5?" and you see that 0 circled and circled and circled in hard, pressed down [fashion]. The emphasis is that I haven't received the help that you as a county said you were going to give me. (School Official A)
>
> Hardest thing? Probably it's consistency. We still don't have a handle on that. Like Teacher A in building 3 is a trained mentor and Teacher B is in this other building, but they may not be doing the same things; they all had the same training. Making sure the program is consistent across the board is probably the hardest. (School Official B)
>
> Consistency across the division . . . some mentors are doing everything. . . . Other mentors are picking and choosing what they want to do . . . and other mentors are choosing not to do [anything] at all. And yet they are all getting the $500 stipend; they're all falling under the same set of expectations . . . (School Official C)

Mentor training and quality, however, were not the only common difficulties. The second most reported problem among the six school officials was more elusive; it involved the nature and structure of education in general. School officials lamented the difficulties they encountered in breaking down the ways in which "school has always been done." The issues of collaboration, instead of isolation; of partnerships between teachers and with administrators, instead of adversary; and the use of formative evaluations in addition to single summative evaluation plagued the mentor teacher programs. As one school official remarked:

> I was thinking that the hardest thing is changing the culture, the whole culture of the field of education. I still see us being too willing to sacrifice neophytes. We aren't willing to back off on our expectations or our assignments. We still give them the toughest assignments and the most committees and the after school duty and no time to prepare . . . there are just too many things that need to be done and too few bodies to do it and so everybody has to multitask all the

time. That's not a good way to do education. And how we change it from a culture of isolation [that] comes together periodically to a true collaborative culture where we're all focused on learning for the kids and learning for the adults, that to me is the biggest [challenge], and that's why I keep at this. It is a challenge.

# Implications

The findings from this one survey and the small series of interviews shed considerable information on the reported state of mentor teacher programs in Virginia. In general, the whole study reveals that the features and practices advocated in research and identified in the *Guidelines* are present at some level in mentor teacher programs in Virginia. However, these data explicate mismatches between reported practices and research-based guidelines in the area of mentor selection and mentor training. Several implications and programmatic suggestions can be drawn from that data.

## 1. KNOW THE PURPOSE OF THE MENTOR TEACHER PROGRAM

Overall, it is important for school divisions to be clear about the intended outcomes of their mentor teacher programs. The purpose of a mentor teacher program is what drives both mentor selection and the responsibilities given to the mentors. If school divisions are focused on familiarizing their new teachers to their policies and procedures, then mentors need to possess one body of skills and personality traits. If, however, the mentor teacher program is designed to foster collaborative, professional skill development, then mentors might possess different qualities and skills. Selection and subsequent training of mentors should fit the intended mentor teacher program outcomes or goals. As Stephen Covey professes, "Begin with the end in mind" (Covey, 1989). Knowing the purpose or intended outcome guides everything that comes before.

## 2. FORMALIZE THE MENTOR SELECTION PROCESS

Most mentors in Virginia are either appointed or volunteer for their positions. Few mentor selection processes entail an application process or any subsequent formal screening of applicants. Formalizing the process can help in two ways. First, informal criteria are more open to personal interpretation and can be applied more inconsistently than formal criteria. Formal standards regarding individual qualifications can guide the mentor selection process. If selection criteria are public and a formal application process is in place, then candidates are able to assess whether they would make good mentors. Also, it validates the fact that not everyone can be a mentor—whether due to lack of skill/disposition or lack of time to commit to the program.

Second, a formalized process sends a message that the mentor teacher program is valued. It recognizes the importance of nurturing new members of the profession and the impact that mentors can have on new teacher socialization. Mentoring deserves more status than mentors being picked as they walk down the hall.

## 3. TRAINING MENTORS REQUIRES THOUGHT, TIME, AND MONEY

Three of every 10 mentors in Virginia assist their new teachers without any training in how to be a mentor or the purpose of mentoring. They have no formal, structured instruction in the duties they are to fulfill or the methods that best affect the positive development of their charges. This is disheartening in light of the influence mentors can play on the new teachers' attitudes and skill development.

Yet, even for those teachers who receive training, misalignment between some training topics and assigned responsibilities exists. Before conducting mentor training, thought must be given to the content and structure of that training. For professional development in general, teachers frequently lament the fact that they receive training pertaining to knowledge and skills that they do not need or use. This is a waste of time and energy. The opposite is just as true: being required to fulfill a task without being taught the skills can be frustrating. In designing training for mentors, it is imperative to know what responsibilities and duties the mentors will be assigned. Thought is required to align training topics to those responsibilities and skills the mentors will need. To achieve this alignment, one must consider the purpose of the mentor teacher program.

Time is another issue related to training mentors. Once the topics of mentor training are identified, it is critical to design instructional strategies that will enhance the mentors' ability to learn the information and skills. Some strategies require more time than others. Mentors need to practice new skills and demonstrate understanding of new information if they are to support the beginning teachers. If the purpose of the mentor teacher programs is to relay policy and procedural information, then instructional strategies such as lecture are appropriate and require less time. If the purpose of the mentor teacher programs is to increase effective teaching behaviors, skills such as observation and feedback are needed; these cannot be taught through lecture alone. Teaching training topics such as observation and feedback requires instructional strategies that allow mentors to practice and reflect upon their newly acquired skills. For these teachers becoming mentors, a single, half-day training session will not promote competence. Depending on the purpose, training teachers to be quality mentors takes time.

Finally, quality mentor training takes money. School divisions should make their mentor teacher programs, complete with quality mentor training, funded programs. Mentor teacher programs that are line-item budget expenditures can quickly be dissolved when school divisions face fiscal dilemmas. Mentor teacher programs can create positive changes in the culture of a school; these programs can support new teachers so they choose to remain in the profession and continue to improve their skills. But, these changes take time. School divisions need to structure their mentor teacher programs to survive any troubled economic times. Funded programs as opposed to line-item expenditures seem to weather budget difficulties better. A long-term financial commitment to these programs must be made.

Mentor teacher programs continue to gain support as vehicles for promoting the development and retention of quality beginning teachers. Certainly mentor selection and mentor training are elements that can enhance the effectiveness of these programs. Research on the structure and content of mentor training could help school divisions make more informed choices about how, when, and for what purpose mentor training should occur. Defining purpose, aligning content, and providing effective training to judiciously selected mentors can enable schools to develop and maintain committed, qualified, and resilient educators.

# References

Andrews, S., & Martin, E. (2003). *No teacher left behind: Mentoring and supporting novice teachers.* Paper presented at the Georgia Association of Colleges for Teacher Education. (ERIC Document Reproduction Service No. ED 481998)

Cave, J., LaMaster, C., & White, S. (1997). *Staff development adult characteristics.* Retrieved November 22, 2004, from http://www-ed.final.gov/linco/staff_adult.shtml.

Covey, S. (1989). *The seven habits of highly effective people.* New York: Simon & Schuster.

DeBolt, G. (1989). *Helpful elements in the mentoring of first year teachers: A report to the state education department on the New York state mentor teacher-internship program for 1988–1989.* New York: New York State Education Department. (ERIC Document Reproduction Service No. ED316501)

Dillman, D. (1978). *Mail and telephone surveys.* New York: John Wiley & Sons, Inc.

Education Commission of the States. (1999). *Beginning teacher mentoring programs.* Education Commission of the States. Retrieved December 10, 2001, from http://www.ecs.org/clearinghouse/13/15/1315.doc.

Evertson, C., & Smithey, M. (2000). Mentoring effects on protégés' classroom practice: An experimental field study. *The Journal of Educational Research, 93*(5), 294–304.

Feiman-Nemser, S., & Parker, M. B. (1992). *Los Angeles mentors: Local guides or educational companions?* East Lansing, MI: National Center for Research on Teacher Learning. (ERIC Document Reproduction Service No. ED350301)

Fuller, F. (1969). Concerns of teachers: A developmental conceptualization. *American Educational Research Journal, 6*(2), 207–226.

Ganser, T. (1999). *Areas of advice seeking among beginning teachers in a mentoring program.* Chicago, IL: Midwestern Educational Research Association. (ERIC Document Reproduction Service No. ED436489)

Ganser, T. (2001, March). *Building capacity of school districts to design, implement, and evaluate new teacher mentor programs.* Paper presented at the annual meeting of the American Association of Colleges for Teacher Education, Washington, DC. (ERIC Document Reproduction Service No. 452168)

Houston, W. R. (1990). *A study of the induction of 300 first-year teachers and their mentors, 1989–1990.* Houston, TX: Houston University. (ERIC Document Reproduction Service No. ED338558)

Huffman, G., & Leak, S. (1986). Beginning teachers' perceptions of mentors. *Journal of Teacher Education, 37*(1), 22–25.

Huling-Austin, L. (1992). Research on learning to teach: Implications for teacher induction and mentoring programs. *Journal of Teacher Education, 43*(3), 173–180.

Kelly, D. K. (n.d.) *Adult learners: Characteristics, theories, motivations, learning environment.* Retrieved November 22, 2004, from http://www.dit.ie/DIT/lifelong/adult/adlearn_chars.pdf.

Moir, E. (2003, July). *Launching the next generation of teachers through quality induction.* Paper presented at the State Partners Symposium of the National Commission on Teaching & America's Future, Denver, CO. (ERIC Document Reproduction Service No. 479764)

National Center for Research on Teacher Learning. (2001). *NCRTL explores learning from mentors: A study update.* National Center for Research on Teacher Learning. Retrieved November 15, 2001, from www.ncrtl.org.

Odell, S. (1986). Induction support of new teachers: A functional approach. *Journal of Teacher Education, 37*(1), 26–29.

Odell, S., & Ferraro, D. (1992). Teacher mentoring and teacher retention. *Journal of Teacher Education, 43*(3), 200–204.

Online Learning. (2000). *Some characteristics of learners with teaching implications.* Rochester Institute of Technology.

Southwest Educational Development Laboratory. (2002). *Mentoring beginning teachers: Lessons from the experiences in Texas.* Austin, TX: Southwest Educational Development Laboratory. Retrieved February 15, 2002, from http://emissary.ots.utexas.edu/wings/mentoring.html.

Tillman, B. A. (2000). Quiet leadership: Informal mentoring of beginning teachers. *Momentum, 31*(1), 24–26.

Virginia Department of Education. (2000). *Guidelines for mentor teacher programs for beginning and experienced teachers.* Retrieved January 15, 2002, from http://www.pen .k12.va.us/VDOE/newvdoe/legislat.PDF.

Virginia Department of Education (2002). *Guidelines for uniform performance standards and evaluation criteria for teachers, administrators, and superintendents.* Retrieved April 16, 2002, from http://www.pen.k12.va.us/VDOE/newvdoe/evaluation.pdf.

Virginia Legislature. (1999). *Code of Virginia 22.1–305.1.* Richmond, VA: Virginia Legislature. Retrieved October 22, 2001, from http://leg1.state.va.us/cgi-bin/legp504 .exe?000 + cod + 22.1–305.1.

Wildman, T. M., Magliaro, S. G., Niles, R. A., & Niles, J. A. (1992). Teacher mentoring: An analysis of roles, activities, and conditions. *Journal of Teacher Education, 43*(3), 205–213.

CHAPTER 12

# There's Nothing Easy about Mentoring

## MENTORS AS TEACHER EDUCATORS IN AN ESTABLISHED PROFESSIONAL DEVELOPMENT SCHOOL

*Catherine K. Zeek*
Lasell College

*Carole Walker*
Texas A&M University–Commerce

Catherine K. Zeek is an associate professor and chair of the Department of Education at Lasell College in Newton, MA. Her research interests include processes of changes in teachers' beliefs and practices and the impact of school/university partnerships on teacher's professional development.

Carole Walker is an associate professor in the Department of Elementary Education at Texas A&M University–Commerce. She has extensive experience at both the school and district levels with the Duval County (Florida) public schools. Her research focuses on the impact of teacher education on mentor teachers' practices.

ABSTRACT

The origin and structure of a well-established professional development school is described, including a recently implemented Induction/Mentoring Academy that highlights the role of mentors as school-based teacher educators. Quantitative measures document its effectiveness through high teacher retention rates, annual performance appraisals on which new teachers meet or exceed professional standards, and student achievement test results that often exceed district and state results. Qualitative measures based on transactional inquiry suggest that mentors have taken on a critical role as teacher

279

educators, taking leadership responsibility for training novice teachers, directing professional development, and altering their school cultures.

"There's nothing easy about mentoring," began a mentor teacher participating in a focus group (Foote, Walker, Filkins, & Zeek, 1997). Her comment eight years ago echoes as we continue to work with mentors, but it is punctuated with mentors' stories of taking pride in their pivotal role in helping novice teachers develop their teaching skills. As teacher educators, we seek to develop effective strategies for supporting new teachers in their initial teaching experiences. Such strategies are intended to increase teacher retention rates, improve teacher quality, and raise student achievement levels. In this paper, we describe one long-established Texas program that supports novice teachers in their final year of teacher preparation and their early teaching experience through an innovative approach to mentoring that affects school cultures. Our data sources include statistics gathered to measure the program's effectiveness, as well as our work with mentor teachers through "transactional inquiry" (Zeek, Foote, & Walker, 2001).

# Background

National attrition rates for teachers have been estimated to be as high as 50% in the first five years, with rates highest for new teachers and the majority of the turnover occurring in the first three years (Curran & Goldrick, 2002; Herbert & Ramsay, 2004; Ingersoll & Kralik, 2004). Researchers have suggested that reducing attrition rates would alleviate reported teacher shortages (Herbert, 2004; Ingersoll, 2003), a critical need amid mandates to provide "highly qualified" teachers for all learners. Formal induction programs for new teachers seek to address the persistent attrition issue by supporting novices in adjusting to school and professional cultures and providing "a 'bridge' from student of teaching to teacher of students" (Ingersoll & Kralik, p. 2). National studies found that after three years, the attrition rate for new teachers participating in formal induction programs was 15%; for those who did not participate in such programs the rate was 26% (U.S. Department of Education, 1997).

In Texas, studies placed three-year attrition rates at 43% (State Board for

Educator Certification [SBEC], 1999), above national rates. Faced with these statistics, in 1999–2000 the state implemented the Texas Beginning Educator Support System (TxBESS) to provide new teachers with a support team, generally consisting of a mentor teacher, campus administrator, and representative from a teacher preparation entity (SBEC, 2003). TxBESS has clearly reduced attrition among new teachers. After one year of support, 89.2% of new teachers participating in TxBESS remained in the profession, compared to 80.8% of new teachers without such support. After two years of support, the retention rate was 84.4%, compared to 75.4% for non-TxBESS teachers (Charles A. Dana Center, 2002).

While formal induction programs vary widely in specific goals and structures, one critical element is the presence of a mentor (American Federation of Teachers, 2000; Charles A. Dana Center, 2002; Curran & Goldrick, 2002; Gold, 1996) who guides novices as they develop the highly diverse skills that make for effective teaching. While pointing to the need for additional documentation of the value added by such programs, studies support the positive link between mentoring and new-teacher retention and suggest that mentors may also benefit (Bahney, 1995; Curran & Goldrick; Gold; Ingersoll & Kralik, 2004; Zeek et al., 2001). Our program, which has evolved during a 14-year partnership, supports novices and their mentors by engaging them in ongoing professional development and building a school culture of collegiality and empowerment.

# Structure of Texas A&M–Commerce Preservice and Induction Programs

Among the largest in the state, the undergraduate teacher education program at Texas A&M University–Commerce is intensively field based; novices learn to teach by working alongside mentor teachers in partner districts. Designed in 1991 by a team of university and public school educators, goals included redesigning preservice teacher education to feature more experience in the public schools, providing ongoing professional development for inservice teachers, and raising the achievement of public school students. The program has also led to exceptionally high passing rates on the state certification tests; within the Texas A&M University system, the passing rates of our students are second only to those of students at Texas A&M–College Station where entrance requirements are more stringent. Increased teacher retention has proven to be another value-added aspect, with graduates of the field-based program showing significantly higher retention rates than graduates of the traditional program (Fleener, 1998).

Following placement interviews with mentors, preservice teachers work as apprentices in two different grade levels for two semesters: two full days per week for 16 weeks in internship and up to five days each week in their residency semester. The other days are devoted to 10 seminar-based courses, designed by university and public school teachers to integrate classroom experience and coursework. The Instructional Leadership Team (ILT) composed of the intern or resident, the two mentors, and the university liaison is the decision-making group guiding the program within the public school. The ILT orients the intern/resident to the school and classrooms, designs teaching experiences, provides formative and summative feedback, and jointly determines course grades during the year in the field.

Since our professional development school was launched in 1991, a variety of data have assisted in making decisions and measuring success. Focus groups highlighted the organic nature (Dixon & Ishler, 1992) of the partnership (Foote et al., 1997; Linek & Sampson, 1996). In May 2003, focus groups from five partner districts composed of mentors, principals, and district-level administrators, responded to a series of questions including *what elements distinguish our program as a quality program*. With remarkable unanimity across districts, the elements they cited aligned with key concepts first identified in 1991. This consensus is noteworthy considering how resistant practice is to substantive change, how strong the forces for reverting to the norm are, and how often state and federal mandates shift our practice. The partners named the importance of the (a) two-semester program, (b) first-days-of-school experiences in the public schools in August before the beginning of the university semester, (c) weekly classroom visits by university liaisons, (d) teaching experiences at two different grade levels with the same two mentors during two full semesters in the field, and (e) solving problems as partners (Walker, Bennett, Cardwell, & Pool, 2004).

Collaborative problem solving prompted program extensions within the PDS. In 2002, through the leadership of a school district administrator, the mentoring structure for preservice teachers was extended into the early years of teaching in one district. The district, situated in a town of 23,000, is about 45 miles from a major metropolitan area. It serves 5,300 students on nine campuses: an early childhood center for four- and five-year-olds, five elementary schools for grades K–fourth, an intermediate school for grades five and six, a middle school for grades seven and eight, and a high school for grades nine through twelve. A design team of mentors, principals, a representative from the regional education service center, and university teacher educators and administrators collaboratively developed an Induction/Mentoring Academy to ease the transition from preservice to inservice teaching and to engage mentors in continued professional growth. Launched at the beginning of the 2002–2003 school year, the Academy had five goals: (a) provide a quality system of support to new teachers, (b) ensure the application of best teaching practices, (c) establish a plan for continued professional growth, (d) reduce the cost of teacher turnover to the school district, and (e) retain high quality teachers. Because of its value to all stakeholders, all first year teachers in the district participate in the Academy.

Now in its third year, the Academy provides novice teachers with 90 hours of seminar-based professional development over two semesters as well as 45 hours of coaching by mentors within the framework of three graduate courses. *The First Days of School* (Wong & Wong, 2004) and *Qualities of Effective Teachers* (Stronge, 2002) suggest best practices. Key Academy components, drawn from the TxBESS framework (SBEC, 2003), are mentoring support within a structured framework of competencies and domains, peer support, and observation of master teachers. Inductees receive $250 stipends to implement action research projects focused on motivating their students, nine semester hours credit toward a master's degree, and professional development hours required for certificate renewal. The mentors receive $500 stipends, peer support, and professional development hours toward certificate renewal.

All first year teachers, both fully certified and those seeking certification through alternative routes, and their mentors belong to the Academy and are also the participants in this study. During its first year (2002–2003) the Academy included 16 inductees teaching in grades PK through ninth and 16 mentor teachers. The next year (2003–2004), there were 16 inductees teaching grades PK through eighth and 24 mentors including eight second year teachers who, with the veterans and inductees, formed mentoring triads following the TxBESS model (SBEC, 2003). In 2004–2005 participants are 34 inductees teaching in grades PK through twelfth, 33 veteran mentors, and 10 second year teacher mentors. A university teacher educator, a veteran liaison in the preservice program, is the teacher-of-record for the seminars through which the graduate credit courses are delivered. Other members of the design team, particularly mentor teachers, are part of the teaching team.

# Evaluation of Program Effectiveness

Both the preservice and induction programs used ongoing quantitative and qualitative evaluation to determine their effectiveness and suggest areas of improvement. Quantitative measures reported teacher retention and satisfaction rates, scores on teacher appraisals, and results of student achievement tests, while qualitative evaluation was based on teachers' narratives of practice and professional growth. Research questions emerged through work within the Academy: (a) Does Academy participation affect teacher retention in the profession and satisfaction with teaching? (b) Does it affect teacher appraisal scores? (c) Does it affect student achievement? (d) Does it affect teacher leadership? Quantitative and qualitative measures and outcomes are discussed in this section.

## QUANTITATIVE MEASURES AND OUTCOMES

Retention rates for new teachers for the first two years of the Academy, obtained from the district's personnel office, served as the first measure of Academy impact. After the first year (2002–2003), 87.5% of inductees remained in the district; after the second year, 75.8% remained. Rates of retention in the profession were also dramatic: 100% after the first year and 96.6 % after the second. Satisfaction with teaching was another measure of impact. Responding to career satisfaction surveys developed in the Academy, 15 of the 16 inductees (93.75 %) indicated in 2003 that they were *very satisfied* (the highest rating); in 2004, 12 (92.3 %) chose *very satisfied* and one (7.7 %) chose *satisfied* (the third highest rating).

The district's annual teacher appraisal process, incorporating classroom observations and teacher-developed portfolios, provided another quantitative measure. Table 12.1 presents ratings for mentors and inductees from the first two years of the Academy. In 2002–2003, the mentors' scores ranged from 95.75 to 100.5 on a 100-point scale, placing all 16 of them in the top category, *exceeds professional standard*. The inductees' scores ranged from 81.73 to 98.64, with the majority (58.3%) in the top category. Mentors' scores for 2003–2004, which included second year teachers in the mentoring triad, ranged from 79.88 to 100. All but two of the mentors, both second year teachers, scored in the top category. Scores for the inductees ranged from 77.46 to 96.97 with half in the top category and half in the middle category, *meets professional standard*.

**Table 12.1    District Mentor and Inductee Teachers' Summative Appraisal Scores**

| Groups | *Exceeds Professional Standard (score of 90–100)* | | *Meets Professional Standard (score of 75–89)* | | *Needs Improvement (score below 75)* |
|---|---|---|---|---|---|
| | *N* | *Percent* | *N* | *Percent* | |
| **2003** | | | | | |
| Mentors | 16 | 100.0% | 0 | 0 | 0 |
| Inductees | 7 | 58.3% | 5 | 41.7% | |
| **2004** | | | | | |
| Mentors | 15 | 87.9% | 2 | 12.1% | 0 |
| Inductees | 6 | 50.0% | 6 | 50.0% | 0 |

The strong results of the mentor teachers were expected. It was, however, beyond our expectations that 100% of the first year teachers would meet or exceed the professional standard. Their results showed that teaching effectiveness was associated with the Academy and raised the possibility that participation had enhanced their effectiveness. Further, teachers who were trained in the professional development school generally outscored those trained in alternative programs (Walker et al., 2004).

Student achievement test results of inductees and their mentors provided another quantitative measure of effectiveness. Reading and math achievement were assessed in all districts each spring in grades 3 through 12 using the standardized, criterion-referenced Texas Assessment of Knowledge and Skills (TAKS), with writing and/or science also assessed at some grade levels. Tables 12.2 and 12.3 present the TAKS results of inductees and mentors where available for the first and second years of the Academy.

In its first year, the Academy included 16 first year teachers in 7 schools, with 9 teaching in TAKS grades. Some of these teachers administered one TAKS test while others administered two, making for a total of 12 tests administered by these beginning teachers. For 5 of the 9 teachers (55.5%), student passing

**Table 12.2   2002–2003 TAKS Passing Rates for Inductee and Mentor Teachers**

| Teachers | | Teacher's Rates (%) | District Rates (%) | State Rates (%) |
|---|---|---|---|---|
| **Inductees (n = 9)** | | | | |
| Inductee 2 | | 88.2 | 72.8 | 79 |
| Inductee 4 | | 89.7 | 72.8 | 79 |
| Inductee 6 | | 55.6 | 65.6 | 74 |
| Inductee 8 | | 86.8 | 83.3 | 88 |
| Inductee 9 | | 65.5 | 83.3 | 88 |
| Inductee 10 | Test 1 | 86.7 | 83.3 | 88 |
| | Test 2 | 43.8 | 80.1 | 88 |
| Inductee 11 | | 49.4 | 63.1 | 73 |
| Inductee 12 | Test 1 | 88.9 | 95.0 | 90 |
| | Test 2 | 88.9 | 91.0 | 89 |
| Inductee 13 | Test 1 | 83.3 | 90.0 | 82 |
| | Test 2 | 83.3 | 60.0 | 82 |
| **Mentors (n = 5)** | | | | |
| Mentor 1 | | 67.6 | 72.8 | 79 |
| Mentor 5 | | 84.3 | 72.8 | 79 |
| Mentor 7 | | 57.6 | 83.3 | 88 |
| Mentor 14 | Test 1 | 90.99 | 0.5 | 88 |
| | Test 2 | 90.9 | 81.4 | 86 |
| | Test 3 | 90.9 | 80.5 | 86 |
| Mentor 15 | | 27.3 | 48.6 | 63 |

**Table 12.3    2003–2004 TAKS Passing Rates for Inductee and Mentor Teachers**

| Teachers | | Teacher's Rates (%) | District Rates (%) | State Rates (%) |
|---|---|---|---|---|
| **Inductees (n = 6)** | | | | |
| Inductee 1 | Test 1 | 100.0 | 91 | 90 |
| | Test 2 | 94.4 | 81 | 91 |
| Inductee 5 | Test 1 | 88.2 | 91 | 90 |
| | Test 2 | 82.4 | 81 | 91 |
| Inductee 15 | | 63.0 | 60 | 69 |
| Inductee 11 | | 13.3 | 47 | 66 |
| Inductee 9 | | 32.9 | 51 | 70 |
| Inductee 8 | | 55.2 | 82 | 89 |
| **Mentors (n = 8)** | | | | |
| Mentor 14 | Test 1 | 86.7 | 92 | 80 |
| | Test 2 | 58.3 | 42 | 83 |
| Mentor 3 | Test 1 | 86.6 | 91 | 90 |
| | Test 2 | 82.4 | 90 | 85 |
| Mentor 7 | | 81.4 | 71 | 82 |
| Mentor 4 | | 88.5 | 71 | 82 |
| Mentor 2 | | 72.7 | 65 | 77 |
| Mentor 10 | | 68.4 | 82 | 89 |
| Mentor 12 | | 100.0 | 47 | 66 |
| Mentor 13 | | 68.2 | 74 | 83 |

rates were higher than the district rates, and for 6 of 12 tests (50%) passing rates were higher than the state rate. TAKS results were available for 5 mentors in 4 schools. Their students' passing rates were slightly better than those of the first year teachers. For 4 of the 7 tests (57%) administered by these mentors, student passing rates exceeded both the district and state rates.

During the 2003–2004 school year there were 14 first year teachers in 6 district schools; 6 taught in TAKS grades, administering a total of 8 tests. On 4 of the 8 tests (50%), the inductees' students exceeded the district passing rates, and for 2 of 8 tests (25%), their passing rates were higher than the state rates. TAKS results were available for 8 mentors in 4 schools, administering a total of 10 tests. Again, their students' passing rates were somewhat higher than those of the first year teachers. In 5 of 10 tests (50%) the passing rates of mentors' students exceeded the district average; in 3 instances (30%) their passing rates exceeded the state average. When we collected the data for analysis, we antici- pated that the passing rates of mentors' students would exceed district and state averages for the majority of the comparisons while those of inductees' students would not. However, passing rates on state tests for the first two years of the Academy show that participation by the inductees in the Academy was associated with enhanced student achievement in more instances than expected, exceeding district averages on 9 tests and exceeding state averages on 8 tests.

Analysis of the quantitative measures, new teacher retention and satisfaction rates, teacher performance appraisal scores, and student passing rates on state achievement tests, documented the effectiveness of the Induction/Mentoring Academy. Retention rates and student passing rates both exceeded statewide figures. Statewide teacher appraisal scores were not reported; however, all of the inductees either met or exceeded professional standards according to district appraisals.

## QUALITATIVE MEASURES AND OUTCOMES

Quantitative measures documented the effectiveness of the preservice and induction programs within this partner district. However, our previous experiences suggested that there was more to the story, and we went beyond the numbers to ask the participants what they found effective. Nearly 10 years ago, in our roles as university liaisons, we initiated conversations with mentors. These teachers were eager to tell their stories of practice and to respond to others' narratives in a collegial setting (Fleener, Walker, Foote, & Zeek, 1998), prompting us to develop a strategy centered on telling and analyzing teachers' stories. Based on narrative inquiry (Clandinin & Connelly, 2000), *transactional inquiry* emphasized teachers' practical knowledge and provided additional information about the impact of the collaborative. The process made visible teachers' often implicit thought processes, engaged them in intentional reflection on actions and decisions, and provided for conversations with other professionals (Clandinin & Connelly; Jalongo & Isenberg, 1995; Lyons & LaBoskey, 2002). It also acknowledged the social constructivist perspective that knowledge is constructed through exploring ideas and in interaction with others.

The transactional inquiry process begins with teachers writing individual narratives of practice, following prompts such as "Tell about an effective lesson you've taught or observed" or "Tell about a lesson you've taught or observed that turned out better than you thought it would." Experienced teachers working in both university and public school settings have read and responded to these narratives of effective practice, suggesting areas of strength and need for the storyteller and identifying strategies for supporting them in their development. Some themes and valuable lessons consistently emerged: (a) teacher leadership grows out of mentoring (Foote et al., 1997), (b) narratives tap teachers' wisdom and document success in a different way than standardized measures

(Foote et al., 1998), and (c) mentor teachers take responsibility for their own professional growth (Zeek & Walker, in press).

Through transactional inquiries within the Academy, we realized that our longtime mentor teacher partners had become teacher educators as they collaborated with university teachers to train preservice teachers during their field-based year and, more recently, in the Induction/Mentoring Academy. For this report, we focused on responses to two narratives purposefully chosen because their richness generated discussion and because they represented differences in subject matter and grade level. One written by *Aidan Lee* (italics indicate pseudonyms), a veteran mentor within the collaborative, told about a math lesson her resident *Tommy Martinez* taught. *Ms. Lee* wrote in part at the beginning:

> I inherited *Tommy* for his residency in the fall after a very bumpy ride during his internship semester in the spring. My story of something interesting he did which turned out better—much better—than I expected is of a lesson on volume measurement . . .

She concluded her story saying,

> The structure of his lesson and the additional exploration time helped the students to develop a strong understanding of the concept of volume. *Tommy's* lesson was a huge success and memorable experience. I gave him great credit for taking a risk I have not yet taken on my own.

The second story was by *Ms. Scott,* also known as *Willis' teacher,* an experienced teacher working toward her master's degree. Her story told about a lesson learned while doing autobiographies with her middle school students and concluded with this paragraph:

> On the last day of school, Willis's mother came to volunteer for field day. Much to Willis's surprise, I had saved his work and printed it out for his mother. She remembered that Willis was asking a bunch of questions about himself as a baby, but she did not have time to sit down and talk. This explained why he didn't start on time. I felt ashamed and thought Willis was only being defiant because he didn't want to participate. In actuality, he did want to write. He just didn't have the information at the time that I had requested. Another lesson learned for *Ms. Scott.*

Sixteen experienced mentors, most of whom had worked with interns and residents and first year teachers, suggested titles for *Ms. Scott* (*Who's Teaching Who?, Finding Willis, Why Didn't I Think to Ask?*); lessons for *Ms. Lee* (mentor teachers can learn from their interns and residents as well as them learning from their mentors—*Tommy* was wise to take the risk, and his mentor was brave to let him); and next steps for *Tommy* (he needs to tell the class eventually what volume equals what—exploring is great, but it all needs to come together at the end); and *Ms. Scott* (use multiple strategies—written, verbal, drama—to stimulate the creative juices; a progressive story as a small group activity may engage those who are reluctant to participate at first).

Reflecting on the insights surfacing during the inquiry process we offered two prompts to mentors: a) Some of the things that teacher educators who are based at the university do are. . . . b) Some of the things that teacher educators who are based at the public school do are. . . . A few mentors listed the traditional theory/practice distinction saying, for example, that those based at the university "provide pedagogical instruction as well as theoretical instruction," while those based in the public school "provide opportunities for students to practice theory and pedagogy" (*Lou Ann Posey*, elementary literacy teacher). However, their lists suggested many more areas of overlap for university-based and public school–based teacher educators (see table 12.4). Some of these veterans suggested that teacher educators in both settings have identical responsibilities to provide feedback, monitor progress, assist in needs, observe and mold teachers, and encourage, while others suggested parallel ideas: University based teacher educators demonstrate/model how a teacher is to act in the classroom and public school–based teacher educators support first year/intern teachers as they assimilate into the public school setting.

# Conclusions and Implications

The established professional development school at Texas A&M University–Commerce relies on organic collaboration between public school and university partners, involving both groups equally in decisions about training and supporting novice teachers. Preservice and induction training years take place in classrooms of experienced mentor teachers, with support from university liaisons. Quantitative data document the effectiveness of the program. Participants in the Induction/Mentoring Academy have higher retention rates than those reported statewide, receive annual appraisals of "exceeds" or "meets" professional standard, and have student passing rates that meet or exceed district and state averages on the state achievement tests. These data support the value added in this PDS. Our results are compelling, but are based on a small sample of teachers and students in one school district. Retention rates are influenced by factors beyond the scope of this study, including family and economic factors. Annual teacher appraisals are subjective, although appraisers receive training to increase

**Table 12.4   Teacher Educators' Work Defined by Mentor Teachers during Transactional Inquiries**

| University-Based Teacher Educators | School-Based Teacher Educators |
|---|---|
| • Demonstrate/model how a teacher is to act in the classroom (*Sean Murphy*, middle school reading)<br>• Provide us with valuable information on how to teach (*Jane*, high school math)<br>• Provide guidance for those wanting to become educators (*Mimi*, intermediate school science)<br>• Guide interns and residents; mentor first year teachers (*Miss Bunny*, 3rd grade)<br>• Teach/prepare mentors; teach/prepare inductees; give advice/direction (*Ernesto Martinez*, 3rd grade)<br>• Team planning (*Sissy*, literacy)<br>• Bases for knowledge to be applied in the classroom (*Lynne*, literacy teacher)<br>• Provide feedback, monitor progress, assist in needs, observe and mold teachers, encourage (*Sherra Adams*, intermediate school math)<br>• Help prepare students to be teachers/ professionals (*Chloe*, kindergarten)<br>• Allow fledgling teachers to teach our students (*Lee Phillips*, teaching methods) | • Support first year/intern teachers as they assimilate into the public school setting<br>• Provide mentees with good advice and suggestions<br>• Provide firsthand opportunities for future teachers to experience the ''real'' classroom<br>• Mentor and work with other teachers<br>• Serve as role models or an example of best practice; give advice/direction<br>• Team planning<br>• Teach classroom management techniques and help student teachers develop these skills<br>• Provide feedback, monitor progress, assist in needs, observe and mold teachers, CHEERLEAD!<br>• Observe and offer feedback . . . to improve teaching skills as well as management skills<br>• Allow fledgling teachers to teach our students |

inter-rater reliability. Additional research should seek comparison groups to extend the results to other settings.

Our inquiry focus has been on the role of mentors in this setting. Years ago the idea that "the mentor teachers teach our teachers to teach" emerged (Foote et al., 1997; Fleener et al., 1998; Foote et al., 1998) through mentor comments such as "They're [interns/residents] my students too. I'm responsible for 22 [children] and this one. You develop a bond. You want to see them succeed and do great things" (Foote et al., 1997). During the past two years, mentors in the Academy repeated this theme. Asked to identify the most interesting thing about mentoring novice teachers, several experienced mentors describe roles and lessons often ascribed to teacher educators: "the opportunity to share (give and take) and help mold professionals to become better; seeing them gain strength and confidence in their ability to manage and teach; watching [them] find a new understanding and love for teaching; stepping aside and giving them the reigns [*sic*] which must happen; and you may not always be perceived as the authority figure."

Describing what they want other teacher educators to know, some mentors point to the value of intentional training with a skilled mentor: "How important teacher training is; Helping new teachers learn from committed educators is the best gift school children can ever have." Others focus on ways in which they grow professionally: "The strength and ability you gain as a teacher by being a mentor justifies and rewards the time, effort and worry you invest in the beginning teacher." Finally, one mentor sums up: "It is always worth it in the end."

These insights from mentor teachers—school-based teacher educators—suggest that their school culture includes ongoing professional development, collegiality, and frequent collaboration. These features grow from the substantive role mentors play in designing and evaluating training for novice teachers. Fullan (1996) discusses the need for restructuring schools, predominantly a top-down, outside-in process, but also for re-culturing schools, a process that must be bottom-up and begin on the inside. The partners in this PDS began restructuring teacher education over a decade ago; re-culturing continues as all partners see its positive outcomes. Our PDS recognizes the essential role that mentors play, as the experts closest to practice, and seeks to engage mentors in thoughtful ways that acknowledge and build their expertise, encouraging partners to continue to connect practice and theory at all levels.

Teacher educators in both university and public school settings need to continually examine our practice. Data from a variety of sources document the value of formal induction programs, while suggesting that a variety of structures may be effective. In each structure, mentors offer crucial support and guidance. Transactional inquiry, in combination with quantitative data collection, offers a structure for encouraging mentors to examine their own practice and beliefs, both about teaching and mentoring and to participate as valued colleagues and teacher educators in the larger conversation about growing new teachers.

# References

American Federation of Teachers. (2000). *Building a profession: Strengthening teacher preparation and induction.* Retrieved October 25, 2004, from American Federation of Teachers Web site: http://www.aft.org/pubs-reports/downloads/teachers/k16report.pdf.

Bahney, J. B. (1995). *Instructional leadership teams: Mentoring in a professional development school.* Unpublished doctoral dissertation, East Texas State University, Commerce.

Charles A. Dana Center. (2002). *Texas Beginning Teacher Support System evaluation report for year three, 2001–02.* Austin, TX: Author.

Clandinin, D. J., & Connelly, F. M. (2000). *Narrative inquiry: Experience and story in qualitative research.* San Francisco: Josey Bass.

Curran, B., & Goldrick, L. (2002). *Mentoring and supporting new teachers.* Washington, DC: National Governors Association, Center for Best Practices. (ERIC Document Reproduction Service No. ED 467748)

Dixon, P. N., & Ishler, R. E. (1992). Professional development schools: Stages in collaboration. *Journal of Teacher Education, 43*(1), 28–34.

Fleener, C. (1998). *A comparison of attrition rates and reasons between graduates of field-based and non field-based teacher education programs in Texas.* Unpublished doctoral dissertation, Texas A&M University–Commerce.

Fleener, C., Walker, C., Foote, M., & Zeek, C. (1998, February). *We thought you'd never ask: Mentor teachers tell their stories.* Paper presented at the meeting of the American Association of Colleges for Teacher Education, New Orleans, LA.

Foote, M., Walker, C., Filkins, K., & Zeek, C. (1997, February). *Leadership development through mentoring: Professional development with—not for—mentor teachers.* Paper presented at the meeting of the American Association of Colleges for Teacher Education, Phoenix, AZ.

Foote, M., Zeek, C., Walker, C., & Fleener, C. (1998, December). *Using stories and "transactional inquiry" to tap the wisdom of teachers: Nonlinear assessment in a standardized world.* Paper presented at the annual meeting of the National Reading Conference, Austin, TX.

Fullan, M. G. (1996) Turning systemic thinking on its head. *Phi Delta Kappan, 77,* 420–423.

Gold, Y. (1996). Beginning teacher support: Attrition, mentoring, and induction. In J. Siluka (Ed.), *Handbook of research on teacher education* (2nd ed., pp. 548–594). New York: Macmillan.

Herbert, K. S. (2004, April). *Production and retention of beginning teachers from 1999 to 2003: A comparison of preparation routes.* Retrieved October 25, 2004, from http://www.sbec.state.tx.us/SBECOnline/reprtdatarsrch/prerptprodretrvsd.pdf.

Herbert, K. S., & Ramsay, M. C. (2004, September). *Teacher turnover and shortages of qualified teachers in Texas public school districts 2004–2005: Report to the Senate Education Committee.* Retrieved October 25, 2004, from http://www.sbec.state.tx.us/SBECOnline/reprtdatarsrch/ReportforSenateEducation Committee.pdf.

Ingersoll, R. M. (2003). *Is there really a teacher shortage?* Retrieved October 25, 2004, from http://depts.washington.edu/ctpmail/PDFs/Shortage-RI-09-2003.pdf.

Ingersoll, R., & Kralik, J. M. (2004). *The impact of mentoring on teacher retention: What the research says.* Retrieved October 25, 2004, from http://www.ecs.org/clearinghouse/50/36/5036.htm.

Jalongo, M. R., & Isenberg, J. P. (1995). *Teachers' stories: From personal narrative to professional insight.* San Francisco: Jossey-Bass.

Linek, W. M., & Sampson, M. B. (1996). Collaboration between public schools and universities: Success through voice and choice. *Illinois Reading Journal, 24*(1), 7–17.

Lyons, N., & LaBoskey, V. K. (Eds.) (2002). *Narrative inquiry in practice: Advancing the knowledge of teaching*. New York: Teachers College Press.

State Board for Educator Certification. (1999). *Overview of Texas teacher supply, demand, and utilization*. Austin, TX: Author.

State Board for Educator Certification. (2003). *TxBESS framework: Beginning teacher performance standards: A developmental continuum*. Austin, TX: Author.

Stronge, J. H. (2002). *Qualities of effective teachers*. Alexandria, VA: Association for Supervision and Curriculum Development.

U.S. Department of Education, National Center for Education Statistics. (1997). *The characteristics of stayers, movers, and leavers: Results from the teacher follow-up survey, 1994–95*. NCES 97450. Washington, DC: U.S. Department of Education.

Walker, C., Bennett, T., Cardwell, M., & Pool, A. (2004, September). *Teacher mentoring/coaching: Value-added research in a school-university collaborative teacher induction program*. Paper presented at the eighth annual Conference on School-University Partnerships, San Antonio, TX.

Wong, H. K., & Wong, R. T. (2004). *The first days of school: How to be an effective teacher* (3rd ed.). Mountain View, CA: Harry K. Wong Publications, Inc.

Zeek, C. K., Foote, M., & Walker, C. (2001). Teacher stories and transactional inquiry: Hearing the voices of mentor teachers. *Journal of Teacher Education, 52*(5), 373–381.

Zeek, C. K., & Walker, C. (in press). Teaching fluently: Exploring teaching practices in divergent certification programs. *Yearbook of the College Reading Association*.

# Summary and Conclusions
## ANALYZING MENTORING PROGRAMS

*Sandra J. Odell*

University of Nevada, Las Vegas

The preceding four chapters present well-characterized mentoring programs that exemplify the major issues that are extant in mentoring today. It is useful to contextualize these programs by reference to the dimensions of quality mentoring (Odell & Huling, 2000) explicated in the introduction to the chapters in this division of the *Yearbook*. Three of the programs, set in school/university partnership contexts, attest to the efficacy of mentoring on outcome measures as varied as the retention of novices, teacher efficacy, and teacher and student performance. Notably, each of these programs is "boutique" like involving relatively small numbers of novices and mentors and financial supports for both novices and mentors. These programs stand in stark contrast to state-wide mandated programs as typified in chapter 11 by Hughes where large numbers of novices/mentors are asked to proceed with fewer extrinsic supports. Each of the programs relates somewhat differently to the dimensions of quality mentoring that serve as our framework for analysis.

## Program Purposes

It is paramount that the purpose of a mentoring program be well articulated to all program participants. The four mentor programs achieve this desideratum variously. In chapter 9 Hayes describes the Ratheon Teaching Fellows (RTF) program at Wichita State University as having the explicit program purposes of enhancing novice teachers' efficacy, performance, and retention. Imbedded in these goals is the humanistic approach of making novices feel more positive, reducing the reality shock that novices may be feeling, and thereby increasing the likelihood that they will remain in teaching. Less explicitly stated is a movement toward standards-based mentoring. The program focuses on the growth and enhancement of rigorously selected math and science preservice teacher education candidates by placing emphasis on their performance and subject matter expertise.

In the Southern Illinois University program (chapter 10) McIntyre, Smith, Gilbert, and Hillkirk state that the program purpose is to encourage self-directed professional development among novices and practicing teachers. This reform-minded focus on the improvement of teaching led to the admirable program requirement that novices reflect on their practice by performing action research. Not surprisingly, surveys indicated that the novices perceived the mentoring program to have enhanced their facility at teacher inquiry.

In chapter 12, Zeek and Walker do not explicitly identify their program purposes. However, one can infer both humanistic and educational companion components from the data they collected on the Texas A&M–Commerce Preservice and Induction Programs. The authors report strong retention rates, annual performance appraisals on which novices and mentors meet or exceed professional standards, and positive student achievement test results. While it might be argued that performance appraisals and achievement tests do not adequately capture the performance of interest, this program is to be commended for going beyond the more typical participant perceptions or testimonials in discerning the efficacy of a mentoring program. Still, subsequent research needs to be designed where the things that mentors do and say get linked to novices' in-class performance and this, in turn, is shown to be causally linked to student outcomes.

Beyond the general goal of having mentor teachers help novices, no specific program purposes are offered for the statewide program described by Hughes in chapter 11. However, it can be assumed that one of the purposes was for mentors to serve as local guides to novices (Feiman-Nemser & Parker, 1992). Mentors in this program are asked, among other things, to acculturate novices into the state system as represented by the Virginia Guidelines for Uniform Performance Standards and Evaluation Criteria for Teachers, Administrators, and Superintendents. While there is no gainsaying that orienting novices to local school system information is an appropriate mentor role, such mentoring does not necessarily enhance the teaching of the novice.

Taking these four programs together, there is considerable emphasis on supporting novices so that they will remain in teaching. Teacher retention has been an appropriate goal of mentoring since the inception of induction programs some twenty-five years ago (Ingersoll & Kralik, 2004). However, for mentoring programs to be fully justified in terms of time and money they need to evolve beyond simply helping novices orient to the school system and enhance their self-efficacy to improving teaching, especially by mentoring toward standards-based practice (Odell & Huling, 2000; Wang & Odell, 2002). All of the programs to more or less a degree place emphasis on novice-teacher performance. The perspective offered here is that each of these programs, and indeed mentoring programs more generally, would benefit by more specific descriptions and information about how mentors are helping novices move toward standards-based practice.

# Mentors

The four programs described herein utilize the expertise of experienced teachers as mentors to guide novices in their practice. Admirably, Wichita State, SIU, and Texas A&M all have preservice programs that involve mentor teachers. By recognizing the importance of having preservice students work in classrooms with mentors they foster connections between theoretical university coursework and the actual practice of teaching. In Wichita and Commerce the preservice programs have been extended to the induction period where beginning teachers graduating from their universities continue to work with mentors. Such continuity between preservice teacher education and teacher induction has the potential of providing a more impactful and consistent entry to the profession for beginning teachers.

Each of the programs has elements of mentor selection and preparation. However, the selection process for math and science mentors at Wichita State is particularly notable. Principals, along with science and math chairs, nominate mentors using specific criteria. The nominees are then sent letters that encourage them to apply, and mentors who are selected attend a course in mentor training during the summer session at WSU. The unique arrangements developed at Wichita State for involving veteran teachers as mentors for preservice teachers, as members of a mentor team, and as consultants to pairs of novices, are creative and exemplify the variety of possible mentor roles that experienced teachers can assume.

In chapter 12, Zeek and Walker describe how preservice novices work alongside mentors in the Professional Development School. The internship and residency semesters for the preservice students are field-based. From a mentor preparation perspective, it is insightful that the mentors' work with these preservice novices is conceptualized as providing ongoing professional development for the inservice mentor teachers in their content areas. Professional development for the mentors is extended through their participation in an induction/mentoring academy that highlights the role of mentors as site-based teacher educators. This view of mentor teachers as site-based teacher educators is particularly appropriate since it establishes their roles as teachers and mentors as professional ones anchored in research-based practice (Association of Teacher Educators, 2005). What is not clear here is the intensity and frequency of the mentor preparation. It is the experience of the author that helping mentors understand the complexities of the site-based teacher educator role can take weekly preparation sessions.

McIntyre, et al. state in chapter 10 that teaching fellows are matched with mentors who have applied to participate in their program and who have been involved previously in one of a variety of mentoring workshops or programs. Because details are not offered regarding the characteristics of those who are chosen as mentors or the extent of the mentor preparation, it is difficult to analyze their practices in this regard. It is noteworthy, though, that the mentors are part of SIUs well-established partnership schools and that they appropriately consider several variables such as work ethic, styles, and philosophy when creating novice/mentor matches.

Selection and preparation of mentor teachers is the major focus of the state-wide mandated Virginia program. It is impressive that Virginia has developed a set of specific guidelines for mentoring programs and for their participants. Specifically, they identify areas for mentor preparation including learning about the state standards and evaluation criteria, understanding formative assessment, developing personal professional development plans, and providing individualized assistance. The structure and format for learning about these topics is left to local districts with suggestions for how long training in these areas should last and how work sessions might be scheduled.

In a survey of 131 public school divisions in the Commonwealth of Virginia, Hughes disappointingly found that implementation of a prescribed mentoring program on a large scale is fraught with difficulties. For example, building principals identified the mentors in 98% of the school districts who responded. This can be problematic since the subjective judgment of principals may be unreliable in identifying competent mentor teachers (Rauth & Bowers, 1986). Over a third did not use, or used informally, years of experience as a criterion for mentor selection even though it was a requirement of the Virginia Department of Education to select mentors with at least three years of experience. Prescribed training for mentors did not occur in about 25% of the districts. Moreover, content for training varied considerably so that consistency across the state was compromised. Hughes concluded that despite broader program goals the mentors in most cases served as local guides to the school system rather than educational companions in learning to teach effectively (Feiman-Nemser & Parker, 1992). This may have resulted from the difficulty in implementing the required training for mentors that was found in almost a third of the districts and the difficulty of finding quality mentors that was found in almost a fourth of the districts. Again, what is striking and enlightening from these results is that even when guidelines for mentor selection and preparation have been specified, the reality of ramping up mentoring programs to implement them on a grand scale is fraught with impediments that must be overcome if mentor programs are going to have an overarching impact on schooling.

# Incentives and Impediments

It is encouraging to note that at least the boutique programs described in this section provide examples of how to reward participants for their work in mentoring programs. In the program at Wichita State, the novices who are preparing to teach math and science are paid a scholarship stipend for their participation in the preservice program, mentors are given three credit hours of credit for attending the mentor training workshop in the summer or receive a stipend in lieu of course credit. The benefits related to mentor and novice learning became apparent in the focus group sessions where mentors and novices reported how much they had grown as a result of social interactions and collegiality that resulted from their involvement in the mentoring program. They also reported how they benefited intrinsically from the humanistic support they received through the mentoring program.

In the SIU program, the novices are provided with excellent financial support in the form of graduate assistantships during the time that they serve as teacher fellows. The assistantship includes a stipend to teach four days each week with a mentor in the mentor's classroom and tuition waivers for work toward a Master's degree. It is interesting that the university provides such support since it is not clear how the university benefits from the expenditure of these funds. In addition, time is provided for a half-day co-planning session for each pair every two weeks. Clearly, providing mentors and novices time to carry out their work is a significant incentive.

Although the chapter by Hughes points out that the early pilot mentoring programs in Virginia were funded, and she indicates the import of funding in her discussion, it is not clear whether the myriad of programs across the Commonwealth provided funding for program implementation. As stated above, Virginia has done more than many states in outlining guidelines for mentor programs. However, it may well be that insufficient ongoing program support and incentives may contribute to the disappointing discrepancies that exist between what is intended for teacher induction across the state and what is actually being implemented.

The program at Texas A&M–Commerce provides mentors with a $500 stipend along with professional development opportunities, and the novices in the induction program receive a $250 stipend to support their efforts with action research in their classrooms. Moreover, the novices receive nine graduate semester hours and professional development hours that can be applied to the renewal of their teacher certification. Obviously, if such a program were to be ramped up to statewide proportions a considerable budget would be implicated. Simply put, quality mentoring at a programmatic level takes money.

Except for the program in the Commonwealth of Virginia, the programs described are fairly small. A total of 158 novices have been prepared across five years in the Raytheon Teaching Fellows Program at WSU, about 16 Teaching Fellows participate in the SIU program each year, and the Texas A&M program supports a small number novices at the induction level, although their student number at the preservice level is among the largest in the state of Texas. (No actual numbers are reported.)

As has become obvious at this point, scaling up small "boutique" mentoring programs is often problematic, even though large university preservice programs and school districts with large numbers of beginning teachers at the induction level could benefit from quality mentoring programs. Impediments such as insufficient funding, overloading already busy teachers with mentoring responsibilities, difficulties in university/school district collaboration, and a lack of incentives often work against efforts to scale up what has been successful with small numbers of participants. The New Teacher Center at the University of California, Santa Cruz (Gless & Moir, 2005) is a national resource dedicated to teacher induction that is involved in numerous local, state, and national partnerships and offers a hopeful structure at the induction level for working with a very large population of mentors and novices. The Educational Testing Service (ETS) PATHWISE teacher induction program is also designed to provide a comprehensive array of professional development activities to assist novices in improving teaching practice and has the capacity for working with large numbers of novices in induction contexts (Educational Testing Service, 2005). Currently, the New Teacher Center and ETS are participating in the federal government's first major evaluation of intensive induction programs being conducted by Mathematica Policy Research, Inc.

# Research

The self-report data collected in the current studies are helpful in suggesting positive outcomes for the programs at WSU, SIU, and Texas A&M–Commerce. Data are generally generated from surveys and focus-group interviews. At WSU, Hayes describes the use of mentor connections logs, a needs assessment survey, and mentor and novice focus groups to glean information about the program.

She uses a creative formula to analyze responses on a needs assessment completed by novices, and uses the mentor logs to track the focus and time of the interactions with novices.

In chapter 10, McIntyre, Smith, Gilbert, and Hillkirk provide some program evaluation and participant testimonials but do not report a process of outcomes-based data collection that could provide even more information regarding the impact of the program. Current and former testimonials by fellows reveal that they believe that participation in the program has helped them to become better teachers and helped with their confidence. Mentor teacher testimonials indicate that participating in the program helps improve their instructional skills; Fellows report that the program helps them to learn how to reflect on their teaching and that the required action research project helps them analyze classroom behavior and student learning in new ways. Still, none of these data provide a direct linkage between mentoring and the impact of novice practice on student learning.

The survey methodology used in the Hughes study of the mentoring programs in Virginia in chapter 11 is appropriate given the goal of assessing programs across 131 public school divisions. She investigates program goals and design and mentor selection and training. The interview questions for administrators in the sub-sample of six districts are included to provide rich descriptions of the ways that programs are designed and implemented.

As reported in chapter 12, Zeek and Walker use the quantitative measure of annual teacher appraisals to rate the teaching effectiveness of mentors and novices and student achievement scores to measure novice and mentor influence on student learning. They also use quantitative measures to determine retention rates that exceeded statewide figures. Finally, to get more qualitative information, they use conversations with participants. These qualitative conversations yield testimonials that support the value added in this professional development school. Taken together, the outcome measures used in this program represent an advancement to sole reliance on self-report measures of efficacy and provide a methodology that other programs might benefit from implementing. Ultimately, if mentor programs are to be justified in terms of their impact on student learning, research methodologies will need to be implemented, probably involving direct observation of mentor/novice behavior, that establish a causal connection between mentors' interactions with novices and novices' subsequent teaching practices in the classroom.

Summing up the lessons to be learned from the current chapters of this ATE *Yearbook*, it seems essential that those working in the area of mentoring develop thoughtful program purposes around mentoring toward standards-based, reform-minded practice. Furthermore, programs need to focus on preparing university faculty, mentors, and principals to do this work, reevaluate structures in schools, establish school/university mentoring partnerships, use funds creatively, and work to eliminate the many impediments that seem to hinder moving beyond small-program examples of quality mentoring. This effort along with more emphasis on quantitative and qualitative research that includes direct observation of mentors and novices learning to teach will move us in the direction of improving the quality of mentoring. No matter the context—schools, higher education, preservice, or induction—we have the challenge as teacher educators to prepare quality teachers. This work requires continued thoughtful interactions with and research related to experienced teachers who are mentors for the novices working in the difficult contexts of today's schools.

# References

Association of Teacher Educators. (2005). *Standards for teacher educators*. Retrieved May 15, 2005, from http://www.ate1.org/pubs/Standards_for_Teac.cfm.

Educational Testing Service. (2005). *The PATHWISE series*. Retrieved May 15, 2005, from http://www.ets.org/pathwise/.

Feiman-Nemser, S., & Parker, M. B. (1992). *Los Angeles mentors: Local guides of educational companions?* East Lansing, MI: National Center for Research on Teacher Learning, Michigan State University.

Gless, J., & Moir, E. (2005). Supporting beginning teachers with heart and mind: A decade of lessons learned from the Santa Cruz New Teacher Project. Retrieved May 15, 2005, from http://www.newteachercenter.org/article7.php.

Ingersoll, R., & Kralik, J. M. (2004). The impact of mentoring on teacher retention: What the research says. *ECS Research Review*, Denver, CO: Education Commission of the States. Retrieved May 15, 2005, from http://www.ecs.org/clearinghouse/50/36/5036.htm.

Odell, S. J., & Huling, L. (Eds.). (2000). *Quality mentoring for novice teachers*. Indianapolis, IN: Kappa Delta Pi.

Rauth, M., & Bowers, G. R. (1986). Reactions to induction articles. *Journal of Teacher Education, 37*(1), 38–41.

Wang J., & Odell, S. J. (2002). Mentored learning to teach and standards-based teaching reform: A critical review. *Review of Educational Research, 7*(3), 481–586.